CONTENTS

ACKNOWLEDGMENTS

We would like to acknowledge all the people who made this book possible, in particular: Mr Philip Galvin, Principal, Crumlin College of Business and Technical Studies, for use of the college computer facilities; the staff and students of Crumlin College for their co-operation, especially computer applications classes for their tireless testing of assignments; Mr A. Clifford, Mr D. Cooney, Mr D. Cox and Mr J.T. Smyth for their advice and encouragement; Mr Hubert Mahony and all the staff of Gill & Macmillan.

From G. Morgan, special thanks to Mary and Oisín, for their support and encouragement.

From S. O'Neill, special thanks to Caroline for her support and encouragement.

Dedicated to our parents

Chapter 1

INFORMATION SYSTEMS

Before deciding to explore the three application areas outlined in this book, we must have some basic background knowledge of computing. To use a comparison: before beginning to drive a car on the road we need to have some idea of the working of gears and other equipment in the car. We also need to know the rules of the road. Similarly, before using computers we should know about the equipment and procedures we are likely to use.

This chapter will cover the following areas:
1. An introduction to information
2. Hardware
3. Data communications
4. Software
5. Data processing
6. The Information Technology environment

1. An introduction to information

1.1 Data and information

The distinction between data and information is important.

Data is the term used to describe basic raw facts about activities of a business. These facts are subsequently used to produce useful information. Examples of data would include the hours worked by an individual, the rate of pay and the quantity of goods ordered by a customer.

Information is obtained when data is assembled or processed in a meaningful and useful way. Examples of information would include the average overtime hours in a year, the total payroll expense for the year and a trading profit and loss account.

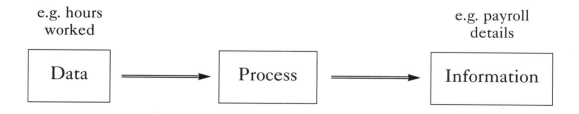

DATA PROCESSING TO PRODUCE INFORMATION

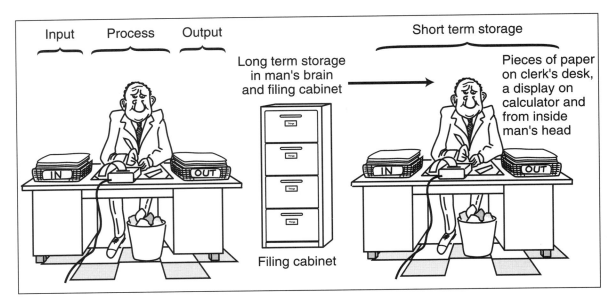

Input   Process   Output

Short term storage

Long term storage in man's brain and filing cabinet

Pieces of paper on clerk's desk, a display on calculator and from inside man's head

IN   OUT

IN   OUT

Filing cabinet

MANUAL DATA PROCESSING

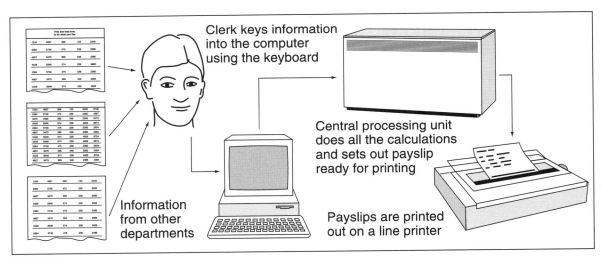

Clerk keys information into the computer using the keyboard

Central processing unit does all the calculations and sets out payslip ready for printing

Information from other departments

Payslips are printed out on a line printer

DATA PROCESSING ON COMPUTER

1.2 Types of information

Information has no value in itself. Its value is derived from its ability to assist and improve decision making. Information is now considered so important that it is regarded as a factor of production in addition to land, labour, enterprise and capital. There are three main reasons why information is needed in organisations.

1. It is necessary to keep a record of events in the company in order to maintain its operational activities. Employees must be paid, invoices must be sent to customers and retained for billing, and statistical information must be kept for the government. This type of information is referred to as **transactional** or **operational information** (see information flows diagram on p. 4).

2. Those responsible for running the organisation need information about what is happening in order to plan and control activities. They need to know the cost of stock, the lead times, machine efficiency and level of sales in order to get an indication of current performance and improve in the future. This information is used by middle management. It is referred to as **tactical information**.

3. Historical information and business environmental information needs to be retained to plan for long term development and forecasts and to maintain competitive advantage. Management need to know summary accounting data, information on competitors and market trends. Using this information long-term decisions can be made, such as how the business should be financed, what business should the organisation be in and how to compete successfully in the market. This type of information is referred to as **strategic information**.

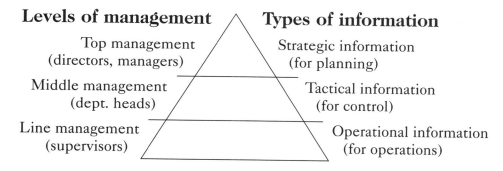

Levels of management   **Types of information**

Top management — Strategic information
(directors, managers) — (for planning)

Middle management — Tactical information
(dept. heads) — (for control)

Line management — Operational information
(supervisors) — (for operations)

As you go down the pyramid:

1. More *structured* information is required
2. More *internal* information is required
3. More *detailed* information is required
4. More *historical* information is required
5. More *repetitive* information is required

THE INFORMATION PYRAMID

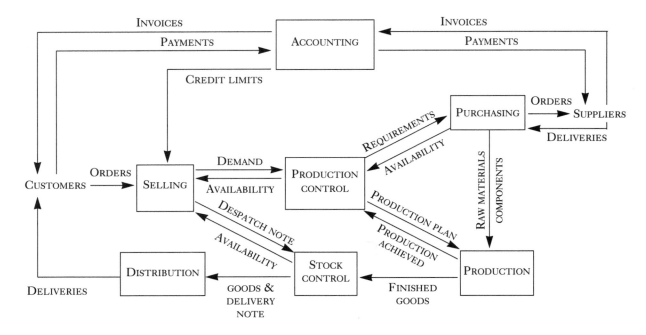

INFORMATION FLOWS (SIMPLIFIED) IN A MANUFACTURING ORGANISATION

1.3 Attributes of good information

Good information is that which is used and which creates value. Good information should have the following characteristics.

Relevant

The information must be relevant for the purpose. Often information given or produced is irrelevant. This can make understanding more difficult.

Concise

The preference is for 'need to know' information rather than 'nice to know information'. The general rule is to give as little information as possible consistent with effective use. This is often called exception reporting, e.g. where only major or important differences between actual figures and budgets are reported.

Accurate

The information must be sufficiently accurate for the purpose. The level of accuracy will depend on the decision level involved. Transactional information may need to be very accurate (down to the nearest penny or second). Strategic information does not need such accuracy.

Complete

The information must be complete. This requires close liaison with information providers and users.

Timing

Good information is that which is communicated in time to be used, otherwise the information will be useless.

Clarity

Clarity is improved by the use of different presentation techniques such as graphs, photographs, insert diagrams and three-dimensional models.

2. Hardware

A computer is a programmable electronic device that can store and process data and information and display the results. The term 'hardware' is used to refer to any physical part of a computer system, such as the keyboard, the monitor, the printer, or the disk drive.

2.1 Types of computer systems

Computer systems are usually divided into three main categories according to their processing capabilities.

Mainframe computers

Mainframe computers (or 'mainframes') are large, powerful computers that many people can use at the same time. They are also the most expensive systems. They are used for very large processing tasks, and perform many important business and government applications.

Minicomputers

These are smaller and more compact systems, and fewer operators can use them compared with a mainframe computer. They are usually found in medium-sized businesses or in divisions within a large organisation, e.g. in government departments.

Microcomputers

Microcomputers — also called 'personal computers' (PCs) — are small, self-contained computers that fit on a desk-top and are usually only used by one person. They are the least expensive type, and are widely used in businesses for a variety of tasks, such as word-processing, small data-base management and spreadsheets. They are also used as home computers, for family budgeting and similar tasks, as well as for games.

For the purposes of this book we will be concentrating on microcomputers. However, much of the information here is also applicable to other computer systems. Also, as computers become more powerful and at the same time smaller, this division by size is becoming less useful. In particular, the distinction between mainframe computers and minicomputers is sometimes hard to draw; while at the same time a number of microcomputers joined together or 'networked' can perform many of the functions associated with minicomputers.

2.2 Parts of a typical microcomputer system

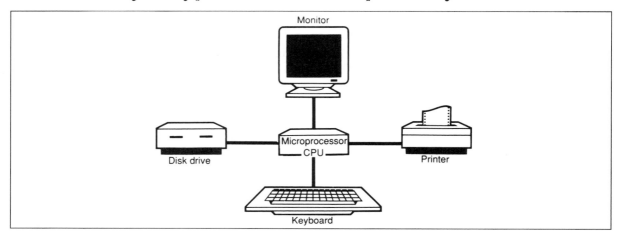

The **keyboard** is used to get the information into the computer. The **CPU** is used to process this information, e.g. to do calculations. The **monitor** is used to display the result and the **printer** produces a copy of this display. The **disk drives** make it possible for the information (and programs) to be stored on disks for further use.

2.3 The four-stage model of a computer

In general, then, we can say that a computer has four main components:
• the hardware used to enter data, called **input devices**
• the hardware that produces results from entered data, called the **processor**
• the hardware that display the results, called **output devices**
• the hardware used to store this information for later retrieval, called **auxiliary storage** or **backing storage.**

All the pieces of hardware outside the processor are called **peripherals**.

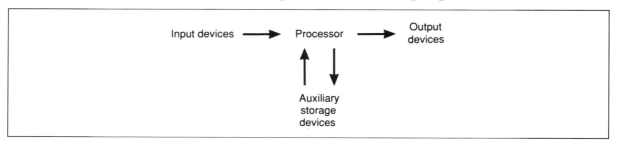

2.4 Input hardware

Keyboard

This is the most common means of entering data. It consists of an array of **keys** or switches, each one producing a particular character on the display when it is pressed. The character keys have a standard layout on all computer keyboards, called the 'QWERTY' layout after the first six letters on the top row; additional keys can include **cursor keys, function keys** and editing keys. The 'enter' key is used to implement a command or, in word-processing, to mark the end of a paragraph. The 'escape' key is often used to cancel an operation.

Mouse

This is a small pointing device connected by a wire to the computer (it vaguely resembles a real mouse!). It is moved about by hand on a flat surface, and the cursor on the screen follows its movements. Buttons on the top of the mouse can also be used to select options. Where used: various 'user-friendly' (easy-to-use) programs, especially graphics.

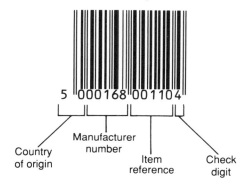

Country of origin · Manufacturer number · Item reference · Check digit

Scanner

Most consumer products now have bar codes on them. A scanner can read these codes by scanning the pattern of lines; this allows the product code to be entered without keyboarding. Scanners are also used for inputting whole pages of text and pictures into a computer. Where used: supermarkets; libraries.

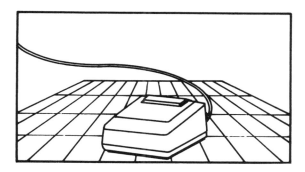

Light-pen

This is another pointing device, resembling a pen with a small light on the end. It is used to point to parts of a display to select options. Where used: some 'user-friendly' applications, especially graphics.

Magnetic card reader

This a machine that reads data from the magnetic strip on a plastic card. Where used: cash dispensing machines; employee access to buildings.

Voice data entry (VDE)

Using a microphone connected to the computer, different commands or letters can be called out and then interpreted by special programs. Major advancements have been made in VDE technology for personal computers in recent times. It is now possible for a user to dictate whole documents and commands directly into the computer. Where used: word-processing application (text entry) laboratories; computers for the physically handicapped.

Optical character recognition (OCR)

This is an input method where a scanner is used to read the text of a document directly into the computer. Special typefaces that the machine recognises can be used, although modern systems can now read ordinary typefaces. Where used: processing of customer bills that have been received with payment; reading of authors' typescripts directly into typesetting systems.

Magnetic-ink character recognition (MICR)

Numerals of a special design can be printed with an ink that contains tiny pieces of magnetisable material, and these can then be read into the computer by a special scanner. The numbers along the bottom of a cheque are used by the computer to update a customer's bank account. They include code numbers representing the bank and branch, the customer account number, the number of the cheque (all of which are printed on each page of the cheque book before it is issued to the customer) and the amount (printed on the cheque after it has been presented to the bank). Where used: cheque books and other bank documents.

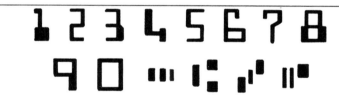

Optical mark recognition (OMR)

With this system a reader connected to the computer can detect the presence or absence of a mark, with the position of the mark determining the value entered. Where used: National Lottery; electricity meter reading; multi-choice examination questions.

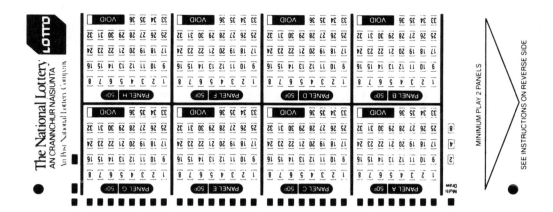

Touch-sensitive screen

The screen displays choices and instructions, and the user simply touches the symbol representing the desired choice. Where used: information screens in banks and shopping centres.

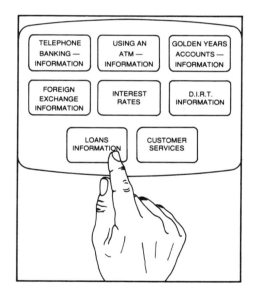

There are many other methods of entering data into a computer for processing. The choice of the most suitable input device depends on the nature of the data to be entered and the environment where the data is generated. A summary of the input devices described above is given on pp. 11–12.

Table — Summary of input devices

	Speed	Volume of input	Advantages	Disadvantages	Where used
Keyboard	Slow	Medium	• Standard QWERTY keyboard which people are familiar with	• Slow • Error prone	• Text/data entry
OCR	Fast	Medium	• No keying required	• Scanner and software are expensive • Quality of document is important	• Archiving • Text entry • Turnaround documents
OMR	Fast	Large	• No keying • Less errors than keying • Easy to complete	• Special stationery required	• Multi-choice examinations • Meter reading • Census recording • Lotto
MICR	Fast	Large	• Used as standard in world-wide banking • Secure as writing over them does not affect the numbers read in	• Need to post code cheques	• Cheques • Giros • Travellers cheques
Bar codes	Fast	Small	• Fast • Less errors	• Expensive hardware and software required	• Retail stores • Libraries

	Speed	Volume of input	Advantages	Disadvantages	Where used
Light-pen	Fast	Small	• Easy to use	• Special screen required • Limited use	• Graphics
Magnetic card	Fast	Small	• Easy to use • Portable • Secure	• Limited amount of data storage on the card	• ATM card • Clock cards
Mouse	Fast	Small	• Easy to use	• Limited – pointing device	• GUI-based software
Touch sensitive screens	Fast	Small	• Very user friendly • No keying required	• Limited – pointing device	• Tourist information • Banks
VDE	Fast	Large	• No keying • Can move around while entering data	• Expensive software • Large memory requirements	• Laboratories • Word processing • Handicapped

Table: **Summary of input devices**

2.5 Processing hardware

The central processing unit (CPU)

This is where all calculations and manipulations of the data are carried out: it could be considered the 'brain' of the computer. The CPU is contained on a tiny integrated circuit or 'microchip' that carries a large number of minute electronic circuits. The speed at which the CPU manipulates data is measured in megahertz (MHz) or the number of million cycles per second. For example, a 33 MHz computer has a clock which 'ticks' and 'tocks' 33 million times each second. Each tick-tock is called a cycle. These cycles co-ordinate the movement of data inside the CPU.

There are three main areas in the CPU: the control unit, the arithmetic and logic unit (ALU) and the main storage or 'memory'.

1. The **control unit** takes instructions in a given sequence (rather like a set of traffic lights at a cross-roads) and controls the movement of data inside the computer.

2. The **arithmetic and logic unit (ALU)** performs mathematical functions and logical decisions, such as deciding whether one number is greater than another.

3. The **main storage or 'memory'** allows data to be stored for processing purposes, and holds the results. It also stores programs or sets of instructions. It similar to our own memory. If you are asked to add three numbers without using pen and paper you would first have to put the numbers into your memory, and then add them. So too with computers. In order to perform any calculations or processes the computer must first have in its memory the data that is required.

A microchip containing the control unit and the ALU is called a **microprocessor**.

Computer memory

There are two types of main storage: **read-only memory (ROM)** and **random-access memory (RAM)**.

The read-only memory (ROM) may not be written to by the computer system. The contents of ROM are entered at the time of manufacture and cannot be changed by the user. When the computer is turned off, this information is not lost; this form of storage is referred to as **'non-volatile memory'**. The information normally only takes up a small amount of the total memory of the computer. There are however some variations of ROM chips, namely PROM and EPROM chips. PROM (programmable ROM) is a chip which can be written to once by the user after its manufacture but is fixed once it has been written to. EPROM (erasable PROM) is a special type of PROM which can be erased using ultraviolet light.

The random-access memory (RAM) is memory that may be read from and written to by the programmer or user. It contains information currently being worked on. In our example above, the three numbers to be added would be contained in RAM while the calculation is being performed. Once the calculation has been completed new data can be entered into RAM. RAM could be compared to an erasable note-pad: the user can read the information from this memory and (unlike ROM) can change its contents. When the computer is switched off, however, this memory is completely cleared; this form of storage is known as **'volatile memory'**. Before you turn off you computer, always make sure to save your data if you want it for another day!

The representation of data

How is the data inside the computer represented? Computers can only understand the numerals 1 and 0 symbolising the presence (1) or absence (0) of an electrical pulse inside the computer. How, then, can computers deal with other numbers, letters, and words? Each character (numeral, letter or symbol) on the keyboard has its own unique code number. For example, the capital letter A has a character number 65. (The character numbers are allocated by an international agreement, which was based on an earlier one called the American Standard Code for Information Interchange (ASCII), and they are often still referred to as ASCII code — pronounced 'askey'.) The character numbers do not have to be known by the user: the computer automatically reads them when each key is pressed. The computer converts each character code into this 1 and 0 form, known as a binary number. For the letter A (character 65) this is 01000001. All the data inside the computer is made up of thousands of these pulses or no-pulses of electricity moving in and out of the memory very rapidly.

Each character is thus represented by a binary number, made up of a series of 1s and 0s. Each single 1 or 0 is called a bit, which is the smallest possible element in a computer memory. A group of bits of the size that a particular computer handles — usually eight — is called a byte.

Memory capacity

Computer capacity is expressed in terms of the maximum number of bytes or characters the computer can hold in RAM at any time for processing. This capacity is measured in a unit of 1,024 bytes (210), called a kilobyte (kb) — sometimes also referred to simply as 'k' — or a unit of 1,024 kilobytes, called a megabyte (Mb) — approximately 1 million bytes. Thus a computer that has a RAM of 32 kb can keep in its memory at any time a maximum of approximately 33,000 characters. Personal computers typically have RAM capacities ranging from 64 kb to 8 Mb.

Having more RAM available in a computer means that it can manage more data and can also accommodate larger applications programs, thus making it more useful for processing purposes. When buying a computer you should be sure that is has adequate memory capacity for your requirements.

A hardware device is said to be on-line when it is connected to the CPU of the computer and under its control. A device is off-line if it is not under the control of the CPU.

2.6 Output hardware

When information has been entered and processed by the computer, we obviously need to see the result. Output devices allow this data to be viewed.

Monitor

The monitor, also called a **visual display unit (VDU)** or **screen**, is the most common means of displaying computer information. There are many sizes and types of monitor. A monochrome screen displays only one colour, often green or amber on black, or black on white, whereas a colour screen can usually display up to sixteen different colours. A low-resolution screen, mainly used to display text, has a relatively small number of 'pixels' (the dots that make up an image). A high-resolution screen, often used to display graphics, usually has more than 30,000 pixels. Examples of high-resolution displays are those of the VGA (video graphics array) or SVGA (super video graphics array) types.

Instead of the traditional cathode-ray tube (CRT), some screens use a liquid crystal display (LCD), like that on digital watches and calculators. These screens are flat and more compact, and are often used for portable ('note book') computers.

The problem with LCD screens is that they cannot be seen if looked at from an angle. With gas plasma screens the display has a glow, allowing it to be seen from any angle, while also being compact.

Printers

The problem with a display is that it is only temporary: when the computer is switched off, the display is lost! Printers allow the information to be put onto paper, creating a permanent and portable display. The output from a printer on paper is called a print-out or sometimes **'hard copy'**.

There are several types of computer printer. They are sometimes classified as impact printers (those that print characters by striking the paper through an inked ribbon: e.g. dot-matrix and daisy-wheel printers) and non-impact printers (those where the print head does not make contact with the paper: e.g. laser and ink-jet printers).

Dot-matrix printers use a series of print combs that strike the ribbon to produce a character made up of a pattern of dots. These printers are cheap, but are quite slow, and do not usually produce high quality. The more dots making up the character the better the image; better dot-matrix printers can produce characters made up of twenty-four or more dots, and this output is described as near-letter-quality (NLQ).

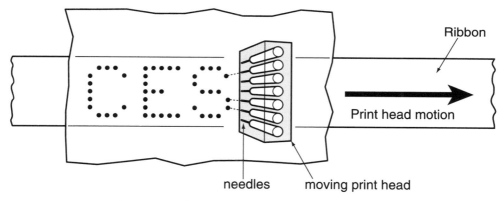

DOT-MATRIX PRINTING MECHANISM (MOVING HEAD)

The characters on **daisy-wheel printers** are moulded on the end of spokes that are arranged in a circle, like the petals of a flower — hence the name! When printing, the wheel rotates until the required character is beneath the hammer in the print head. The hammer strikes the character, which in turn strikes the paper through the ribbon. The output from these printers is said to be 'letter-quality': this means that the characters are fully formed, continuous lines produced to the standard of a traditional typewriter.

Ink-jet printers are very popular at present. They work by sending a finely controlled jet of ink onto the paper to produce the required characters. They are very quiet and produce excellent quality print.

The mode of operation of **laser** (**l**ight **a**mplification by **s**timulated **e**mission of **r**adiation) printers is similar to that of photocopiers. They produce very high-quality printing and are extremely fast; however, they are expensive to buy and to run.

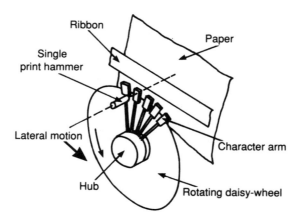

DAISY-WHEEL

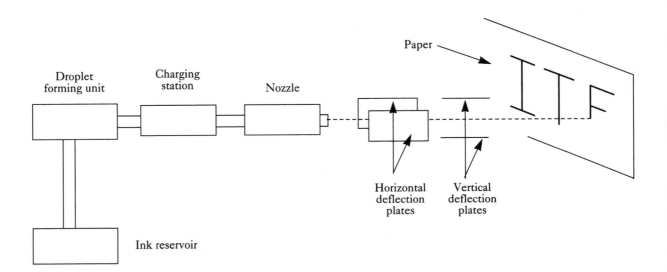

INK-JET PRINTER

Drum printers contain characters on a metal drum. The drum hits the ribbon which then produces the image. They are called line printers as the entire character set is repeated 180 times across the drum.

Chain printers contain characters on a fast revolving metal chain. Again they are impact printers.

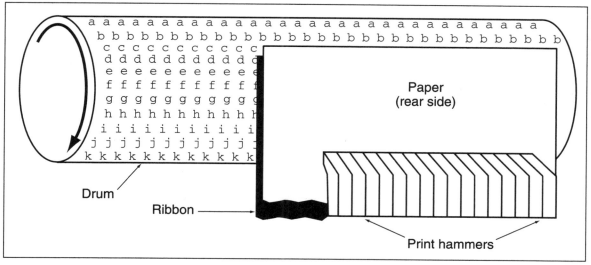

DRUM PRINTER

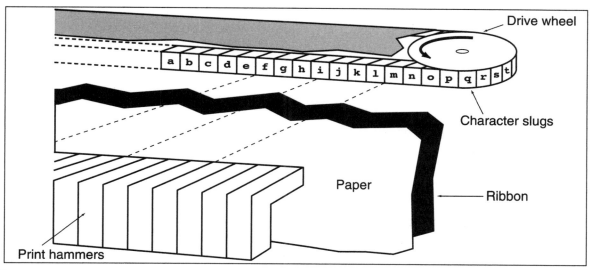

CHAIN PRINTER

Plotters

These are output devices which allow lines to be drawn using different colour pens. There are two basic types: the **flatbed** type where the pen moves up, down, across or to the side along a flat surface and the **drum plotter** where the paper is wrapped around a drum.

The output of low-speed printers is measured by the number of characters they can print per second (cps). The output of high-speed printers is usually measured in lines or pages per minute (lpm or ppm).

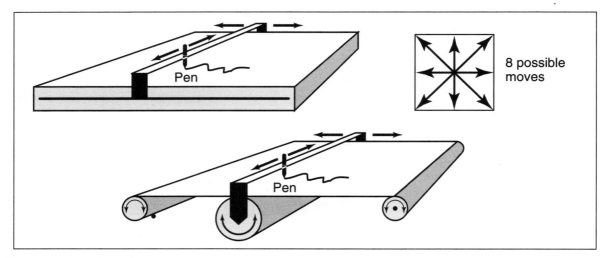

8 possible
moves

FLATBED PLOTTER (ABOVE) AND DRUM PLOTTER

Printer paper

Most printers can use two types of paper: fan-fold paper, and sheets.

Fan-fold paper consists of one long sheet perforated at intervals and folded alternately backwards and forwards on the perforations. It is fed into the printer by means of the small holes on the side of the paper (this is called 'tractor feed'). After printing, the sections are pulled apart to form pages of standard (usually A4) size.

Using a 'form feeder', individual sheets of paper, usually A4 size, can be fed into the printer from a tray like that on a photocopier.

Computer output on microfiche/film

This is where output is produced on film. This is done by means of a photographic technique where output is projected in a reduced form onto film. The film is not readable by the naked eye and requires a special magnifying reading device.

Example of a hardware specification

Advertisements often display the specifications of computers. When considering the purchase of a computer it is important that these specifications are understood. An example is given below, followed by an explanation of each term.

Hardware specification:
Pentium 90 MHz CPU
16 Mb RAM
850 Mb hard disk
CD–ROM drive
3.5" floppy disk drive
15" SVGA VDU
Windows preloaded

The Pentium chip is a type of Intel central processor.

90 MHz is the clock speed of the CPU, 90 million cycles per second. The higher the speed the quicker the computer can perform tasks. Graphic User Interface-based software requires fast CPU speeds.

16 Mb RAM means 16 million bytes or characters of information can be contained in the Random Access Memory of the computer. This memory is used by both the operating system and application software (discussed later). Again, the larger the RAM the better, especially for graphics-based applications. Windows software will require at least 4 Mb of RAM.

850 Mb hard disk means **850** million bytes or characters can be stored on the hard disk for later use.

SVGA VDU stands for Super Video Graphic Adapter Visual Display Unit. This is a high-resolution screen and will display graphics very clearly.

CD-ROM drive is a special drive used to read compact disks (see p. 22).

3.5" floppy disk drive is a disk drive which can use 3.5" floppy disks.

Windows is operating software, developed by Microsoft, which uses menus and icons for command options.

◈ Table	*Summary of output devices*					
	Relative speed*	**Volume of output**	**Quality**	**Advantages**	**Disadvantages**	**Where used**
Daisy-wheel printer	Slow	Small	LQ	• Cheap to run • Good quality	• Limited to text output • Noisy	• Low volume/ high quality text
Dot-matrix printer	Slow	Small	NLQ	• Cheapest type of printer • Text and graphics output possible • Very cheap running cost	• Very slow • Very noisy • Quality can vary	• Draft work
Ink-jet printer	Slow	Medium	LQ	• Excellent quality • Quiet	• Running costs expensive • Relatively slow	• Low volume/ high quality output

	Relative speed*	**Volume of output**	**Quality**	**Advantages**	**Disadvantages**	**Where used**
Summary of output devices						
Laser printer	Fast	Large	LQ (best)	• Best quality • Very fast • Quiet	• Running costs expensive	• High volume/ high quality output
Drum printer	Fast	Large	Varies	• Multiple copies possible • Very fast	• Quality can vary	• High volume multiple copy output
Chain printer	Fast	Large	Varies	• Multiple copies possible • Very fast	• Quality can vary	• High volume multiple copy output
Plotters	Slow	Small	LQ	• Attention to detail • Different colours and pens	• Slow • Expensive software and hardware	• Graphics • Designs
VDU	Fast	Small	LQ	• No media expense	• Temporary display • VDU omissions	• Temporary output • Enquires
COM	Fast	Large	LQ	• Large volume output on small media (space saving/ easier to distribute)	• Need special viewing equipment • Cannot be edited by hand	• Libraries

*SLOW = 10 CPS TO 300 LPM; FAST = 300 LPM TO 3000 LPM.

2.7 Auxiliary storage

All computer systems can store information for later retrieval. Magnetic disks of various types and sizes are the most common storage medium.

Diskettes or 'floppy disks'

Diskettes are small disks made of flexible plastic that is coated with a magnetisable material. These disks are removed from the disk drive when not in use, and can be copied, filed, carried around, or even sent through the post.

The first microcomputer disks had a diameter of 130 mm (5.25 in.) and were enclosed in a strong but flexible plastic envelope (hence the term 'floppy disk'). The modern standard disk has a diameter of 90 mm (3.5 in.) and is completely enclosed in a rigid plastic cartridge — although disks of the earlier type continue to be used side-by-side with the newer ones.

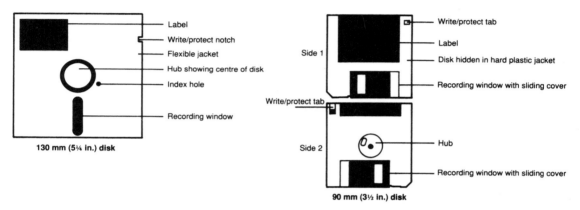

The information on the disk is stored in the form of spots of magnetisable material, each spot representing one bit (magnetised = 1, unmagnetised = 0). This information is stored on tracks or concentric rings or circles on the disk. There are usually forty tracks on a 130 mm disk and eighty tracks on a 90 mm disk.

Most disks are double-sided (2S), i.e. they have a usable surface on both sides. The amount of information that can be packed onto a disk varies: for example, a 130 mm (5.25 in.) double-sided double-density (2S-2D) disk usually holds about 360 kb; a 90 mm (3.5in.) 2S-2D disk usually holds about 720 kb. A high-density (HD) disk holds approximately 1.5 Mb.

Fixed disks or 'hard disks'

Fixed disks (usually called 'hard disks', in contrast to 'floppy disks') are permanently installed inside the case of the computer. They are made of a hard metal alloy with a magnetisable coating on both sides. These disks can store very large quantities of information (up to 1 gigabyte (Gb) — 1000 million bytes). They can also access this information much faster than floppy disks.

Optical disks

Optical disks are physically similar to the compact disks (CDs) used by the recording industry. They can store up to a hundred times the amount of information on a fixed disk. The only problem with these disks is that the user can only read information from the disk (read only — CD ROM): it is not possible to record your own information on them. However, there are CDs being developed which can be written to but they are very expensive at present.

Formatting a disk

A disk is formatted only once — before using it for the first time — and this simply divides the disk into sectors or slices. The procedure is similar to dividing a city into postal districts: the sectors allow data to be stored on specific areas on the disk for easy retrieval. Note: Some floppy discs are pre-formatted when purchased.

Here is an example to illustrate the retrieval method (simplified). When a file or document is stored on the disk it will have to be given a file name. Along with this name the computer will keep a record of where it recorded that file on the disk. For example, the file might be named 'CAR.doc'. When this file is saved the file name will be recorded on the outer track ('file allocation table' ,FAT) of the disk as CAR.doc 712. The number 712 is used to tell the computer where it has stored the file on the disk: 7 means the seventh sector and 12 means the twelfth track. When the computer needs to retrieve this data it will immediately position the read-write head (like the stylus of a record player) at the twelfth track in the seventh sector.

This method of positioning the read-write head exactly on the spot where the data is stored is called **direct access system (DAS)**. This allows information to be retrieved from disks very rapidly.

Care of disks

Magnetic disks must be treated with great care. For this reason, and because of possible loss of data from wear and tear on disks or power failure or hardware problems, you should keep contingency or 'back-up' copies of all data and program files. Back-up disks (which are exact copies of original disks) should be regularly updated, and used only in an emergency.

Other storage media

Magnetic tape, similar to that used in tape recorders, can also be used to store computer information. For some small home computers, audio tape cassettes can be used in a standard tape recorder-player. For business use, reel-to-reel tapes are sometimes used.

The main disadvantage of tapes is that only serial access is available, compared with the direct access possible with disks. This means that the tape must be wound forward until it reaches the spot where the information is stored, which can take several minutes in certain circumstances.

Magnetic tape is not used very often with business microcomputers, except occasionally for contingency or 'back-up' purposes.

E C A Table	Summary of backing storage devices			
	Floppy disk	**Hard disk**	**Magnetic tape**	**CD-ROM**
Approx. access speed	200 milliseconds (ms)	50 ms	Varies	100 ms
Capacity	360 K, 720 K 1.44 Mb, 2 Mb	40 Mb to 5 Gb	120 K to 1.25 Mb	650 Mb to 10 Gb
Method of operation	DAS (direct access system)	DAS	SAS (serial access system)	DAS
Where used	Microcomputer systems, also to backup	Micro, miniframe, mainframe	Mainframe,	Micro, mini, mainframe

3. Data Communications

The basic requirements of any communications systems are:
- a sender of the information
- a receiver of the information
- an encoding system
- a decoding system
- a medium to transmit the message.

Taking the example of two persons communicating over the phone the five requirements or components would be:
- the person making the call
- the person receiving the call
- the language used would be the encoding system
- the decoding system would be the ability of the person receiving the call to comprehend the language
- the medium would be the telephone line.

When communicating via a computer the components would be:
- the sending computer
- the receiving computer
- the **modem** would be the encoding system (the modem converts digital signals from the computer to telephone signals which can be sent over telecommunication lines (**modulation**)
- the decoding would be done by a modem on the other end which converts the telephone signal to digital form to be interpreted by the computer (**demodulation**)
- the medium would be the telephone line.

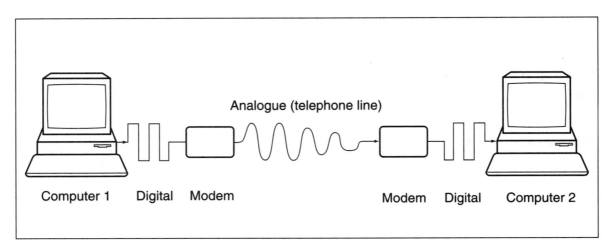

Analogue (telephone line)

Computer 1   Digital   Modem   Modem   Digital   Computer 2

DATA TRANSMISSION AND THE USE OF MODEMS

3.1 Communications hardware

Modem

A modem (short for modulator/demodulator) is the piece of hardware required to allow two computers to communicate over the normal telecommunication lines. It has a dual function:

- to translate digital information into telephone signals (modulation)
- to translate telephone signals into digital signals (demodulation).

The data transfer rate is the amount of information that can be transmitted along a data channel. The rate is referred to the **baud rate**. The baud rate is the number of bits that can be transmitted per second. As a character is normally composed of eight to ten bits a 300 baud line would be capable of transmitting 30 characters per second. Modern modems should have a minimum 14,400 to 28,800 baud rate.

Multiplexor

This is a hardware device which combines data from several sources for transmission down a single line. It can also split data from one line to several other internal communication lines.

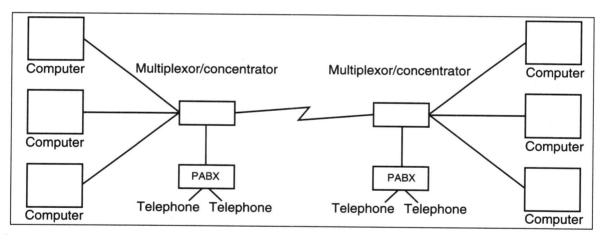

DATA COMMUNICATION LINKS VIA A MULTIPLEXOR

Communication ports

At the back of most computers there are a number of connecting points called ports. These allow the computer to be connected to the keyboard and printer and to other peripheral devices. There are two types of port: serial and parallel.

A **serial port** is a connection point that sends information to or from the CPU one bit after another. This port is usually used to connect the mouse or a modem to the computer.

A **parallel port** is a connection point that sends information one byte at a time, i.e. in groups of eight bits. This port is usually used to connect a printer to the computer.

3.2 Data transmission terms

Simplex link is where communication is possible in one way only (e.g. printer connection).

Half duplex link is where two-way communication is possible but only in one direction at a time (not simultaneously).

Full duplex link allows simultaneous two-way communication.

Synchronous transmission is where bits are sent down the line and this is timed to coincide with the clock pulse of the computer.

Asynchronous transmission is a high-speed method of transmitting data which is not synchronised by a pulse but requires special start and stop bits.

SERIAL TRANSMISSION

$$0 \leftarrow 1 \leftarrow 0 \leftarrow 0 \leftarrow 0 \leftarrow 0 \leftarrow 0 \leftarrow 1$$

PARALLEL TRANSMISSION

$$\leftarrow 0$$
$$\leftarrow 1$$
$$\leftarrow 0$$
$$\leftarrow 0$$
$$\leftarrow 0$$
$$\leftarrow 0$$
$$\leftarrow 0$$
$$\leftarrow 1$$

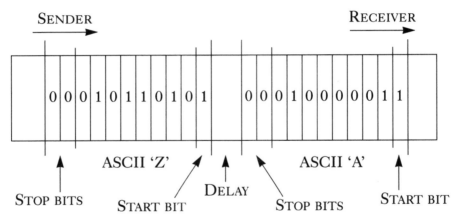

ASYNCHRONOUS TRANSMISSION

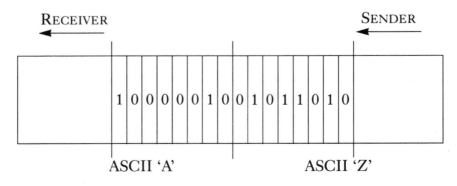

SYNCHRONOUS TRANSMISSION

3.3 Networks

A network is a linked set of computer systems capable of sharing computer power and resources. The advantages of networking computers are:

- the ability to share expensive resources such as disks, software, printers and processing power
- the ability to share information, thus avoiding unnecessary duplication
- the ability to communicate directly with others on the network
- the network allows local processing and central control.

Types of network

Local area network (LAN)

This is a network which is confined to one local site. External telephone lines are not used. Local cabling such as coaxial or twisted pair cable is used to connect the network.

Wide area network (WAN)

This is a network which is spread over a wide geographical area. It involves the use of telecommunication lines and satellites to connect the computers. These networks are often used to connect external databases or services.

Two methods of transmission are used in WAN communication. **Circuit switching** involves a circuit being made and maintained for the duration of the transmission. Delays often occur when setting up transmission and the line is monopolised for the duration of the transmission. An alternative is to use a method called **packet switching**. This method involves the sending of fixed chunks (packets) of information down the link. It is not necessary to establish a connection with the recipient as the message can be stored forward.

Network topologies (configuration)

Star network

The computers are all connected to a central file server through which all messages pass.

ADVANTAGES

- Supports dumb terminals
- Central control
- More secure
- Failure of one node will not affect the network

DISADVANTAGES

- Central computer failure means the entire network will be dysfunctional
- Complex software required at hub

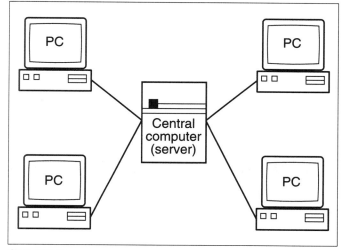

STAR NETWORK

Bus Network

Each mode on the network uses a linear communication line (bus) to transmit information. The bus line is not in a loop. It has a terminal box at the end of the bus.

ADVANTAGES
- Less cabling required compared with star network
- Fast communication

DISADVANTAGES
- Security problems as data is on the bus all the time (no central control)

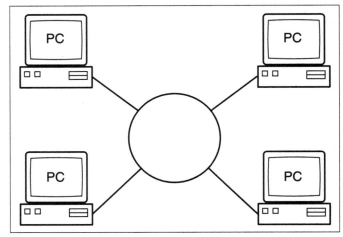

BUS NETWORK

Ring network

All nodes are connected together in a ring where none has overall control. Messages are constantly revolving around the loop until they are picked up.

ADVANTAGES
- No dependence on central device
- High-speed transmission

DISADVANTAGES
- One-way traffic only
- Repeater to boost the signal often required

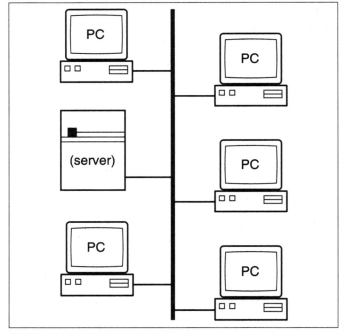

RING NETWORK

3.4 Modern communication methods

Telephone

Despite the increasing popularity of E-mail the telephone remains the most popular and important method of communications in the office. Telephone technology is also advancing rapidly with such developments as mobile phones, digital phones and PABX exchanges.

PABX switchboards

These allow an interface between a group of telephones extensions, teletext devices and computers. They are essentially muliplexors.

Telex

This is a twenty-four-hour communication system. It permits telex users to transmit information to another telex users. All telex messages are received and printed out. Cost is based on an annual rental and a cost per communication.

ADVANTAGES
- Printed record of all messages
- Messages may be received when the office is closed
- Legal standing

DISADVANTAGES
- The number of telex users is limited
- Only text can be transmitted

Facsimile transmission (fax)

This is an extremely popular and effective means of communication. Most businesses today have fax machines. These allow pictures, diagrams and text to be transmitted from place to place via the telephone lines. Fax operates in the same way as a photocopier and is often described as a long distance photocopier.

ADVANTAGES
- Very fast
- Messages can be received outside office hours
- Text, photos and diagrams can be transmitted
- Very reliable

DISADVANTAGES
- Print quality can vary considerably
- Point-to-point connection must be maintained (no store forward facility)
- The transmission is a copy and hence has no legal standing

Electronic mail (E-mail)

This is the use of computers to transmit information to other computer users. This can be directly to another computer or to a central E-mail box held on a central computer. All E-mail allows for a message to be stored for retrieval at the user's convenience. To send a message the user must have the E-mail address of the receiver.

ADVANTAGES
- Paperless
- Store forward facility
- Fast
- Text editing facility available

DISADVANTAGE
- Computer required by both sender and receiver

ViewData

This is the name given to any system which provides information through the telephone lines to a television or terminal screen. The system is interactive, i.e. the user can transmit as well as receive information through the ViewData network. Most ViewData allow access to vast data-bases such as stock markets, business information and reservation systems. Examples include Prestel in the UK and the Minitel system in France.

ADVANTAGES
- Provides access to large data-bases
- No need to own a computer to use the system (only television and adapter required)

Teletext

This is a one-way system where information can be received and displayed on a television screen. A telephone is not required. The information is transmitted across the airways. Examples include CEEFAX, Oracle and Aertel. A teletext adapter must be available in the television but there is no additional charge for the service. The information available on these data-bases includes weather reports, news, sports reports, subtitles for some programs, jokes and advertising.

ADVANTAGES
- No usage fee
- Large data-bases available without the need for a computer

DISADVANTAGE
- Not interactive, can only receive data

The Internet

The Internet (also known as the 'Net') is the world's largest computer network. There were thirty million users world-wide in 1995 and it is growing by more than 10% every month. There is a large range of different services available on the Internet. To be connected to it there are four requirements: a modem, an account with an Internet provider (a company that connects customers to the Internet, similar to the role of Cablelink for television connections), a computer and a telephone line. The following are some of the services available on the Internet.

- **Electronic mail:** you can exchange E-mail with millions of people all over the world. E-mail is used for anything that might be on paper mail or the telephone such as gossip, recipes, business, love letters etc.
- **Information retrieval:** this is done on the **World Wide Web (WWW)**. This is a system which allows information to by retrieved by a browser program. This information includes pages of text, graphics, sound and even video. The WWW is the largest library in the world and includes information from thousands of libraries, government offices and businesses.. Searching for and looking through information on the Web is called 'surfing'. The information available includes government publications, news, finance, art and music to mention a few types.
- **UseNet:** this allows users to set or access discussion or interest groups. There are currently 15,000 groups dealing with a very wide range of interests. It is possible to access any of these groups' information or send messages to the group. Whether the interest is technical or simply how to bake a cake there is an interest group to answer your query.
- **Shopping:** almost 200,000 companies currently advertise their products or services on the Internet. For example, it is possible to browse through all the titles in a particular book store and order a book through the Internet using a credit card number.
- **FTP:** file transfer protocol allows software to be downloaded.

ADVANTAGES
- Information can be retrieved from anywhere in the world for the cost of a local call
- Huge volume of information available
- Advertising on the Internet is to a very large audience world-wide and is cheaper than other forms of advertising

DISADVANTAGES
- Control: there is no controlling authority on the Internet
- Security: sending credit card numbers over the Internet is subject to abuse by hackers
- Undesirable groups can distribute information on the Internet

4. Software

So far we have discussed the machinery or equipment that makes up a computer system: the 'hardware'. The problem is that if we had all this equipment available to us the computer would still be useless. So what is missing? The answer is programs or 'software'.

The software is the set of instructions that enables the computer to perform its function. A car is useless without instructions to go fast or slow, stop or start. So too a computer is useless without the instructions for performing a particular task. For example, if we want to extract a trial balance from a computer we must first have the accounting program (instructions) in the computer's memory.

4.1 Types of software

There are two types of software that need to be in place before we can use the computer: the **operating system** and **application programs**.

The operating system

This is the set of instructions that looks after the internal running of the computer. Its functions include the following:

- providing a user interface to allow the user to give the computer instructions
- managing the memory of the computer as efficiently as possible
- error reporting and error handling
- handling the operation of input, output and backing storage devices
- running application software
- running utilities programs for displaying information on the screen, reading from disks, listing the contents of the disk, formatting disks, copying disks or files and so on.

A common operating system used with IBM microcomputers and other computers based on this design is the Microsoft Disk Operating System (MSDOS — pronounced 'em-ess-doss'). This operating systems has been recently transformed to have a graphic user interface where icons (graphic symbols) and pull-down menus are used to select commands. The new operating environment is called Microsoft Windows. Other types of microcomputers, such as the Apple Macintosh, have their own operating systems.

These instructions must be in the computer's memory before any other software can function. Programs work by communicating requests to the operating system, which acts as a kind of secretary to the application software.

Application programs

Application programs are computer programs that are written to make the computer perform specific tasks, such as:

- word-processing
- spreadsheets
- graphics
- data-base management
- financial accounting
- sales order processing.

Programs that perform specific functions such as these are often called applications (to distinguish them from programs that make the computer itself work more effectively, called the operating system as outlined above). Application programs are written in computer programming languages by large specialist companies, such as Microsoft, Lotus, Claris and Ashton-Tate, and these programs can then be bought 'off the shelf' from computer suppliers. Alternatively, computer programs can be specially written (or customised) for a particular company's needs: this kind of program can be very expensive.

Easy-to-use (user friendly) programs

Greater emphasis is placed nowadays on programs that are easy to learn and to use, or 'user-friendly' programs. Some or all of the following features may be found with such programs.

Sound: Sound may be used to signal to the user that a mistake has been made. Sound may also indicate that a task is complete or that the computer is awaiting more data.

Colour or contrast: Colour can highlight displays and improve the presentation of information. With a monochrome monitor changes in contrast can be used instead to highlight various options.

Help facility: The use can give a special command to request help if needed. With some programs, if an error occurs the computer will automatically give the required explanation and offer ways to remedy the mistake. This is called 'on-line help'.

Icons: These are small symbols displayed on the screen to represent commands or options, and are usually selected by using a mouse. This means that complex commands do not have to be remembered.

Menus: The use of menus means that the user is guided through the application.

Program prompts: At no stage during the operation of a program should the user be left not knowing what to do next or in what form the information should be entered. Program prompts are messages telling the user the next action to take or offering choices, such as 'Press any key to continue' or 'Do you want to exit the system (Y/N)?' or 'Do you want to save before exiting?'.

On the other hand poor choice of sound, graphics or colour may not enhance the ease of use of a particular program. Frequent beeps may be a source of irritation to the user, and may distract others working in the same room. The graphics and colour chosen may only serve to cause eye discomfort.

4.2 Programming languages

As a computer can only interpret binary code it is necessary for all programs to be broken down or translated into this form (called the **object program**). All software is generated using programming languages (referred to as the **source code**). There are four generations of programming language, as shown in the table on pp. 34–35.

ECA Table	*Generations of programming languages*			
Generation	**First**	**Second**	**Third**	**Fourth**
Known as	Machine code	Assembler language	Procedural languages	Non-procedural
Description	A machine understandable code which is expressed in 1s and 0s	Symbolic language which largely corresponds to machine code	Common language based code	Menu and command based languages designed to speed up software development (code is automatically produced)
Level	Low	Low	High	High
Translated by	None required	Assembler software	Compiler software (or interpreter software for small PCs)	Compiler software
Where used	• Where speed and strict control of hardware is important, e.g. control of machine controls	• Computer games • As for machine code	• Most application software • Training	• Rapid development of software • Development of prototypes • Non-specialist uses
Examples	10101011010	ADD, SUB MULT	BASIC COBOL PASCAL C	DBASE LOTUS123 EXCEL Program Generator

◈ E C A ◈ *Table*	*Generations of programming languages*			
Generation	**First**	**Second**	**Third**	**Fourth**
Advantages	• Fastest running time (as no translation time) • Very detailed control over the hardware	• Fast running time • Detail control • Easier to understand than machine code	• Easy to learn and understand • Machine independent language • Detailed knowledge of hardware not required	• Very quick development time • User friendly • Non-procedural
Disadvantages	• Error prone • Difficult to understand and learn • Machine dependent • Detailed knowledge of hardware required	• Translation required which slows down execution • Machine dependent • Detailed knowledge of hardware required	• Less control over hardware • Slow execution time	• Often inefficient programs produced

5. *Data processing concepts*

5.1 *Elements of a computer file*

A **file** is a collection of records.
A **record** is made up of a collection of related fields.
A **field** consists of a number of characters.

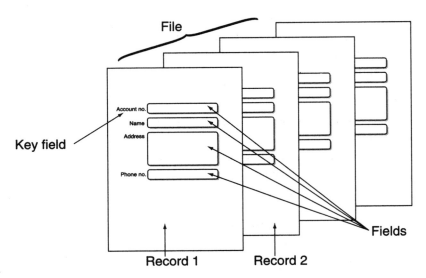

THE ELEMENTS OF A FILE

Key field

The key field is a field within a record that uniquely identifies the record, e.g. a bank account number.

5. 2 *Types of record*

Fixed length records

Every record of this type in the file will have the same fixed number of fields, and characters. The maximum size of the fields is always specified. The main advantage of this type of record is that it is easier for programmers to use. The main disadvantage is that some space allocation may be wasted.

Variable length records

With this type of record not all records in the file are the same size. The number of fields may vary or the amount of characters in a particular field may vary. The main advantage of this type of record is that it is a better use of space. The main disadvantage is that programming can be difficult.

5.3 Types of file

Transaction file
This consists of records that relate to individual transactions that occur from day to day, e.g. sales invoices, orders.

Reference file
This contains reference data that is normally altered or updated infrequently, e.g. price lists, company regulations. It does not contain any transaction data.

Master file
This consists of reference data and transaction data that is built up over time, e.g. the payroll master file would contain reference data such as PRSI numbers and cumulative totals of pay and tax to date.

5.4 File Organisation

File organisation refers to the way records are held on file. Usually a key field, e.g. student number or account code, is used to identify each record. The various types of file organisation are outlined below.

Serial
The key fields are stored one after the other but not in any logical order. This method is usually used for recording transaction data initially.

Sequential
Records are ordered by the the key field. Often transaction files are ordered sequentially before master files are updated.

Index sequential
Records are held sequentially but are accessed by means of an index.

Random
Records are not stored in any particular order. They are stored in addressable locations which are calculated based on the key field.

5.5 Updating a tape file

To update a master file it is not possible to write back the extra information to the same portion of the tape. The method used requires a new master file on a new reel of tape.

Updating consists of the following steps:
- The transaction file must be sorted into the same order as the master file.
- The sorted transaction file data and master file data are read into memory.
- The transaction data and master file data are matched and updated in the memory and transferred to the new master file. If no update is required for a particular record the original record on the master file will be copied unaltered to the new master file. Usually three generations of master tape are retained for back-up purposes. This is known as the **'grandfather–father–son'** concept, the son being the most up-to-date tape.

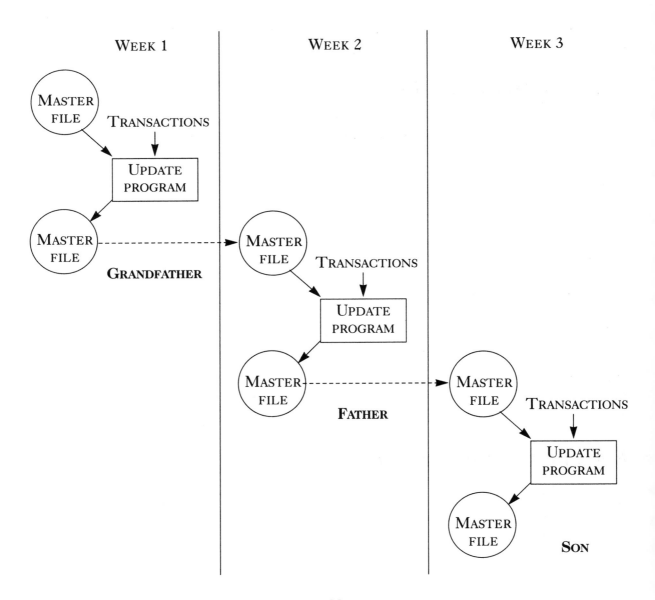

5.6 *Updating disk files*

Individual records on a disk are addressable directly (DAS). It is possible to write back to and update a record to the same place from which it was read. This involves overwriting the existing information with the new information. This is often referred to as **updating by overlay** or in **place**.

Updating consists of the following sequence:
* The transaction file data and master file data are are read into main memory.
* The transaction data and master file data are matched and updated in the memory and transferred to the same place on the master disk.

5.7 *Stages of data collection*

1. *Data collection*
Data may be collected on manually prepared source documents, e.g. invoices, orders etc., or the data could be captured in a machine sensible form at source, e.g. bar codes.

2. *Data transmission*
This involves sending source documents to a central location by post, telephone, electronic mail or fax for processing.

3. *Data preparation*
This can involve transcription of data from the source documents to a machine sensible form if there is no direct data capture and verification. **Data verification** is the process of checking that the original source information has been correctly transcribed. It is essentially a process of checking that the data input is identical to the source documents.

A common method of verification is to have the data rekeyed by another person and compared with the first entry. Misspelling and transposition errors can be detected. Tranposition errors are those where characters are mixed up, e.g. code 2343 is keyed in as 2334.

4. *Input*
The verified data is then subject to validation checks before processing. **Data validation** is a process which checks verified data before processing. Common validation checks are outlined below.

Range check: checks whether the input data is within specific allowable ranges, e.g. accounts code are only allowed between 0000 and 9999

Limit check: certain numbers are not allowed to be above or below a certain level, e.g. 24 hours in a day

Existence check: data is checked to ensure that all necessary fields are present.

Format check: data is checked to ensure that it contains only characters of the correct type, e.g. there should only be numbers in numeric fields.

Reasonablesness check: checks that numbers are not unusually high or low. There have been cases of householders getting electricity bills for thousands of pounds due to a meter reading error.

Check digits: these are used to check codes for validity. The computer calculates a check which is added to each code for validation purposes.

For example: calculation of the check digit using 11 as the division factor.

Original code: 9564

Multiply each digit by a weight starting one greater than the number of digits: 5432.

Product 　　 $9 * 5 = 45$
　　　　　　 $5 * 4 = 20$
　　　　　　 $6 * 3 = 18$
　　　　　　 $4 * 2 = 8$

Sum the product = 91

Divide by 11 = 8 and remainder of 3

Subtract the remainder from 11 = 8 (11–3)

8 is the check digit

New code is 95648

When the new code number is input to the computer a weighting system is used. One is used for the rightmost digit and two for the next and so on. The product is calculated and summed. It is then divided by eleven and the remainder should be zero. If the remainder is not zero the code is not valid.

New code: 95648

Product 　　 $9 * 5 = 45$
　　　　　　 $5 * 4 = 20$
　　　　　　 $6 * 3 = 18$
　　　　　　 $4 * 2 = 8$
　　　　　　 $8 * 1 = 8$

Sum = 99

Divide by 11 =9 and remainder 0

Thus this code would pass the validition test.

Note: an original code giving rise to check digit of '10' is normally discarded.

5. 8 Methods of data processing

Batch processing

This involves individual source documents being grouped or batched manually or on computer and processed at a predetermined interval of time. For example, in an accounting system all the invoices for a week could be entered into the computer but not processed (updating the accounts) until the end of the week. At the end of the week all accounts relating to the batch would be processed in one run.

ADVANTAGES
- Better control
- More efficient use of processing time
- Large tasks can be broken down into small batches
- Access to the computer not always required

DISADVANTAGES
- Random enquires not possible as files are not constantly up-to-date
- Causes peaks and lows in computer use
- Only applicable to certain applications

APPLICATIONS SUITED TO BATCH PROCESSING
- Payroll
- Accounting updates
- Sales statistics

On-line transaction processing

This involves processing of transactions as they occur. An example would be an airline booking system. As bookings are received they are immediately reserved on the system.

ADVANTAGES
- Files always up-to-date
- No data preparation necessary
- Random enquiries possible

DISADVANTAGES
- Computer power must always be available
- Back-up systems vital

APPLICATIONS SUITED TO ON-LINE PROCESSING
- Airline booking system
- Electronic point of sale systems using bar code readers
- ATMS

5.9 Data processing department

The data processing department is like any other department in any business in that it usually has a structure where diffferent people have specific tasks to perform. The typical structures for two sizes of data processing departments are given on p. 42. The number and nature of the tasks performed by these staff will vary with the size and nature of the business. A list of the common tasks performed by data processing staff is also outlined.

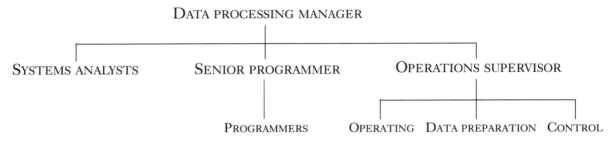

A SMALL DATA PROCESSING DEPARTMENT

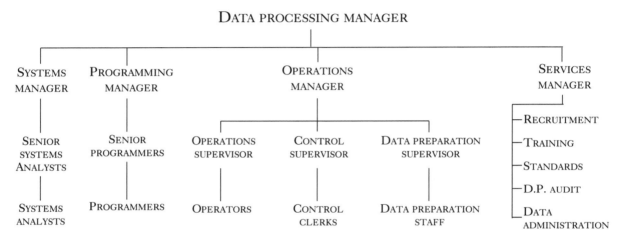

A LARGE DATA PROCESSING DEPARTMENT

The data processing manager/IT manager

ROLE
- In charge of the DP department
- Leadership and motivation of systems and programming and operations work

QUALITIES REQUIRED
- Leadership skills and experience
- Up-to-date knowledge of current computer technology
- Probably experience in all areas of the department

Systems analyst

ROLE
- Designing new information processing systems
- Improving existing systems
- Liaison with programmers and computer users

QUALITIES REQUIRED
- Good business experience
- Programming and computer knowledge and experience
- Interpersonal skills

Programmer

ROLE
- Writing programs according to specifications
- Testing programs
- Assisting the systems analyst
- Documenting all programs

QUALITIES REQUIRED
- Programming qualifications or knowledge
- Logical mind and attention to detail

Operations manager

ROLE
- Responsible for the smooth running or operation of the computer systems

QUALITIES REQUIRED
- In depth knowledge of computers
- Leadership qualities

Operator

ROLE
- Data entry
- Maintaining back-ups

QUALITIES REQUIRED
- Accuracy
- Speed
- Ability to work to deadlines
- Computer application knowledge

Computer librarian

ROLE
- Responsible for all program disks
- Responsible for all data disks
- Responsible for all back-up disks
- Filing and labeling disks
- Issuing disks when required
- Physical security of all magnetic media

Data-base administrator

ROLE
- Design and maintenance of a large data-base and integration of new applications into the data-base
- Documentation of the data-base
- Back-up procedures for the data-base
- Monitoring performance

6. The information technology environment

The aim of this section is to describe ways to minimise risks to the information technology environment.

6.1 Definitions

The **security** of computer systems 'is the establishment and application of safeguards to protect data, software and computer hardware from accidental or malicious modification, destruction or disclosure' (The British Computer Society).

The **privacy** of computer systems is a part of overall security and involves methods of protection against unauthorised access or disclosure.

6.2 Risks to computer systems

1. Input fraud
This involves entering false or misleading information into a computer system. This is the most common method of fraud because the majority of users have input access.
Examples are:
- use of 'ghost' or fictitious employees on a payroll system
- creation of fictitious suppliers
- positive falsification, i.e. inserting additional data which is false
- negative falsification, i.e. where data is suppressed (not shown).

2. Alteration of programs
This is less common as very technical skills are required to alter commercial programs. The most common form of alteration is where a small slice or portion of an account is redirected into a secret account. This is called salami programming.

3. Output fraud
This is where computer output is suppressed, stolen or altered. Slow output devices mean that data is sometimes exposed to fraudulent attempts in a data queue.

4. Unauthorised access

5. Computer viruses
These are computer programs, designed as a prank or to damage data, which can copy themselves by attaching to other programs.

6. Physical damage from fire, flood and break-ins
7. Environmental factors such as dust, dampness and heat
8. Power supply cut-off
9. Loss of data and programs
10. Poor personnel procedures

6.3 Methods of minimising the risks to the information technology environment

There are three main types of method:
- physical
- logical
- procedural.

Physical methods
- Air conditioned rooms, especially for mainframe computers
- Dust-free rooms
- Controlled temperature systems
- Back-up power supply (generator)
- Surge controller, to control any variations in power going into computer systems
- High-security locks on computer room doors
- Limited access to keys
- Locks on computer equipment

Logical methods
These involve the use of computer programs to minimise risks.

- Use of non-display passwords for access to programs or data.
- The use of passwords to limit what the user can do on the system, e.g. the system manager's password will normally allow access to all areas whereas the computer operator may be resticted to data entry only.

- Built in user monitor programs. These are programs which monitor the activities of every user of the system. Information such as log-on time, update activities, files read, menus visited, log-off time etc. is stored for future reference. Printed summaries of this information are taken at regular intervals.
- Virus protection programs prevent viruses from infecting the computer. An alarm is usually sounded when a virus is present. These programs must be updated regularly to keep up with the many new viruses.
- Virus destruction software enables the user to delete or remove certain viruses if detected on a disk.
- Screen blank programs. These programs are time activated. After a set period of time of non-activity the screen will blank off. To reactivate the screen the password must be given.

Procedural methods
Good personnel procedures are very important for minimising risks to computer systems

- Back-up copies of data should be regularly made. These back-up copies (on disk or tape) should be stored in separate locations in fire-proof safes.
- Proper log-out procedure should be adhered to. The computer should not be switched off before logging out.
- Audit trials should be carried out randomly (once or twice yearly) and at regular intervals (twice a year). The audit trial will perform a full check on the working of the system and is particularly useful for detecting input fraud, program alterations and output fraud.
- Computer output should be shredded if not required or if confidential.
- Personnel should sign for important documentation
- Proper care of floppy disks:
  - store away from electrical devices
  - store in disk boxes
  - never insert a disk in the disk drive before switching on the computer
  - always take the disk out before turning off the computer
  - never take a disk out when the drive is active
  - do not touch the surface of the disk
  - disks should be labelled clearly.
- Digruntled staff should be closely monitored.
- No employee should be put into a situation where there is a 'conflict of interest', e.g. a bank employee updating his/her own account.
- Personnel must follow legislation regarding data storage, e.g. The Data Protection Act 1988.

The Data Protection Act 1988
The eight principles of The Data Protection Act 1988 are as follows:
1. Personal data should be obtained and processed fairly and lawfully.
2. Personal data should only be held for a lawful purpose.
3. Personal data should not be disclosed.
4. Personal data should be adequate, relevant and not excessive.
5. Personal data should be accurate and kept up-to-date.
6. Personal data should not be kept longer than deemed necessary.
7. An individual is entitled at reasonable intervals and without undue delay to find out
   - whether information is held about that individual
   - what the content of the information is
   and where appropriate, the individual can have the data edited or erased.
8. Appropriate measures should be used to limit access to personal data or for the destruction of personal data.

To ensure adherence to this Act the following procedures should be adopted:
- Store only essential information.
- Improve the security of data using methods outlined above.

- Identify data elements which are sensitive, in particular, personal details and monetary data.
- Adopt a policy of regularly updating information.
- Anticipate change — when designing or purchasing new software ensure that it takes into account future anticipated changes or that it is flexible.

6. 4 Improving the Information Technology Environment for Users — Ergonomics

Ergonomics is the study of work environments with a view to improving employee comfort and in turn employee productivity.

Ergonomic considerations were thought of as luxuries in the past. Today ergonomic considerations are now a management responsibility , enforceable by law. This is especially true with the passing the of the EC directive (90/270/EC) on Display Screen Equipment which came into force on 1st January 1993.

The regulations have six major requirements.

1. Analysis of workstations

Every employer must perform a suitable and sufficient analysis of user workstations to assess the risks which they may pose for the health and safety of users. Any risks identified must be reduced.

Common risks are:
- eyes (strain and glare)
- musculoskeletal (posture)
- mental stress
- space problems.

An ergonomics checklist can be very useful for analysing the workstations.

2. Requirements for workstations

These include:
- equipment should be adjustable
- glare-free working conditions
- software suitable for the task.

3. Daily routine for users

Users should where possible have a mix of screen based and non-screen based work or, if this is not possible, the provision of breaks in work routine is essential.

4. Eyes and eyesight

Users have the right to request an eyesight test at their employers expense. If it is found that corrective appliances are required for display screen work, then the employer is liable for the cost.

5. Provision of training

All users of work stations must be provided with adequate training in the areas of software use and health and safety issues.

6. Provision of information

All employers are required to ensure that all relevant information available is provided to users of work stations.

The diagram below shows a workstation that is ergonoically designed.

AN ERGONOMICALLY SOUND WORK STATION

Questions

MCQ · *Multi-choice questions*

1. Which of the following is the smallest computer system?
   (a) megacomputer
   (b) minicomputer
   (c) mainframe
   (d) microcomputer

2. A monitor is —
   (a) an output device
   (b) an input device
   (c) a peripheral device
   (d) an item of hardware
   (e) all of the above

3. The CPU consists of —
   (a) control unit, ALU and main storage
   (b) ROM, RAM and ALU
   (c) main storage
   (d) chips

4. ROM is —
   (a) non-volatile
   (b) storage
   (c) permanently required
   (d) all of the above

5. Typically, how many bits are there in one byte?
   (a) 4
   (b) 2
   (c) 65
   (d) 8

6. Which of the following disks holds most information?
   (a) 130 mm (5.25 in.) disk
   (b) 90 mm (3.5 in.) disk
   (c) fixed (hard) disk
   (d) optical disk

7. Formatting a disk is usually done —
    (a) once before using a new disk
    (b) every time something is saved on the disk
    (c) every time the disk is full
    (d) to make a back-up copy of a file

8. The instructions that enable a computer to function are called —
    (a) hardware
    (b) applications
    (c) software
    (d) instructions

9. Which one of the following printers cannot produce letter-quality printing?
    (a) laser printer
    (b) ink-jet printer
    (c) dot-matrix printer
    (d) daisy-wheel printer

10. Which pair are the most commonly used input and output devices?
    (a) mouse, printer
    (b) keyboard, printer
    (c) VDE, monitor
    (d) keyboard, monitor

11. The information needed for long-term planning is called —
    (a) tactical
    (b) transactional
    (c) operational
    (d) strategic

12. Which of the following is not a utility?
    (a) copy file
    (b) format a disk
    (c) directory of contents of a disk
    (d) memory management

13. Where records are stored in order of their key fields the file organisation method is called —
    (a) index sequential
    (b) serial
    (c) sequential
    (d) random

14. Which of the following generations of languages requires the most detailed knowledge of computer hardware?
  (a) first generation
  (b) second generation
  (c) third generation
  (d) fourth generation

15. The software used to translate second generation languages to binary form is called —
  (a) assembler
  (b) compiler
  (c) interpreter
  (d) translator

16. The person who is responsible for the design of new computer systems is known as —
  (a) systems programmer
  (b) data processing manager
  (c) systems analyst
  (d) database administrator

17. Aertel is an example of —
  (a) teletex
  (b) teletext
  (c) telex
  (d) viewdata

18. A PABX is a form of —
  (a) telephone
  (b) modem
  (c) multiplexor
  (d) file server

19. The check digit for the code 4214 using division by 11 is —
  (a) 6
  (b) 5
  (c) 1
  (d) 39

20. Which of the following would not be used to combat input fraud?
  (a) passwords
  (b) monitoring disgruntled employees
  (c) virus protection
  (d) monitoring programs

sAQ · *Short-answer questions*

1. Name three types of computer system, and give an example of where each system is normally used.
2. What is an input device? Name six different input devices.
3. How is data inside the computer's memory represented?
4. What unit is computer capacity measured in?
5. What is a port?
6. What type of paper can a printer use?
7. List conditions likely to damage disks.
8. What is the function of the operating system, and how does it differ from application software?
9. What do the terms 'on-line' and 'off-line' mean? Give examples of on-line and off-line devices.
10. Explain the functions of ROM and RAM, and how they differ.

sQ · *Structured questions*

1. Information in an organisation is often classified as strategic, tactical and operational.
   (a) Take an organisation with which you are familiar (e.g. a company or college) and explain the nature of the strategic, tactical and operational information giving examples.
   (b) When communicating information to management, give five rules that should be observed so as to ensure that management will be satisfied with the information.
2. What method of data capture would you recommend as input to computer systems in each of the following situations:
   • time recording for employees in a company
   • multi-choice examination answers
   • sales orders in a mail order business.
   (a) Describe the main features of each method you would recommend for the applications given above.
   (b) Give possible advantages and disadvantages of each method described.
3. Describe the main features of any three output devices (other than printers) and indicate the most suitable application for each device.
4. (a) Explain what you understand by the term the 'modern electronic office' and explain the principal hardware features of such an office.
   (b) List the possible benefits of the modern electronic office.
5. Owing to a combination of errors including an electrical fault and an error made by an inexperienced operator the master file containing details of 10,000 insurance policy holders was destroyed.
   (a) Describe how this situation could be rectified if the master file was (i) on tape and (ii) on disk.
   (b) Describe what precautions should have been taken so that the above situation could have been avoided.

6. 'Computer networks are becoming extremely popular in business organisations today'.
   (a) List the main reasons why companies set up computer networks.
   (b) Describe, using diagrams, three network topologies.
   (c) Discuss the relative merits and demeritsof each topology.

EQ · *Examination questions*

National Council for Vocational Awards

Sample Paper 1994

Information Systems Level 2

Section A: Sample Objective Questions

1 For which of the following would a Batch Processing System be suitable?
   (i)   Testing interactive software
   (ii)   Preparing a payroll output
   (iii) Handling an on-line sales order system
   (iv)   Training by stimulation

2 The job of a systems programmer is to
   (i)   develop and maintain programs which are used by the operating system
   (ii)   assist the systems analyst in the design of computer systems, such as payroll
   (iii) develop and maintain programs written in a high level language, such as Cobol
   (iv)   document existing computer programs and systems, such as accounts packages

3 The purpose of spooling is to
   (i)   read or write to tape
   (ii)   rewind tape
   (iii) to make more efficient use of the CPU
   (iv)   compact tape contents

4 One result of the use of the Grandfather–Father–Son technique is that
   (i)   storage space is saved
   (ii)   security copies of files are saved
   (iii) the computer can work more quickly
   (iv)   the operator can work more quickly

5 In a disk pack, what is the name given to the total area which can be written to or read from with one setting of the read/write heads?
   (i)   Sector
   (ii)   Block
   (iii) Cylinder
   (iv)   Track

6 Which one of the following features describes a database management system?
- (i) Common data shared by programs
- (ii) Programs designed for managers
- (iii) Data owned by programs
- (iv) Data updated remotely

7 Which phrase describes a computer word?
- (i) A memory location containing characters
- (ii) A basic grouping of non-numeric data
- (iii) An unrelated collection of bytes contained within a CPU
- (iv) A basic grouping of bits handled as one unit

8 Which one of the following should query a date of '31st June' correctly keyed from a source document?
- (i) Verification
- (ii) Validation
- (iii) Compilation
- (iv) Interpretation

9 Which of the following sequences applies to batch processing?
- (i) Merge, sort, update, verify
- (ii) Validate, verify, sort, update
- (iii) Verify, validate, sort, update
- (iv) Verify, merge, archive, create

10 A multi-programming environment is one in which
- (i) Several users share the same peripherals
- (ii) A CPU performs two or more tasks simultaneously
- (iii) Two or more CPUs are connected together
- (iv) A CPU divides its time between several jobs

Section B: Sample Structured Questions

Q.1 Information Technology is at the heart of many modern business systems, which require many different types of information in order to be able to carry out their functions. Levels of Information within an organisation are sometimes referred to as being Tactical, Strategic or Operational.

(a) Outline the role of each of the following attributes of Information
- (i) Relevancy
- (ii) Timeliness
- (iii) Completeness
- (iv) Clarity

(b) Explain the differences between the terms Tactical, Strategic and Operational Information.

(c) Explain the concept of 'feedback', in regards to an organisation and its information requirements, illustrating, by means of an example, its importance.

Q.2 Your department has been allocated a sum of money to purchase a new printer. Having scanned the trade journals, looking for a suitable machine within the price range specified, a number of terms such as 'page printer', 'Letter-quality', 'inkjet', 'non-impact printer' and 'consumables' have caused some confusion to those responsible for selecting a printer.
(a) Explain the terms underlined above.
(b) Describe two printers that would be suitable, providing they meet the criteria: (i) relatively noiseless, (ii) able to produce both high quality graphics and text.

Q.3 Your organisation has decided to investigate data communications technology with a view to facilitating the transfer of data between other branches, customers' computers etc. You have been chosen to liaise between your own staff and the investigation team.
(a) Explain the terms 'Parallel interface' and 'Serial interface'.
(b) Explain what is meant by a Modulator/Demodulator, and why they are still necessary parts of most data communication systems.
(c) Identify a device used to enable more than one terminal/user access a single communications line.

Q. 4 Your organisation stores the majority of its data and information on magnetic disk. Access to this data is required to be provided both on a 'Batch-Processing' and 'On-Line' basis. Access rights will be dependent on the role of the user in the organisation, with security of the data-base a top priority.
(a) Explain the terms 'Batch Processing' and 'On-Line'.
(b) Explain what is meant by the terms 'Access Rights' and 'Data-base'.
(c) Provide four examples of threats to the security of data and recommend techniques or methods of counteracting these threats.

Q.5 There is a large variety of relatively new backing storage media available to the PC user currently, each of which offers advantages in comparison to its rivals. The available devices and the media include CD-ROM, WORMS, and Optical Erasable Disk. Your organisation is interested in exploring the potential of such media, as it requires the ability to store large amounts of textual data for archival purposes, as cheaply as possible, and with the ability to access stored data quickly.
(a) Explain what is meant by each of the underlined terms above
(b) Briefly compare and contrast CD-ROM and Optical Eraseable technologies, focusing on such factors as typical areas of use, average capacities and re-usability.
(c) Given the requirements that your organisation has for data storage and access, as specified above, select one of the three types of media mentioned, justifying your choice.

AQ · *Additional sample questions*

Q.1(a) Explain the terms: bit, byte, MB.
  (b) Compare and contrast the use of floppy disks and hard disks as secondary storage devices.
  (c) How much disk space would be required to store the personnel records of a large company which employs 10,000 people? Each record is 200 characters long.

Q.2 Compare and contrast dot matrix and laser printers under the following headings:
   (i)   method of operation
   (ii)   speed
   (iii) cost
   (iv)   quality
   (v)   advantages/disadvantages

Q.3 Describe what you understand by sequential and direct access file organisation. List the advantages, disadvantages and uses of each.

Q.4 Write notes on each of the following:
   (i)   Control Unit
   (ii)   ALU
   (iii) ASCII
   (iv)   RAM
   (v)   ROM

Q.5 What is an operating system?
   Describe the main functions carried out by an operating system.

Q.6 What is a computer network?
   What advantages has a network over stand alone computers?
   Describe three types of computer network.
   What is the most common type of PC network?

Q.7 (a) Describe the roles of the following data processing personnel:
        (i)   Computer Operator
        (ii)   Programmer
        (iii) System Analyst
    (b) Describe the main points of the Data Protection Act.

Sample Questions for Information Systems Examination 1994

1. In order for the output of a data processing system to be termed 'Information', it must possess attributes such as (fill in the blanks)
        (a) <   >
        (b) <   >
        (c) <   >
        (d) <   >

2. Information used by a manager to assess requirements, over the next few months, for bought-in terms and materials in a company which manufactures electrical appliance is known as <   > information.

3. Explain what is meant by 'feedback' in regards to an information system, and briefly outline its importance to the smooth operation of that system, including an example.

4. Explain, in no more than a sentence for each, the function of each of the main component parts of a CPU.

5. Write short notes on each of the following:
    (i)   MICR
    (ii)   Magnetic stripe cards
    (iii)   Bar codes
    (iv)   Dot matrix printers
    (v)   Microfiche

6. Compare and contrast barrel and laser printers, in relation to type and speed of output, overall versatility and areas of use.

7. Write short notes on each of the following:
    (i)   Cylinders
    (ii)   Update by overlay
    (iii)   Trailer labels
    (iv)   Hard sectored disks
    (v)   WORM storage

8. CD-ROM stands for <   >, can hold up to <   > bytes of data, and is normally used to contain <   > or <   > material.

9. Compare and contrast:
    (i)   RAM and ROM
    (ii)   Binary and decimal
    (iii)   Index sequential and random access file organisation
    (iv)   Systems and applications software

10. Describe four of the main functions carried out by an operating system.

11. Dot matrix printers are regarded as <   > printers, and have a major advantage over non-impact printers, such as laser printers, in that they can <   >.

12. Briefly describe at least four errors that could be caught by the use of data validation techniques.

13. Describe four methods that can be used to secure a system against threats, indicating the type of threat that each is designed to foil.

14. Compare and contrast the operation of an acoustic coupler with that of a modem.

15. Write short notes on each of the following:
    (i)   Rotational delay
    (ii)   Variable length records
    (iii)   Multiuser computers
    (iv)   Utility programs

16. Compare and contrast the two network types, star and bus, particularly in relation to the advantages and disadvantages of each system.

17. Compare and contrast data security and data integrity.

18. The Database Administrator is responsible for:
    (a) <   >
    (b) <   >
    (c) <   >
    (d) <   >

19. Write short notes on each of the following:
    (i)   Intelligent terminals
    (ii)   Electronic mail
    (iii)   Half duplex
    (iv)   Packet switching systems

20. Compare and contrast serial and parallel interfaces.

National Council for Vocational Awards

Information Systems Level 2, 1994

Section A
Answer all 20 questions

1   The capacity of a $3\frac{1}{2}$" DD floppy disk is
     a   360 K
     b   720 K
     c   1.2 MB
     d   1.44 MB

2   One Gigabyte is
     a   103 bytes
     b   104 bytes
     c   105 bytes
     d   106 bytes

3   A computer word is
     a   a memory location containing characters
     b   a basic grouping of non-numeric data
     c   an unrelated collection of bytes within a CPU
     d   a basic grouping of bits handled as one unit.

4   A boot or system disk is
     a   a new unused floppy disk
     b   a disk containing the FORMAT program
     c   a disk that can be used to start the computer
     d   a CD-ROM.

5   A laser printer cannot
    a   print text
    b   print graphics
    c   use multi-part stationery (NCR)
    d   print bar codes.

6   Which of the following is not system software
    a   COBOL compiler
    b   BASIC interpreter
    c   FORMAT program
    d   payroll package.

7   A program that converts a high level language into the 1s and 0s that can be understood by the computer is called
    a   an application package
    b   an operating system
    c   a compiler
    d   a function.

8   A multiprogramming environment is one in which
    a   several users share the same peripherals
    b   a CPU performs two or more tasks simultaneously
    c   two or more CPUs are connected together
    d   a CPU divides its time between several jobs.

9   A database management system is
    a   one large file containing all the company data
    b   a software system which maintains a database
    c   a series of separate files containing data
    d   a company payroll file.

10   Which of the following is usually an interpreted language?
    a   COBOL
    b   BASIC
    c   PASCAL
    d   C

11   Which of the following file organisations is most suitable for an airline reservation system?
    a   serial
    b   sequential
    c   index sequential
    d   direct access

12   Which of the following is not the job of a systems analyst?
    a   examining the feasibility of potential computer applications
    b   analysing existing computer requirements

c   maintaining the operating system

d   designing computer systems

13   One result of the Grandfather–Father–Son technique is that

a   storage space is saved

b   security copies of files are saved

c   the computer can work more quickly

d   the operator can work more quickly.

14   In a disk pack, what is the name given to the total area which can be written to or read from with one setting of the read/write heads?

(a)   sector

(b)   block

(c)   cylinder

(d)   track

15   For which of the following would a Batch Processing system be suitable?

a   testing interactive software

b   preparing a payroll output

c   handling an on-line sales order system

d   training by simulation

16   A modem is a piece of equipment used to connect

a   a mouse to a computer

b   a printer to a computer

c   a light pen to a computer

d   a computer to another computer via a telephone line.

17   The unit for measuring the speed of operation of a modem is

a   baud

b   bit

c   byte

d   ohm

18   A parallel interface is normally used to

a   connect a printer to a computer

b   allow simultaneous use of two computers

c   connect a mouse to a computer

d   convert an audio signal to a digital signal.

19   A file server is

a   a hard disk used to store user files

b   a computer connected to a file server

c   the computer on which the network software runs

d   a magnetic tape unit

20   Which of the following is not true of a FAX machine?
a   it must be connected to a computer
b   it is used to transmit text
c   it is used to transmit graphics
d   it must be connected to a telephone line.

Section B
Answer any four questions

1   Information systems are an integral part of the working of modern business. Good information is necessary for the efficient and profitable operation of a company.
(a)   Describe four characteristics of good information.
(b)   Typically information within an organisation can be classed into three levels. Name the three levels and explain the differences between them.

2   The following advertisement for a PC appeared in a national daily newspaper.
33 MHz 486SX
4 MB RAM
Super VGA
170 MB/15 ms access time hard disk drive
3 $\frac{1}{2}$" HD floppy disk drive
DOS 6.2, Windows 3.1 and mouse
A friend of yours wants to buy a PC for word-processing. He does not know a lot about computers and has asked you to
(a)   Explain the following terms and their significance:
MHz
RAM
VGA
Access time
Windows
(b)   Explain the difference between a hard disk drive and a floppy disk drive.
(c)   Decide if the above PC would be adequate for his word-processing needs. He needs to mix text, graphics and mathematical symbols in his documents. Give your reasons.

3   A small company is in the process of installing two PCs - one for word-processing and the other for doing the company's accounts. You have been given the job of buying two printers - one for each computer. Output from the accounts package needs to be printed on multi-part continuous stationery whereas the company secretary needs to print large volumes of high quality text and graphics.
(a)   What type of printer would you recommend for each application? Give your reasons.
(b)   Describe the method of operation of the types of printer you recommend.
(c)   Compare both types of printer under the following headings:
(i) Cost

(ii) Speed

(iii) Quality

(iv) Noise levels

4   You are employed by a company which specialises in networking. Your company has been approached by the manager of a small business which currently has 5 stand alone PCs. These are used for word-processing, spreadsheets, database and accounts. Somebody has told her that she should install a network. She wants you to explain to her:

(a)   What is a network?

(b)   What advantages does a network have over stand alone PCs?

(c)   What types of network are available?

(d)   Which type she should go for and why?

5   The new human resources manager in your company has been asked to recruit some staff for the data processing department and also to set up an employee database. Unfortunately she is not well versed in information technology and needs you to assist her. She needs you to:

(a)   Describe the roles of the following data processing personnel

(i)   Computer Operator

(ii)   Database Administrator

(iii) Programmer

(b)   Acquaint her with the main points of the Data Protection Act and its implications for the employee database she is setting up.

6   Your organisation stores most of its data on magnetic disk. This data is used in both 'Batch-Processing' and 'On-Line' modes. Access rights are dependent on the position of the user within the organisation, with security of the data a priority.

(a)   Explain the terms 'Batch-Processing' and 'On-Line'.

(b)   What is meant by 'Access Rights'?

(c)   Give four examples of threats to the security of data and recommend ways of counteracting these threats.

National Council for Vocational Awards

Information Systems Level 2, 1995

Section A
Answer all 20 questions

1   The capacity of a $3\frac{1}{2}$" HD floppy disk is

a   360 K

b   720 K

c   1.2 MB

d   1.44 MB

2   One Gigabyte is
   a   106 bytes
   b   107 bytes
   c   108 bytes
   d   109 bytes

3   Which of the following commands is used to format a boot or system disk?
   a   FORMAT A:
   b   FORMAT A:/b
   c   FORMAT A:/S
   d   FORMAT A:*B

4   Which of the following memory types **cannot** be changed once written?
   a   RAM
   b   ROM
   c   PROM
   d   EPROM

5   The capacity of a CD-ROM is approximately
   a   400 MB
   b   600 MB
   c   800 MB
   d   1000 MB

6   Which of the following is **not** part of MS-DOS?
   a   FORMAT program
   b   DISKCOPY program
   c   DEL command
   d   LS command

7   Which of the following is **not** applications software?
   a   payroll program
   b   spreadsheet
   c   database
   d   C compiler

8   A byte is a group of
   a   4 bits
   b   8 bits
   c   16 bits
   d   32 bits

9   Which of the following is **not** a direct access storage device?
   a   floppy disk
   b   hard disk
   c   magnetic tape
   d   CD-ROM

10 Seek time is
    a   the time to position the read/write heads of a magnetic disk
    b   the time to search a database
    c   the time to dial up a bulletin board
    d   the time to log in to a network

11 Which of the following is **not** a high level language?
    a   ASSEMBLER
    b   COBOL
    c   BASIC
    d   RPG

12 Which of the following file organisations is most suitable for a travel agent's holiday booking system?
    a   serial
    b   sequential
    c   index sequential
    d   direct access

13 Who in the following list would perform system backups?
    a   computer manager
    b   computer operator
    c   database administrator
    d   programmer

14 What type of system is most suitable for controlling the environment in a green house?
    a   batch
    b   on line
    c   real time
    d   time-sharing

15 In a disk pack, what is the name given to the total area which can be written to or read from with one setting of the read/write heads?
    a   sector
    b   track
    c   channel
    d   cylinder

16 Which of the following is the RTE teletext service?
    a   CEEFAX
    b   MINITEL
    c   AERTEL
    d   EIRPAC

17 Duplex is a data transmission term which means that
    a   transmission is possible in one direction only

b   transmission is possible in both directions, but not simultaneously

c   transmission is possible in both directions simultaneously

d   transmission is not possible

18   Which of the following does **not** translate source code into object code?

a   assembler

b   compiler

c   interpreter

d   multiplexor

19   The instruction set of a computer consists of

a   the set of machine instructions which the computer can perform

b   the language compilers that will run on the computer

c   the operating systems that will run on the computer

d   the operating system commands that are available

20   In which of the following microprocessor has a bug been discovered recently?

a   386 DX

b   486 SX

c   486 DX

d   Pentium

Section B
Answer any four questions

1   Generally there are three levels of management in an organisation:- top management, middle management and junior management. Each management level requires good information.

(a)   Explain the meaning of the term information.

(b)   Name and describe the type of information that is required by each management level.

(c)   List five characteristics of good information.

2   Your brother is studying data processing as part of his accountancy course. He is having difficulty in understanding the various components of a computer system. He has asked you to help him. In particular he wants you to

(a)   Explain the functions and operation of the components listed below

(i)   Control unit

(ii)   Main Storage

(iii) ALU

(iv)   Backing store

(b)   Give two examples, other than the keyboard, of input devices. In each case describe where the input device might be used and give its advantages/disadvantages.

3   The three main types of printer supplied with micro computers are - laser, dot matrix and ink jet. As prices fall laser printers are becoming more popular but there are still valid reasons for buying the different types.

(a)   For each printer describe
    (i)   mode of operation
    (ii) quality of output
    (iii) typical speeds
    (iv) typical costs
(b)   Describe the advantages/disadvantages of each type of printer and give examples of situations where the different types are most suitable.

4   A computer without software is of no use. An operating system is necessary to allow the user to interact with the computer and language translators are necessary for software development.
(a)   Describe the main functions carried out by an operating system.
(b)   Identify the four generations of programming languages and list the advantages/disadvantages of each.

5   Companies are becoming increasingly dependent on the data contained in their computer systems. This data needs to be accurate and secure.
(a)   Describe four validation techniques which could be used at the data entry stage to guard against incorrect data being entered.
(b)   Give four examples of threats to the security of data and recommend ways of countering these threats.

6   The data communications consultancy for which you work was commissioned to recommend how a large company with offices in different locations might computerise its business. The report which was prepared contains terminology which the company managing director does not understand. You are to
(a)   Explain what a network is and describe the benefits of networking.
(b)   Describe the difference between a LAN and a WAN.
(c)   Explain what a modem is.
(d)   Explain what a serial interface is and indicate where it might be used.

Glossary of computer terms

access time: the amount of time to retrieve data from a storage device, measured from the instant of executing the command to retrieve data to the moment when the data is stored in a specified location.

ALU (arithmetic and logic unit): the part of the CPU that performs mathematical functions and logical decisions, such as deciding whether one number is greater than another.

application software: programs to perform specific tasks, such as word-processing or database management, as distinct from system software (operating system), which maintains and organises the computer system.

ASCII (American Standard Code for Information Interchange): a term sometimes used to describe the system of allocating code numbers to different characters.

assembler: software that translates low level languages to binary code.

auxiliary ('backing') storage device: hardware used to store information for later retrieval.

bar code: a distinctive pattern of lines printed on a product or label, usually containing a code for the product number and capable of being entered into the computer by means of a suitable scanner.

binary number: a number system using only the digits 1 and 0, and therefore capable of being represented inside a computer by means of the presence (1) or absence (0) of an electrical current or magnetic charge.

bit: one digit in a binary number, either 1 or 0; the minimum unit of information in a computer system.

block: a group a records or words treated as a logical unit of data.

byte: a collection of bits, usually eight, to represent a single character.

catalogue: a listing of details of the files stored on a disk.

character: any of the signs used in creating text, whether a letter, a numeral or a symbol.

compiler: software that translates high level languages to binary code.

computer: a machine that processes data and supplies results.

contingency ('back-up') copy: a duplicate of data or program files kept in case of loss of this information; should be up-dated regularly and only used in an emergency.

control unit: the part of the CPU that takes instructions in a given sequence and controls the movement of data inside the computer.

corruption: the accidental alteration of data stored on any storage medium.

CPU (central processing unit): the part of the computer that decodes instructions and controls the hardware used to execute them; it consists of the control unit, arithmetic unit, and main storage (memory).

cursor: a movable mark on the screen that shows where the next character will be displayed.

cursor keys: a group of keys that move the cursor left, right, up or down the display.

data: unprocessed source material.

default: an automatic option or value in a program that is used unless an alternative is specified (this term should not be confused with a fault of any kind).

direct access: a type of access used when reading information from a disk; the read–write head goes directly to the place on the disk where the data is stored.

directory: another term for 'catalogue'.

disk drive: an auxiliary storage device that enables data and programs to be stored and retrieved.

diskette/'floppy disk': a flexible plastic disk coated with a magnetisable material and enclosed in a plastic envelope or case.

dot-matrix printer: a printer that produces characters made up of patterns of dots.

dumb terminal: a VDU and keyboard link to a network. It has no local processing capability.

editing keys: a group of keys that perform specialised functions such as page up, page down, go to end of file, etc.

electronic mail (E-mail): facility to send messages directly from one computer to another or to a specific 'mail box'.

EPROM: erasable PROM (see below).

ergonomics: the study of the environment of work in order to improve efficiency.

file server: a computer which controls the sharing of resources in a network.

fixed (hard) disk: a rigid, non-removable disk coated in a magnetisable material.

formatting: the procedure used to prepare a blank disk before use for a particular computer; it divides the disk into sectors so that information can be stored and retrieved.

function keys: a group of keys that can be programmed to execute commands or to choose options.

hardware: the physical components of a computer system.

hit rate: the percentage of master file records that are updated in a update run.

information: processed data

input device: any hardware device that enables data to be transmitted from the source into the computer.

intelligent terminal: a VDU, CPU, keyboard link to a network. It has local processing capability.

inter block gap: a blank space between blocks of information on a magnetic tape.

interpreter: a line by line translator of high level languages to binary code (used mainly on small microcomputers).

keyboard: an input device with a systematic arrangement of keys, used for entering instructions and data.

kilobyte (kb): a unit of 1,024 bytes (sometimes rounded to 1,000).

laser printer: a high-quality printer that uses a method of reproduction similar to a photocopier and prints whole pages at a time.

light pen: an input device used in conjunction with a screen to choose commands or data.

local area network (LAN): a network confined to one local site.

mainframe computer: the largest type of computer, capable of being used by many people at the same time.

megabyte (Mb): a unit of 1,0048,576 bytes (sometimes rounded to 1 million).

menu: a list of the options available at any stage in the execution of a program.

MICR (magnetic-ink character recognition): an input system that allows magnetic characters (usually found on cheques) to be read into a computer.

microcomputer: a self-contained desk-top computer built around a microprocessor and that can be used by only one person at a time; sometimes called a 'personal computer' (PC).

microprocessor: an integrated circuit or 'microchip' that contains the ALU and control unit of a computer.

minicomputer: a medium-sized computer system, usually used by one department or a medium-sized company.

modem (modulator/demodulator): hardware required to convert a digital signal to a telephone signal and vice versa.

monitor: an output device like a television set that shows the stages in the operation of a program and displays the results; sometimes called a 'visual display unit' (VDU).

mouse: an input device housed in a palm-sized case used for pointing to commands or icons on the screen; the movement of the mouse on the desk-top corresponds to the movement of the cursor on the display, and one or more buttons on the mouse can be used to select options or execute commands.

multiplexor: hardware used to split and connect different communication lines.

network: a group of computers linked together to communicate or share resources.

NLQ (near-letter-quality): a simulation of high-quality printing on a dot-matrix printer.

OCR (optical character recognition): an input system that reads printed or typewritten characters.

off-line: not under the direct control of the CPU.

OMR (optical mark recognition): an input device that can recognise the presence or absence of a mark.

on-line: under the control of the CPU.

operating system: all the software used to operate and maintain the computer system and utilities.

operational information: information required for day-to-day operations.

optical disk: an auxiliary storage device similar to a compact disk.

output device: any hardware device that enables computer data to be displayed, transmitted or printed.

parallel port: a communications port that allows information to be received or transmitted in groups of bits.

parity bit: a bit appended to a byte. The state of the bit is such as to ensure that the parity is consistently either even or odd.

port/communications port: an external socket allowing peripheral devices to be connected to a computer.

printer: an output device that produces printed text or graphics on paper.

PROM: programmable ROM (see below).

RAM (random-access memory): an area of electronic storage inside the computer used to hold current data and programs; information is constantly read from and written to this memory area.

ROM (read-only memory): an area of electronic storage used to hold instructions essential to the running of the computer; it is not possible to write to this area.

scanner: a method of access used with magnetic tape, where files are stored one after another and information is retrieved by rapid winding or rewinding until the required files are found.

sector: a storage area on a disk.

seek time: the amount of time taken by a disk drive to move its head from one track to another.

serial port: a communications port that allows bits of data to be received or transmitted one after the other.

software: another name for programs.

strategic information: information required for long-term planning.

tactical information: information required to plan for the medium term.

teletext: one-way information service using the television airways.

track: one of the concentric rings of data on a magnetic disk.

utility program: part of operating software which allows the user to carry out standard procedures such as formatting, copying files etc.

validation: a procedure carried out by a computer to check if the data is complete and reasonable.

VDE (voice data entry): an input system that responds to the human voice.

VDU (visual display unit): another name for a monitor.

verification: a method of checking that the original data has been correctly entered. It often involves rekeying data.

viewdata: interactive information service via telephone connection.

wide area network (WAN): a network which spans over a wide area and is connected using telephone lines and other communication links.

Chapter 2

INTRODUCTION TO DATA-BASES

What is the next available flight to New York? What is the current exchange rate for the Canadian dollar? Are there any rooms available at a certain hotel?

To answer these questions we may have to consult a travel agent, a bank clerk, and the hotel receptionist, respectively. It is unlikely, however, that they will know these answers immediately. They may have to consult their respective data-bases.

What is a data-base?

A data-base is an organised collection of related information. It usually consists of one or more files that may be related to one another.

What is a file?

A file is a collection of similar records.

An employment agency, Bestmatch Recruitment, holds a personnel file on people looking for suitable employment. For simplicity, we will assume that there are only six people on the agency's file at present:

Table

NAME	ADDRESS	PHONE_NO	SEX	JOB	YEARS
MURPHY P	6 GREENORE PK	4449234	M	SECRETARY	2
HOPKIRK L	16 KILKENNY RD	8349042	F	SECRETARY	3
MAHER K	56 MAIN ST	8899593	M	CHEF	0
GREENE A	55 WICKLOW RD	5231772	F	ACCOUNTANT	10
BURNS J	57 HAZEL RD	7783924	M	CHEF	2
OWENS M	56 ASHE ST	4931448	F	PHARMACIST	4

The information on each of the people seeking employment is arranged under these headings:

NAME: the person's name (surname and initial);
ADDRESS: the person's home address;
PHONE_NO: the person's home telephone number;
SEX: the person's sex;
JOB: the job sought;
YEARS: the number of years' experience the person has of this work.

(Note that there is an underline character rather than a space in 'PHONE_NO': this is because some data-base programs need the parts of a heading to be joined together so that the computer can treat them as one word, and this character is the one usually used.)

What is a record?

A record is a complete unit of related data items organised in named fields. In our example, the information held on each person seeking a job is stored in a separate record. The third record in our file holds information on Kevin Maher.

What is a field?

A field is a space for a specified item of information in a record. In our example, 7783924 (a specific item of information) is held in the PHONE_NO field of the fifth record of the file. The content of a field is often referred to as a **data item**.

Why is information now stored in computer data-bases?

Information, stored in a computer data-base, can be:

(a) found extremely quickly, e.g. the number of three-bedroom houses in a certain area can be extracted from an estate agent's file;

(b) sorted and re-sorted quickly and efficiently, e.g. a personnel file can be sorted in chronological order of the date that each employee joined a company;

(c) kept up-to-date very easily, e.g. adding new member and erasing lapsed member details on a golf club membership file;

(d) used by other applications, e.g. the names and addresses of customers in a customer file can be extracted and used in producing mailshots by a word processor.

In summary, a data-base may consist of one or more files. Each file consists of a number of records, and each record comprises a number of fields.

Holding a data-base on computer

In order to hold a data-base on computer, we need a data-base program or **data-base management system** (DBMS). On a microcomputer, this is a program that allows us to store information in a data-base, as well as to edit, organise or retrieve that information.

The data-base program is like our own private librarian, who looks after our data-base and carries out any editing, organising or retrieval requests from us.

We now examine how to set up a data-base on a computer and how we can carry out various activities on the file, under the following headings:

1. Defining the data entry form
2. Entering data into the file
3. Editing the file
4. Searching the file
5. Displaying selected fields
6. Sorting the file

7. Indexing the file
8. Changing the record structure
9. Performing mathematical operations
10. Creating reports

1. Defining the data entry form

Before we enter a new file into our computer data-base, we must define the data entry form.

A data entry form is a screen layout resembling a form that displays only one data record a time, which makes it easier to enter and edit data.

We must decide the following:

(a) the heading of each field within the record structure, e.g. NAME, ADDRESS;

(b) the maximum width of each field. The longest address is 16 KILKENNY RD, so we must define a field width of 14 for the ADDRESS field to accommodate this address;

(c) the data type: **alphabetic** (letters only), **numeric** (numbers only), or **alphanumeric** (a combination of letters and numbers). In our example the NAME field is alphabetic, the YEARS field is numeric and the ADDRESS field is alphanumeric.

We would now give our data-base program the following information about our personnel file:

FIELD	FIELD NAME	FIELD WIDTH	DATA TYPE
			Table
1	NAME	9	Alphabetic
2	ADDRESS	15	Alphanumeric
3	PHONE_NO	7	Numeric
4	SEX	1	Alphabetic
5	JOB	10	Alphabetic
6	YEARS	2	Numeric

This is the record structure for the file. The corresponding data entry screen is displayed below:

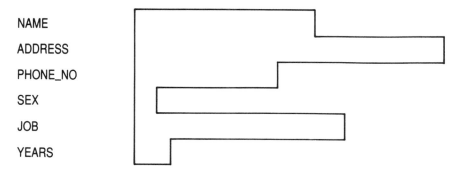

2. Entering data into the file

Once we have defined our data entry form, we must now enter data into the file. It is usually entered without punctuation.

It is important that data be entered consistently: in the YEARS field you must not enter '2' in one record and 'two' in the next. This can cause problems when you wish to search or sort the file later. You must take care at this stage, as incorrect data can be entered accidentally.

When you have entered all the data, the file can be displayed on the screen, or printed, and should appear as follows:

Table

NAME	ADDRESS	PHONE_NO	SEX	JOB	YEARS
MURPHY P	6 GREENORE PK	4449234	M	SECRETARY	2
HOPKIRK L	16 KILKENNY RD	8349042	F	SECRETARY	3
MAHER K	56 MAIN ST	8899593	M	CHEF	0
GREENE A	55 WICKLOW RD	5231772	F	ACCOUNTANT	10
BURNS J	57 HAZEL RD	7783924	M	CHEF	2
OWENS M	56 ASHE ST	4931448	F	PHARMACIST	4

3. Editing the file

Once we have set up our file on computer, we can add new records or delete unwanted records. We can also change the contents of individual records in the file.

Adding and deleting records

Let us assume that we have just received the following information about a person who is looking for a job:

Table

Name	Address	Phone	Sex	Job	Years
Aidan McCann	32 Shannon Park	8568264	M	Mechanic	7

We can select the command or option in our data-base program to add a new record to the file. A data entry form appears on the screen, and we simply enter the appropriate details. Let us also say that Kevin Maher finds a suitable job and no longer requires the agency's services. We can delete his record from the file by using the command or option to delete a record in our data-base program.

The file will now appear as follows:

NAME	ADDRESS	PHONE_NO	SEX	JOB	YEARS
MURPHY P	6 GREENORE PK	4449234	M	SECRETARY	2
HOPKIRK L	16 KILKENNY RD	8349042	F	SECRETARY	3
MAHER K	56 MAIN ST	8899593	M	CHEF	0
GREENE A	55 WICKLOW RD	5231772	F	ACCOUNTANT	10
BURNS J	57 HAZEL RD	7783924	M	CHEF	2
OWENS M	56 ASHE ST	4931448	F	PHARMACIST	4
MCCANN A	32 SHANNON PK	8568264	M	MECHANIC	7

Changing the contents of records

Using the appropriate command or option, we can display a record and then delete or insert various items of information.

Let us say that Aisling Greene has moved to 68 Shannon Park, and her new telephone number is 8568234. Also, a mistake was made in the name field of the second record: the name should be Hopkins, not Hopkirk.

When we have made these changes, the file will appear as follows:

NAME	ADDRESS	PHONE_NO	SEX	JOB	YEARS
MURPHY P	6 GREENORE PK	4449234	M	SECRETARY	2
HOPKINS L	16 KILKENNY RD	8349042	F	SECRETARY	3
MAHER K	56 MAIN ST	8899593	M	CHEF	0
GREENE A	68 SHANNON PK	8568234	F	ACCOUNTANT	10
BURNS J	57 HAZEL RD	7783924	M	CHEF	2
OWENS M	56 ASHE ST	4931448	F	PHARMACIST	4
MCCANN A	32 SHANNON PK	8568264	M	MECHANIC	7

4. Searching the file

One of the really useful features of having files stored on a computer data-base is the ease and speed with which we can search for information. As records are numbered according to their position in a file, we can cause a particular record to be displayed. We can also display or print all those records that meet a certain condition or set of conditions.

Searching for records by their position in the file

We can select the appropriate command or option to display record 3 in the personnel file:

RECORD NO.	NAME	ADDRESS	PHONE_NO	SEX	JOB	YEARS
3	GREENE A	68 SHANNON PK	8568234	F	ACCOUNTANT	10

Searching for records using one condition

Let us say that Bestmatch Recruitment get a telephone call from a company's personnel officer looking for a secretary. We can search the file for the records containing details of secretaries. We follow these steps:

(a) select the option or command for searching the file;

(b) choose the correct field for our search: the JOB field;

(c) enter the job we are searching for: SECRETARY;

(d) some programs may then require the user to give an 'execute' command to start the search.

The results of this search may appear as follows:

NAME	ADDRESS	PHONE_NO	SEX	JOB	YEARS
MURPHY P	6 GREENORE PK	4449234	M	SECRETARY	2
HOPKINS L	16 KILKENNY RD	8349042	F	SECRETARY	3

Searching for records using more than one condition

We can obtain details of those people on our file who are female and who have more than three years' experience in their chosen career, by carrying out the following steps:

(a) select the option or command for searching the file;

(b) choose the field for our first search condition: the SEX field;

(c) enter the sex for which we are searching: FEMALE;

(d) choose the field for our second search condition: the YEARS field;

(e) select the greater-than operand (>) and enter 3;

(f) some programs may then require the user to give an 'execute' command to start the search.

Once the request has been carried out, the results may appear as follows:

NAME	ADDRESS	PHONE_NO	SEX	JOB	YEARS
GREENE A	68 SHANNON PK	8568234	F	ACCOUNTANT	10
OWENS M	56 ASHE ST	4931448	F	PHARMACIST	4

Searching for records using variable symbols

Sometimes we may have to search a file without knowing the precise conditions under which we are performing the search. This can be done by using **variable symbols** (sometimes called 'wild cards'). These are characters (for example ? or *) that the program interprets as 'any character'.

Let us say that someone whose details are on the personnel file has just phoned the agency. The receptionist takes the caller's telephone number and assures her that the manager will return the call within the hour. The manager, however, loses the telephone number, but remembers the first three digits: 834. The data-base program will allow him to search the file for the details of any person whose telephone number starts with 834.

The steps taken to carry out this type of search on most data-base programs are as follows:

(a) select the option or command for searching the file;
(b) choose the correct field for the search: the PHONE_NO field;
(c) enter the portion of the data entry that we know: 834;
(d) fill the remainder of the field with the variable symbol: ****;
(e) some programs may then require the user to give an 'execute' command to start the search.

The result of this search on th personnel file will be displayed as follows:

HOPKINS L	16 KILKENNY RD	8349042	F	SECRETARY	3

5. Displaying selected fields

Another feature of a data-base program is its ability to display only a certain number of fields. This is useful when our records contain a large number of fields.

We may wish to display only the NAME, JOB and YEARS fields of all the records in the file. These are the steps we take:

(a) select the option or command that enables us to select the fields that we want displayed;

(b) select the fields in the order in which we would like them displayed;

(c) then select the command or option to execute the 'display selected fields' facility.

The result should appear as follows:

NAME	JOB	YEARS
MURPHY P	SECRETARY	2
HOPKINS L	SECRETARY	3
GREENE A	ACCOUNTANT	10
BURNS J	CHEF	2
OWENS M	PHARMACIST	4
MCCANN A	MECHANIC	7

It is possible to combine the 'display selected fields' and search facilities.

We may wish to display the NAME, ADDRESS and JOB fields of all those records belonging to the males on file. In order to carry this out we must:

(a) select the fields to be displayed: NAME, ADDRESS and JOB;

(b) select the option or command for searching the file;

(c) choose the field for the search condition: the SEX field;

(d) enter the sex for which we are searching: MALE;

(e) some programs may then require the user to give an 'execute' command to start the search.

The result should appear as follows:

NAME	ADDRESS	JOB
MURPHY P	6 GREENORE PK	SECRETARY
BURNS J	57 HAZEL RD	CHEF
MCCANN A	32 SHANNON PK	MECHANIC

6. Sorting the file

Another useful feature of our computer data-base is the ease with which we can sort the records. In this section we examine the following methods:

• alphabetic sorting
• numeric sorting
• reverse sorting
• multi-level sorting
• group sorting.

Most data-base programs would normally allow us to sort a file in the following way:

(a) select the option or command for sorting;

(b) select the key field (this is a field chosen by the user on which sorting will be carried out);

(c) use the option or command to choose whether we wish to sort the records in ascending order (with text this is the same as alphabetical order) or descending order. The default setting in most data-base programs is ascending order.

Alphabetical sorting

Let us assume that we wish to sort the records by name, in alphabetical order. The NAME field will thus be the key field. The results of this sort may be displayed as:

NAME	ADDRESS	PHONE_NO	SEX	JOB	YEARS
BURNS J	57 HAZEL RD	7783924	M	CHEF	2
GREENE A	68 SHANNON PK	8568234	F	ACCOUNTANT	10
HOPKINS L	16 KILKENNY RD	8349042	F	SECRETARY	3
MCCANN A	32 SHANNON PK	8568264	M	MECHANIC	7
MURPHY P	6 GREENORE PK	4449234	M	SECRETARY	2
OWENS M	56 ASHE ST	4931448	F	PHARMACIST	4

Numeric sorting

We can sort the file by number of years' job experience of each person. The YEARS field will be chosen as the key field. The sorted file will then appear as follows:

NAME	ADDRESS	PHONE_NO	SEX	JOB	YEARS
MURPHY P	6 GREENORE PK	4449234	M	SECRETARY	2
BURNS J	57 HAZEL RD	7783924	M	CHEF	2
HOPKINS L	16 KILKENNY RD	8349042	F	SECRETARY	3
OWENS M	56 ASHE ST	4931448	F	PHARMACIST	4
MCCANN A	32 SHANNON PK	8568264	M	MECHANIC	7
GREENE A	68 SHANNON PK	8568234	F	ACCOUNTANT	10

Reverse sorting

The file, as it appears above, is sorted in ascending order of number of years' job experience of each person. We can also sort the file in descending order, again using the YEARS field as the key field. The sorted file will now appear as:

Table

NAME	ADDRESS	PHONE_NO	SEX	JOB	YEARS
GREENE A	68 SHANNON PK	8568234	F	ACCOUNTANT	10
MCCANN A	32 SHANNON PK	8568264	M	MECHANIC	7
OWENS M	56 ASHE ST	4931448	F	PHARMACIST	4
HOPKINS L	16 KILKENNY RD	8349042	F	SECRETARY	3
MURPHY P	6 GREENORE PK	4449234	M	SECRETARY	2
BURNS J	57 HAZEL RD	7783924	M	CHEF	2

Multi-level sorting

In our examples we have been sorting on one field: either the NAME field or the YEARS field. It is possible, however, to sort on a number of fields at the same time.

If we are sorting on two fields, the first field we select is the **primary sort field** and second is the **secondary sort field**. We can now sort our file using the SEX field as the primary key field and the NAME field as the secondary key field. The result would be as follows:

Table

NAME	ADDRESS	PHONE_NO	SEX	JOB	YEARS
GREENE A	68 SHANNON PK	8568234	F	ACCOUNTANT	10
HOPKINS L	16 KILKENNY RD	8349042	F	SECRETARY	3
OWENS M	56 ASHE ST	4931448	F	PHARMACIST	4
BURNS J	57 HAZEL RD	7783924	M	CHEF	2
MCCANN A	32 SHANNON PK	8568264	M	MECHANIC	7
MURPHY P	6 GREENORE PK	4449234	M	SECRETARY	2

As F comes before M in the alphabet, all the female entries are listed first, in alphabetical order, then the male entries in alphabetical order.

Group sorting

We can select a particular group of records from the file and display this group sorted on one or more fields. We may wish to have all records of those people who have more than two years' experience sorted alphabetically by name, and then displayed.

Some data-base programs may allow us to sort the file using the NAME field as the key field and then search the sorted file for all those people with more than two years' experience. Other programs may allow us to extract the records of those people with more than two years' experience and then sort these records into alphabetical order. The result, in either case, should appear as follows:

ECA Table

NAME	ADDRESS	PHONE_NO	SEX	JOB	YEARS
GREENE A	68 SHANNON PK	8568234	F	ACCOUNTANT	10
HOPKINS L	16 KILKENNY RD	8349042	F	SECRETARY	3
MCCANN A	32 SHANNON PK	8568264	M	MECHANIC	7
OWENS M	56 ASHE ST	4931448	F	PHARMACIST	4

7. Indexing the file

When we sort a data-base file, the records are physically sorted by the computer into the order required. We have seen, in an earlier example, that the records are numbered according to their position in the file.

ECA Table

NAME	ADDRESS	PHONE_NO	SEX	JOB	YEARS
BURNS J	57 HAZEL RD	7783924	M	CHEF	2
GREENE A	68 SHANNON PK	8568234	F	ACCOUNTANT	10
HOPKINS L	16 KILKENNY RD	8349042	F	SECRETARY	3
MCCANN A	32 SHANNON PK	8568264	M	MECHANIC	7
MURPHY P	6 GREENORE PK	4449234	M	SECRETARY	2
OWENS M	56 ASHE ST	4931448	F	PHARMACIST	4

We can get a print-out of the file sorted on the NAME field:

Many computer data-base programs offer an alternative to sorting, namely **indexing**. We can get a computer print-out of our unsorted file:

RECORD NO	NAME	ADDRESS	PHONE_NO	SEX	JOB	YEARS
1	MURPHY P	6 GREENORE PK	4449234	M	SECRETARY	2
2	HOPKINS L	16 KILKENNY RD	8349042	F	SECRETARY	3
3	GREENE A	68 SHANNON PK	8568234	F	ACCOUNTANT	10
4	BURNS J	57 HAZEL RD	7783924	M	CHEF	2
5	OWENS M	56 ASHE ST	4931448	F	PHARMACIST	4
6	MCCANN A	32 SHANNON PK	8568264	M	MECHANIC	7

If we index our file using the NAME field, the records themselves are not ordered. Instead, the numbers of the records are ordered in a small file called an 'index file'. As BURNS would head the list in alphabetical order, the first number in the index file would be 4, because this person's record is the fourth record in the file. The index file in this case would contain the following list of numbers: 4, 3, 2, 1, 6, 5.

When we activate this index file and then request a print-out, we would obtain the following:

RECORD NO	NAME	ADDRESS	PHONE_NO	SEX	JOB	YEARS
4	BURNS J	57 HAZEL RD	7783924	M	CHEF	2
3	GREENE A	68 SHANNON PK	8568234	F	ACCOUNTANT	10
2	HOPKINS L	16 KILKENNY RD	8349042	F	SECRETARY	3
6	MCCANN A	32 SHANNON PK	8568264	M	MECHANIC	7
1	MURPHY P	6 GREENORE PK	4449234	M	SECRETARY	2
5	OWENS M	56 ASHE ST	4931448	F	PHARMACIST	4

The records are printed according to the order of the numbers in the index file. Frequent data-base users rarely use sorting and prefer indexing, as index files can be activated very quickly. Sorting a large file can take some time.

Another advantage of using indexing rather than the sorting facility is that some database programs, when sorting a file, set up a completely new file, and copy the records across to this new file in sorted order. We would then have two files containing exactly the same information stored on our disk — one sorted and one unsorted. In this case indexing is obviously preferable to sorting, as index files will take up a much smaller amount of disk space than sort files. The indexing facility is not available on all data-base programs.

8. Changing the record structure

Sometimes, after we have defined the record structure of a file and entered information into it, we may wish to change the record structure. This could be for one or more of the following purposes:
- adding a new field
- deleting an existing field
- changing the order of fields
- widening fields
- changing field names.

The commands and techniques to change the record structure vary, depending on the data-base program you are using. As you proceed through this section you should check the appropriate command or technique to undertake a particular change to the record structure.

Changing the field width

The field width of the NAME field in our example was set at 9 in order to accommodate the longest name, which was HOPKINS L. The field is not wide enough, however, to allow us to include the first names. If we include the first name instead of the initial, Aisling Greene has the longest name: we need a field width of 14 to accommodate this name.

When we have redefined the field width of the NAME field to 14 and edited the file to include the first names, it will appear as follows:

NAME	ADDRESS	PHONE_NO	SEX	JOB	YEARS
BURNS JOHN	57 HAZEL RD	7783924	M	CHEF	2
GREENE AISLING	68 SHANNON PK	8568234	F	ACCOUNTANT	10
HOPKINS LIZ	16 KILKENNY RD	8349042	F	SECRETARY	3
MCCANN AIDAN	32 SHANNON PK	8568264	M	MECHANIC	7
MURPHY DANIEL	6 GREENORE PK	4449234	M	SECRETARY	2
OWENS MARY	56 ASHE ST	4931448	F	PHARMACIST	4

Deleting a field from the record structure

As we have the telephone number of each person on file, there is little need for a field that includes the address. We will use the commands specific to our data-base program to deletethis field from the record structure. The file would then appear as follows:

NAME	PHONE_NO	SEX	JOB	YEARS
BURNS JOHN	7783924	M	CHEF	2
GREENE AISLING	8568234	F	ACCOUNTANT	10
HOPKINS LIZ	8349042	F	SECRETARY	3
MCCANN AIDAN	8568264	M	MECHANIC	7
MURPHY DANIEL	4449234	M	SECRETARY	2
OWENS MARY	4931448	F	PHARMACIST	4

Adding a new field to the record structure

As companies often phone the agency from various towns looking for staff in their own area, we might include a TOWN field for the home town of each person on file. When we have set up this new field and included the appropriate details, our file would appear as follows:

NAME	TOWN	PHONE_NO	SEX	JOB	YEARS
BURNS JOHN	TRIM	7783924	M	CHEF	2
GREENE AISLING	NAVAN	8568234	F	ACCOUNTANT	10
HOPKINS LIZ	DROICHEAD NUA	8349042	F	SECRETARY	3
MCCANN AIDAN	MONAGHAN	8568264	M	MECHANIC	7
MURPHY DANIEL	CAVAN	4449234	M	SECRETARY	2
OWENS MARY	TRALEE	4931448	F	PHARMACIST	4

Changing a field name

We can change the name of the field that includes each person's occupation from JOB to CAREER.

Changing the order of fields

We may wish to move the YEARS field so that it appears second in the record structure. When we have made these final two changes to our record structure, our personnel file will now appear as follows:

NAME	YEARS	TOWN	PHONE_NO	SEX	CAREER
BURNS JOHN	2	TRIM	7783924	M	CHEF
GREENE AISLING	10	NAVAN	8568234	F	ACCOUNTANT
HOPKINS LIZ	3	DROICHEAD NUA	8349042	F	SECRETARY
MCCANN AIDAN	7	MONAGHAN	8568264	M	MECHANIC
MURPHY DANIEL	2	CAVAN	4449234	M	SECRETARY
OWENS MARY	4	TRALEE	4931448	F	PHARMACIST

Careful planning

The facilities for changing a record's structure are very useful but should be used sparingly. A prudent data-base user will always plan the record structure of a new file on paper before defining it on computer. A little early planning with field names and field widths will save a lot of alterations to the record structure later.

9. Performing mathematical operations

Two useful facilities offered by most data-base programs are:
(a) the ability to perform one of the four basic mathematical operations (add, subtract, multiply or divide) on the data items of two or more numeric fields and to place the result in another field;
(b) the summation function.

Performing mathematical operations on data items

Set up the following file on your computer. It contains details of goods that are for sale at Jim's Electrical Superstore. The file consists of five records, and each record has four fields:
ITEM: the name of the electrical item;
COST: its cost price;
QUANTITY: the number in stock;
RETAIL: its retail price.
The file's contents are as follows:

ITEM	COST	QUANTITY	RETAIL
WASHING MACHINE	250.00	7	318.00
REFRIGERATOR	400.00	3	625.00
VIDEO RECORDER	290.00	8	428.00
TELEVISION	350.00	4	520.00
VACUUM CLEANER	180.00	2	245.00

We can quite easily change the record structure to include two new fields:
PROFIT: the data item in this field will be the profit obtained on the sale of one item, and can be obtained by the simple formula 'retail minus cost', which subtracts the contents of the COST field from the contents of the RETAIL field for each of the five records; VALUATION: the data item in this field will be the total value of all items of a particular type, for example the total value of all television sets. The valuation is obtained by a formula, 'cost multiplied by quantity', which multiplies the contents of the COST field by the contents of the QUANTITY field for each of the five records.

When you have set up the file containing the two fields, it should look like this:

⬧E⬧C⬧A⬧ *Table*					
ITEM	COST	QUANTITY	RETAIL	PROFIT	VALUATION
WASHING MACHINE	250.00	7	318.00	68.00	1750.00
REFRIGERATOR	400.00	3	625.00	225.00	1200.00
VIDEO RECORDER	290.00	8	428.00	138.00	2320.00
TELEVISION	350.00	4	520.00	170.00	1400.00
VACUUM CLEANER	180.00	2	245.00	65.00	360.00

The summation function

Most data-base programs have a summation function, which allows us to sum fields. Let us say that someone wishes to buy all five of the items listed in the file. We can use the summation function to obtain the total value of the data items in the RETAIL fields of the five records. We get:

> 5 records summed on the RETAIL field
> Total = £2,136.00

As we will see in the next section, the summation of fields can be carried out automatically when we generate reports.

10. Creating reports

A report is any meaningful information retrieved from a data-base and displayed or printed. Strictly speaking, all the output from the two files outlined in this chapter are reports. Most data-base programs, however, are equipped with a **report generator**. This is a facility that allows us to design the presentation of the output from a data-base file. The report generator can also total columns of numeric data automatically.

The following is a print-out of a report generated on the electrical shop file:

	ECA Table				

JIM'S ELECTRICAL SUPERSTORE VALUATION REPORT

ITEM	COST	QUANTITY	RETAIL	PROFIT	VALUATION
WASHING MACHINE	250.00	7	318.00	68.00	1750.00
REFRIGERATOR	400.00	3	625.00	225.00	1200.00
VIDEO RECORDER	290.00	8	428.00	138.00	2320.00
TELEVISION	350.00	4	520.00	170.00	1400.00
VACUUM CLEANER	180.00	2	245.00	65.00	360.00
TOTAL		24			7030.00

SUMMARY

In this chapter we have examined the main facilities of a data-base program. Most of these facilities should be available on your program.

We have dealt with the simplest type of data-base, the **flat-file** data-base. This is one where all the files are treated individually by the program and are not linked in any way.

Glossary of data-base terms

batch processing: the technique of updating a file at one time with all the transactions that have occurred in a given period.

data-base: a collection of related information about a subject, organised in a way that provides the means for retrieving and sorting the information, drawing conclusions and making decisions.

data-base management system (DBMS): a computer program used for creating data-bases and that provides the tools for inserting, retrieving, modifying and deleting information and for producing relevant reports from the data-base.

data entry form: a form layout on the screen that facilitates the entering of information into a data-base file. Only one record is displayed at a time, and the fields within each record are usually listed vertically.

field: a space for a specified piece of information in a record.

file: a collection of similar records.

fixed-length field: a field that is capable of holding a predetermined maximum number of characters.

fixed-length record: a record that is capable of holding a predetermined number of fixed-length fields.

flat-file data-base: a data base in which all the files are treated individually by the program and are not linked in any way.

flat-file data-base program: a program that stores, organises and retrieves information from one file at a time.

index: a small file containing 'pointers' or information about the physical location of records in a data-base file. When searching or sorting, the data-base program uses the index rather than the full data-base.

microfiche: a form of microfilm in which documents are photographically reduced and copied onto small sheets of film.

microfilm: an information storage system in which documents are photographically reduced and copied onto 16 mm film strip.

multi-level sort: a sort that uses two fields, a primary sort field and a secondary sort field, to determine the order in which records are arranged.

multi-user system: a system that allows more than one person to have access to the data-base program and files at the same time.

programmable data-base: a data-base system that has its own programming language, allowing the user to structure files and reports according to specific needs.

random access: a method that allows the system to retrieve information by going directly to a specific part of a disk rather than having to go through all the preceding tracks and sectors.

real-time processing: the technique of updating a file when the operator is 'on-line' to the CPU and the updating is carried out immediately by the computer.

relational data-base: a data-base system that can link two or more files together through at least one common field. Such a program allows the user to update two or more linked files simultaneously in the same operation.

sequential file: a file in which the records are arranged in a particular order, usually ascending or descending order of key field.

serial file: a method in which the records in a file are not physically arranged in any particular order on a disk or tape.

sort: an operation that arranges data in a particular order.

variable-length field: a field whose length varies according to the contents of the field at a particular time.

variable-length record: a record in which the number of fields may vary from that of other records in the same file. Variable-length records usually consist of variable-length fields.

Chapter 3

PRACTICAL DATA-BASE ASSIGNMENTS

These assignments are graded, and we advise that you work through them in the order in which they are given.

Guidelines for students

Unless the actual assignment specifies otherwise, the following guidelines apply.

1. The data entry screen

A properly formatted data entry screen must be created for each assignment.
- All fields must have suitable field names.
- There should be two fields per line on the data input screen. (In the case of an odd number of fields, the last field will obviously stand alone.)
- The input screen should have a centred title at the top.
- There is no need for borders or other effects.

2. Entering data

Care must be taken when entering data into a file and the following rules apply:
- Commas in numbers must not be entered, e.g. enter 10300 instead of 10,300.
- Currency amounts must be entered as values in numeric fields, e.g. enter 2.85 instead of £2.85.
- Where field names consist of two separate words these should be joined by an underscore, e.g. Age Profile should appear as Age_Profile.

3. Creating reports

Assignment 12 onwards specifies the production of report formats.
- The field names used on data entry screens will suffice as column headings in reports.
- Do not, unless specifically asked, perform any mathematical calculations on any numeric fields (e.g. averaging or totalling).

Functions and commands required

As you progress through these assignments you will need to check the commands, functions, icons and pull-down menus specific to your data-base program. You will also be practising commands and techniques learned in earlier assignments. (Note: if you do not have access to a printer, you can display the result of the task instead.)

The new work involved in each assignment is as follows:

ASSIGNMENT 1
- Creating a file
- Designing the data entry form
- Entering data
- Editing the contents of individual records
- Adding a new record
- Deleting an existing record
- Saving the file

ASSIGNMENT 2
- Consolidation assignment

ASSIGNMENT 3
- Consolidation assignment

ASSIGNMENT 4
- Searching on one condition

ASSIGNMENT 5
- Searching on two conditions

ASSIGNMENT 6
- Searching on three conditions
- Displaying selected fields for all records

ASSIGNMENT 7
- Combining the 'displaying selected fields' facility with a one-condition search

ASSIGNMENT 8
- Combining the 'displaying selected fields' facility with a two-condition search
- Sorting a file in alphabetical order on one field

ASSIGNMENT 9
- Sorting a file in ascending numerical order on one field
- Using the global replace facility

ASSIGNMENT 10
- Searching on four fields
- Sorting a file in descending numerical order on one field
- Organising a file on one field using the indexing facility (if possible)

ASSIGNMENT 11
- Deleting a field
- Inserting a new field
- Creating and saving a subset of a file

ASSIGNMENT 12
- Producing a report format

ASSIGNMENT 13
- Sorting a file chronologically
- Developing mailing labels

ASSIGNMENT 14
- Sorting on primary and secondary fields

ASSIGNMENT 15
- Producing a grouped report format

ASSIGNMENT 16
- Consolidation assignment

ASSIGNMENT 17
- Consolidation assignment

ASSIGNMENT 18
- NCVA sample data-base methods examination paper

ASSIGNMENT 19
- NCVA data-base methods past examination paper

ASSIGNMENT 20
- NCVA data-base methods past examination paper

ASN · *Assignment 1*

You are required to set up a file containing information on eight students. The information on each student falls under the following six headings: name, age, sex, telephone number, area and class.

In data-base language you must set up a file of eight records, each record consisting of six fields. When defining the record structure, the field name and width for each field are as follows:

Field	Field name	Width
1	Name	10
2	Age	2
3	Sex	1
4	Phone	7
5	Area	11
6	Class	3

Once you have set up your record structure **and** designed a suitable data entry screen with the heading 'Student Record', you should enter the following information into the file:

Name	Age	Sex	Phone	Area	Class
Maher R	17	M	5612431	Ballyfermot	LW1
Andrews K	16	F	2977116	Dundrum	AC2
Stephens G	18	F	8346002	Beaumont	LW1
O'Brien P	17	F	4977701	Rathgar	ST1
Byrne S	18	M	7679061	Sutton	CM1
Williams M	19	M	4511782	Kimmage	AC2
Conway C	16	F	8360890	Glasnevin	ST1
Doyle E	18	M	4566102	Crumlin	CM1

Carry out the following tasks:
Save:
1. all the details to a file called STUDENT1.
Make the following alterations to the relevant records:
2. Andrews is male and lives in Rathmines.
3. Conway is 17 years old.
4. E Doyle is a student in ST1 and not CM1.
Delete:
5. P O'Brien's record from the file.
Add:
6. the following information on a new student who has just joined the school: D Ryan, 16, male, 8453222, Cabra, LW1.

Save:

7. this edited version of the file as STUDENT2.

ASN · *Assignment 2*

The following is a list of information on eight films that are available for rental from Leisure Video Ltd:

Title	Category	Lead	Length	Cert	Price
Jurassic Park	Thriller	Sam Neill	120	15	£2.00
Pretty Woman	Comedy	Julia Roberts	115	12	£1.50
Schindler's List	Drama	Ben Kinglsey	187	18	£2.50
Speed	Action	Keanu Reeves	111	15	£2.00
The Lion King	Cartoon	Simba	101	12	£1.50
Unforgiven	Western	Clint Eastwood	125	15	£2.50
Forrest Gump	Comedy	Tom Hanks	136	12	£2.50
Circle of Friends	Drama	Minnie Driver	115	15	£2.00

The information on each film includes its title, category, leading actor or actress, running time, suitability certificate and rental cost. You are required to transfer this information to a data-base file on your computer. The record structure for the file is as follows:

Field	Field name	Width
1	Title	17
2	Category	9
3	Lead	14
4	Length	3
5	Cert	2
6	Price	5

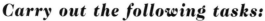

Carry out the following tasks:

Save:

1. the file to disk as FILM1.

Make the following alterations to the relevant records:

2. *Jurassic Park* is best described as an *adventure* film.

3. The leading role in *Schindler's List* was played by *Liam Neeson*.

4. The running time for *The Lion King* is only *87* minutes.

5. The cost of renting *Forrest Gump* is only *£2.00*.

6. Leisure Video Ltd have withdrawn *Unforgiven*. Erase the record on this film from the file.

Add:

7. the following information on two more films:

ᴇ ᴄ ᴀ Table

Title	Category	Lead	Length	Cert	Price
The Flintstones	Comedy	John Goodman	87	12	£2.50
Wyatt Earp	Western	Kevin Costner	183	15	£2.00

Save:

8. this edited version of the file as FILM2.

ᴀꜱɴ · *Assignment 3*

Getaway Travel Ltd, specialists in sun holidays, have just given you the following details on available bookings:

ᴇ ᴄ ᴀ Table

Country	Resort	Price	Day	Time	Flight	Places
Turkey	Kusadasi	445	Thursday	08:00	TK63	19
Portugal	Faro	610	Sunday	15:00	PO71	6
Spain	Marbella	390	Friday	00:30	SP16	0
Greece	Kos	575	Tuesday	06:30	GR95	3
Malta	Valetta	525	Friday	11:00	MA52	8
Spain	Salou	435	Sunday	18:00	SP23	12
Cyprus	Limassol	480	Saturday	09:30	CY48	2
Morocco	Agadir	415	Sunday	14:30	MO91	15

You are required to transfer this information to a data-base file on your computer.

Carry out the following tasks:

Save:

1. the file to disk as HOLIDAY1.

Make the following alterations to the relevant records:

2. The departure time for the Portuguese holiday should be 19:00.
3. The price of the holiday in Malta should only be £385.
4. There are only 8 places left on the Spanish holiday in Salou.
5. The holiday in Cyprus should be in Paphos and not Limassol.
6. The departure day for the Moroccan holiday should be Friday.
7. As the holiday in Marbella, Spain is fully booked, delete this record from the file.
8. Information on two other holidays must be added to the file. The details are as follows:

◇E◇C◇A◇ Table

Country	Resort	Price	Day	Time	Flight	Places
Greece	Corfu	460	Thursday	21:00	GR97	23
Portugal	Penina	585	Saturday	17:30	PO73	18

Save:

9. this edited version of the file to disk as HOLIDAY2.

ASN • Assignment 4

Express Couriers Ltd, based in Dublin, delivers items nationwide. Articles are classified as high (H), medium (M) or low (L) priority and are billed accordingly. Sandra Cosgrave, the managing director of the company, wishes to hold delivery details on a computer data-base file. You are requested to create the file and enter the following details:

◇E◇C◇A◇ Table

Item	Sender	Location	Recipient	Cost	Priority
Garden shed	Davy's DIY	Galway	P O'Dea	£42.00	M
Books	Reader's Heaven	Birr	T Dooley	£16.00	L
Wedding dress	Zoe's Boutique	Sligo	A Walsh	£50.00	H
Computer	Bits & Bytes Ltd	Galway	S O'Sullivan	£55.00	H
Dog kennel	Pet Mansions Ltd	Cork	G Dillon	£28.00	L
Satellite dish	DS Electrical Ltd	Dundalk	D McDonnell	£22.00	L
Contact lenses	Vision Care Ltd	Tralee	L Sheehy	£30.00	H
Cello	Endless Chords	Limerick	R Patterson	£36.00	M
Sunbed	Body Tones	Cork	O Hayes	£25.00	L
Safe	MD Security Ltd	Cavan	M O'Reilly	£45.00	H

Carry out the following tasks:

Save:

1. the file as COURIER1.

Make the following alterations to the relevant records:

2. Padraig O'Dea ordered a lawn-mower and not a garden shed.
3. The charge for the delivery to Birr should be £19.00.
4. The satellite dish is a high priority delivery and the charge should be £42.00.
5. The Cello is to be collected from Waltons.
6. The sunbed should be delivered to O Hynes in Tuam.
7. The computer delivery has been cancelled. Remove this record from the file.

Add:

8. the following details on a new delivery to the file:

Item	Sender	Location	Recipient	Cost	Priority
Water cooler	Oasis Coolers	Galway	P Brogan	£65.00	H

Save:

9. this edited version of the file as COURIER2.

Display all the details of those deliveries:

10. which are high priority.
11. which go to Galway.
12. where the cost is less than £30.00.

ASN · Assignment 5

A hotelier who specialises in angling holidays has compiled information for her guests on all the lakes within 12 km of her hotel. She can give the name of any lake, its distance from the hotel, the presence of trout in the lake, the year it was last restocked with young fish, its floor type, its depth and the availability of boats.

The information available is as follows:

Lake	Distance	Trout	Restocked	Lake floor	Depth	Boat hire
Tully	4.0	N	1996	Sand	10.2	N
Gulladoo	3.7	Y	1995	Sand	13.5	Y
Carrigallen	0.5	N	1996	Mud	8.5	N
Garadice	11.3	Y	1994	Sand	15.4	Y
Woodford	4.6	Y	1996	Mud	11.9	N
Glasshouse	2.6	Y	1995	Mud	10.3	Y
Keeldra	6.4	N	1994	Sand	9.6	N
Errew	13.8	Y	1996	Sand	13.0	Y
Killegar	3.2	N	1996	Mud	8.8	N
Cullies	4.4	N	1994	Mud	11.3	N

You are required to set up a data-base file on your computer containing the above information, using the headings given above as field names.

Carry out the following tasks:
Save:
1. the file as LAKES1.
Make the following alterations to the relevant records:
2. The distance to Tully lake, as given in the file, is by an old unapproved road. The actual distance from the hotel to this lake by the new road is 5.5 km, and this distance should be given in the file.
3. Trout are not present in Woodford lake but are present in Cullies lake.
4. Keeldra lake was last restocked with young fish in 1996.
5. The maximum depth of Garadice lake has been measured incorrectly. Members of a visiting sub-aqua club have discovered an underwater channel with a depth of 24.3 m, and this must now be reflected in the file as the maximum depth of this lake.
6. Errew lake is more than 12 km from the hotel and should not be listed. Erase this record from the file.
7. The hotelier, when compiling the information, overlooked an excellent trout lake that is only 7.2 km from the hotel. You must include its details in the file. The information is as follows:

Lake	Distance	Trout	Restocked	Lake floor	Depth	Boat hire
Calloughs	7.2	Y	1996	Sand	14.1	Y

Save:
8. this edited version of the file as LAKES2.

Display all the details of those lakes:

9. where trout are present.
10. that have a lake floor of sand.
11. that are less than 4 km from the hotel **and** have boat hire.
12. that are more than 10 m deep **and** have a lake floor of mud.

Aꜱɴ · Assignment 6

The marathon, a race over 26 miles, is held each year in a certain city. To aid efficient running of the event the organisers hold the following information on each entrant: the athlete's name, vest number, age, sex, club, wheelchair user (Y/N), number of previous marathons run and the athlete's personal best time in a marathon.

 You are requested to set up a data-base file on computer containing the following details on ten marathon entrants using the headings given as field names:

⟨E C A⟩ Table

Athlete	Number	Age	Sex	Club	Wheelchair	Marathons	Time
P Brady	6783	19	M	Cavan	N	1	3.2
O Murphy	2910	24	F	Wexford	N	5	2.8
K Nugent	3420	37	M	Portlaoise	Y	6	3.1
R O'Brien	8003	21	F	Santry	N	8	3.0
C Murtagh	4430	29	F	Trim	N	2	3.9
H Greene	7821	36	M	Drimnagh	N	11	2.7
S Daly	9926	44	M	Longford	N	6	3.3
R McCann	3418	18	F	Tuam	Y	4	2.9
F Lynch	1099	32	M	Santry	N	7	3.5
M Quinn	6225	23	F	Thurles	N	9	3.1

Carry out the following tasks:
Save:
1. the file as MARATHON.
Display all the details of the entrant(s) who:
2. has vest number 4430.
3. are from the Santry club.
4. are more than 30 years of age.
5. have personal best times of less than 3 hours.

6. is male **and** is a wheelchair user.
7. is more than 30 years of age **and** has a personal best time of less than 3 hours.
8. are female **and** have run more than five marathons.
9. are under 25 years of age **and** are not wheelchair entrants **and** who have run more than one marathon to date.
10. Display the Athlete, Age and Club fields **only** for all the entrants in the file.

ASN · *Assignment 7*

Noeleen's Newsagents stock a wide range of magazines. Noeleen Mooney, the owner of the shop, holds the following information on each magazine in stock:
- the magazine name
- its category and price
- its frequency (weekly or monthly)
- quantity on order
- day of issue
- the number of copies which must be reserved
- whether the magazine is imported or not.

Noeleen wishes to hold the magazine details in a computer data-base file. You are employed to set up this file containing the information given below. You can use the headings given as field names.

ECA *Table*

Magazine	Category	Price	Frequency	Quantity	Day	Reserved	Import
RTE Guide	TV	£0.85	W	80	Wed	15	N
Vogue	Women's	£4.96	M	45	Wed	12	Y
Runner's World	Sport	£2.87	M	10	Mon	5	Y
PC Direct	Computing	£2.93	M	30	Tue	8	Y
TV Times	TV	£0.69	W	25	Sat	0	Y
Touchdown	Sport	£3.00	M	20	Mon	6	Y
U	Women's	£1.65	M	35	Wed	11	N
Carsport	Sport	£2.35	M	8	Fri	0	N
PC Plus	Computing	£4.56	M	50	Mon	25	Y
Garden Answers	Gardening	£2.18	M	25	Fri	3	Y
Irish Cycling	Sport	£1.50	M	5	Thu	0	N
Best	Women's	£0.68	W	20	Tue	5	Y

Carry out the following tasks:

Save:

1. the file as MAGAZINE.

Display all the details of the magazine(s) that:

2. are issued on a Wednesday.
3. are produced in Ireland.
4. are women's magazines **and** cost more than £1.00.
5. are issued weekly **and** are imported.
6. cost less than £1.00 **or** more than £3.00.
7. is issued on a Monday **and** costs less than £3.00 **and** is in the sport category.

Display:

8. the magazine name, category and price of all the magazines in the file.
9. the magazine name, category, price and quantity details of all the computing magazines in the file.
10. the magazine name, frequency, quantity, day and number reserved details of all the magazines that are reserved .

A$N • Assignment 8

Leinster Coach Hire Ltd, established in 1995, offers carefree and cost effective access to any part of the country. Each booking is recorded, at present, in the company's day log book. The following table shows the details of 12 separate bookings:

E C A Table

To	Purpose	Organiser	Date	Group	Age profile	Cost	Previous use?
Cork	Holiday	Greene P	04/10/96	22	1	£190.00	N
Knock	Pilgrimage	O' Connor K	15/09/96	83	5	£520.00	Y
Mosney	School tour	Daly T	14/06/96	38	3	£140.00	Y
Roscommon	Wedding	Cox D	18/08/96	14	2	£115.00	N
Killarney	Holiday	Cooney D	10/07/96	8	2	£85.00	Y
Blarney	Holiday	Mahon D	03/06/96	20	4	£175.00	N
Lough Derg	Pilgrimage	Galvin P	23/08/96	51	2	£330.00	N
Cavan	Fishing trip	Brennan M	25/07/96	12	2	£72.00	N
Belfast	School tour	Smyth J	28/06/96	60	3	£365.00	Y
Knock	Pilgrimage	Jones R	07/08/96	90	5	£600.00	N
Doolin	Field trip	Elsdon H	18/09/96	27	4	£280.00	Y
Galway	Holiday	Dunne C	18/08/96	9	1	£110.00	Y

Each booking shows:
- destination
- purpose of the coach hire
- organiser
- date of proposed trip
- number in the group
- age profile of the passengers
- cost of the booking
- whether a previous booking has been made by the organiser.

The age profile is recorded using a 1–5 code system: 1 — old age pensioners, 2 — adults, 3 — children, 4 — students and 5 — mixed.

You are required to set up a data-base file on your computer containing the information in the table above. You should use the headings given in the table as field names.

Carry out the following tasks:

Save:
1. the file as COACH.

Display all the details of the booking(s):
2. where there are more than 10 in the group **and** the age profile of the intending passengers is adult.
3. that were made for August.
4. that are either pilgrimages **or** holidays.
5. that are neither pilgrimages **nor** holidays.
6. where there are more than 50 intending passengers in the group **and** the cost is less than £500.00 **and** where previous bookings have been made.
7. made for a group of old age pensioners in October.

Display:
8. the destination, organiser, date and group details for any wedding bookings.
9. the destination, date and cost details for any bookings where the age profile of the group is either adult **or** mixed.

Sort:
10. the entire file in alphabetical order of the organiser's name.

Save:
11. this sorted file as COACH2.

ASN · Assignment 9

A maternity hospital holds the following information on new mothers:
- mother's name
- ward
- mother's age
- date of the birth
- sex of the baby

- weight of the baby in kilograms
- the number of children born to the mother
- VHI membership (Y or N)
- attending doctor.

Set up a data-base file on your computer holding the details on the ten mothers listed below. You can use the headings given as field names.

Mother	Ward	Age	Date	Sex	Weight	Child	VHI	Doctor
Mills D	St Peter's	22	3/9/96	F	2.9	1	Y	Dr Wilcox
O'Dea F	St Clare's	34	6/9/96	F	3.2	4	Y	Dr Evans
Willis P	St Anne's	29	6/9/96	M	3.0	1	N	Dr Evans
O' Hare Y	St Anne's	30	2/9/96	F	3.6	2	Y	Dr Kent
Sammon M	St. Anne's	41	3/9/96	M	2.9	5	Y	Dr Wilcox
O' Neill A	St Clare's	25	5/9/96	M	4.2	2	Y	Dr Kent
Molloy K	St Peter's	19	1/9/96	F	2.5	1	N	Dr Evans
Byrne L	St Anne's	33	5/9/96	M	3.7	1	Y	Dr Kent
Conway T	St Peter's	24	4/9/96	M	3.4	2	Y	Dr Kent
Quinn A	St Peter's	27	6/9/96	F	4.0	3	N	Dr Wilcox

Carry out the following tasks:

Save:
1. the file as BABY1.

Replace:
2. the ward name *St Peter's* with *St Mark's* in the file by using the global replace facility of your data-base program

Display all the details of the mother(s) who:
3. had baby girls and are in St Mark's ward.
4. are 30 years old or more **and** are being attended by Dr Kent.
5. had a baby girl weighing less than 4 kilograms on 6 September.

Sort:
6. the file into alphabetical order of mothers' names.

Save:
7. the sorted file as BABY2.

Display from the BABY2 file:
8. the name, age and attending doctor of those mothers who are not members of the VHI.

Sort:
9. the BABY2 file into ascending order of babies' weights.

Save:
10. this file as BABY3.
Display from the BABY3 file:
11. the name, ward, sex, weight and child details of those mothers whose new baby weighed 4 kilograms or less **and** who have more than one child.

ASN · *Assignment 10*

The Denver Pizza Company, established in 1996, supplies succulent American-style pizzas to homes all over Dublin. Nine items of information are held on each order received. Rick Baker, the owner of the company, wishes to transfer these order details to a computer database file. The information held on each order is as follows:
- customer's name and address
- the exact time that the order was placed
- the pizza type
- the pizza size — large (L), medium (M) or small (S)
- the base type — deep pan (DP) or light and crispy (LC)
- the number of toppings (Tpns) requested
- the price of the pizza
- whether or not the pizza was delivered.

Set up the data-base file on your computer containing the details in the table below. The headings in the table can be used as field names.

ECA Table

Customer	Address	Time	Pizza	Size	Base	Tpns	Price	Delivery
O' Brien G	4 Seacliff Rd	18:33	Hawaiian	L	DP	8	£10.15	Y
White M	51 Idrone Dr	17:51	Hot & Spicy	L	DP	3	£8.55	Y
McCann F	3 Elkwood St	18:55	Mighty Meaty	S	LC	5	£2.85	N
Wilson H	15 Wood Ct	18:03	Full House	L	LC	4	£6.20	Y
Brady A	9 Hill Gdns	18:24	BLT	M	LC	7	£4.25	Y
McHugh M	121 Myrtle St	17:46	Veggie's Delight	M	DP	3	£5.80	N
O'Reilly P	67 Russell Ave	18:15	Hawaiian	S	LC	8	£4.05	Y
Foley K	19 Kincora Rd	16:40	Original	L	DP	5	£8.80	Y
Cummins B	4 Church Ave	17:05	Bombay Double	S	DP	4	£5.20	N
Dowd P	22 Ludford Pk	18:37	Sicilian	S	LC	3	£2.05	Y
Maher R	156 Barry Rd	17:30	Mighty Meaty	L	DP	6	£8.90	N
Colgan E	10 Hilltop St	16:51	Original	M	DP	5	£6.55	Y

Carry out the following tasks:

Save:
1. the entire file as PIZZA1.

Display all the details of the order(s) for any:
2. medium original pizza.
3. large pizzas with five toppings or less.
4. small pizzas delivered after 18:00.
5. large deep pan pizzas that were delivered and cost less than £9.00.

Sort:
6. the file into chronometric (time) order.

Save:
7. the sorted file as PIZZA2.

Display:
8. the customer's name and address, the pizza type and the order time for all light and crispy pizzas that were delivered.

Sort:
9. the file into descending order of pizza prices.

Save:
10. this sorted file as PIZZA3.

Display:
11. the customer's name, the pizza type, size and price for all orders listed except those for Hawaiian **and** Original pizzas.
12. Produce, using the indexing facility of your program (if possible), a display of the entire file organised in alphabetical order of customer names.

ASN · *Assignment 11*

You are required to set up a data-base file containing information on the twelve countries listed below. The information on each country includes:
- the name of the country
- its population
- its area (in square kilometres)
- the capital city
- the principal language
- its unit of currency
- the highest point above sea level in metres (HP)
- the type of government (Govt)
- the main religion (Rel).

In the table, abbreviations have been used for the government types and main religions. The abbreviations for government types are as follows:
- constitutional monarchy — Cm
- federal republic — Fr
- constitutional republic — Cr

- Islamic republic — Ir
- multiparty republic — Mr

The abbreviations for the religions are:

- Christianity — Ch
- Islam — Is
- Judaism — Ju.

You can use the headings in the table as field names.

Country	Population	Area	Capital	Language	Currency	HP	Govt	Rel
Ireland	3,509,000	70,284	Dublin	English	Punt	1,041	Cr	Ch
UK	57,376,000	244,100	London	English	Pound	1,343	Cm	Ch
Germany	77,754,000	356,755	Berlin	German	Mark	2,963	Cr	Ch
USA	250,941,000	9,372,614	Washington	English	US dollar	6,194	Fr	Ch
Pakistan	122,666,000	796,095	Islamabad	Urdu	Rupee	8,611	Ir	Is
Brazil	150,368,000	8,511,965	Brasilia	Portuguese	Cruzeiro	3,014	Mr	Ch
Israel	4,616,000	20,770	Jerusalem	Hebrew	Shekel	1,208	Mr	Ju
Argentina	32,880,000	2,766,889	Buenos Aires	Spanish	Austral	6,960	Fr	Ch
Iran	56,923,000	1,648,000	Tehran	Farsi	Rial	5,604	Ir	Is
Peru	22,332,000	1,285,216	Lima	Spanish	Inti	6,768	Mr	Ch
Morocco	25,228,000	458,730	Rabat	Arabic	Dirham	4,165	Cm	Is
Sweden	8,523,000	449,964	Stockholm	Swedish	Krona	2,111	Cm	Ch

Carry out the following tasks:

Save:

1. the file as COUNTRY1.

Display all the details of any:

2. non-English speaking countries where Christianity is the main religion.
3. countries that are either constitutional **or** multiparty republics with populations of less than 50 million people.

Delete:

4. the field containing the details for the highest point above sea level from the file.

Insert:

5. a new field between the Currency and Govt fields to hold the per capita gross national product details for each country. The latter is expressed in US dollars. Use GNP as the field name.

Enter:

6. the following per capita GNP details for each country into the new field in each record: Ireland — $8,500, UK — $14,570, Germany — $20,750, USA — $21,100, Pakistan —

$370, Brazil — $2,550, Israel — $9,750, Argentina — $2,160, Iran — $4,500, Peru — $1,090, Morocco — $900, Sweden — $21,170.

Sort:

7. the file into descending order of per capita GNP.

Save:

8. the sorted file as COUNTRY2.

Extract:

9. from the COUNTRY2 file all the details of countries whose per capita GNP is less than $US 10,000.

Save:

10. this subset to a new file called COUNTRY3.

Recall:

11. the original COUNTRY1 file to the screen.

Sort:

12. this file into alphabetical order of country names.

Save:

13. this sorted file as COUNTRY4.

Print:

14. the entire COUNTRY4 file.

ASN · *Assignment 12*

MountainView Business Park is home to twelve different companies. Pat Cash, the manager of the park, holds the following details on each company:

Company — the company's name

Business — its line of business

Owner — the owner of the company

Established — the year that the company was set up

Type — whether it is a service (S) or manufacturing (M) company

Employees — the number of staff

Premises — whether the company's premises are owned (O) or rented (R)

Export — whether the company exports its products (Y or N).

You must enter the details in the table on p. 107 into a data-base file using the italicised words above as field names.

Absel Drilling	Concrete drilling	Stone D	1992	S	12	R	N
HomeWorld	Kitchens	Brady P	1996	M	7	O	N
Curtex Blinds	Window blinds	Curtain R	1994	M	21	O	Y
Moo-moo Foods	Dairy Products	O' Grady K	1992	M	43	O	Y
Elegant Rooms	Interior design	Ashley A	1996	S	5	R	N
P Murtagh & Co.	Architects	Murtagh P	1990	S	9	O	N
GA Ices	Ice cream	O' Grady K	1995	M	18	O	N
Cans and all	Recycling	Tidy D	1993	M	26	R	N
Which Way?	Brass signs	Knowles S	1995	M	8	R	N
Little Ones	Children's clothes	McEniff B	1994	M	35	O	Y
EasyClean	Carpet cleaning	Waters B	1996	S	4	R	N
Jetwash	Pressure washers	Richards M	1996	M	15	R	Y

Carry out the following tasks:

Save:

1. the file as COMPANY1.

Display:

2. the company names and owners for all companies set up prior to 1996.

Insert:

3. a new *telephone* field after the owner field.

Enter:

4. the telephone number of each company: Absel Drilling — 21988, HomeWorld — 32751, Curtex Blinds — 30887, Moo-moo Foods — 21997, Elegant Rooms — 32880, P Murtagh & Co. — 20017, GA Ices — 31634, Cans and all — 24119, Which Way? — 31772, Little Ones — 30955, EasyClean — 32859, Jetwash — 30910.

Sort:

5. the file into descending order of the number of staff employed.

Save:

6. the sorted file as COMPANY2.

Extract:

7. from the COMPANY2 file all the details of the non-exporting companies who own their own premises.

Save:

8. this subset to a new file called COMPANY3.

Print:

9. the COMPANY3 file.

Recall:

10. the original COMPANY1 file to the screen.

Sort:

11. the file into alphabetical order of company name.

Save:

12. this sorted file as COMPANY4.

Create:

13. a report format, using the COMPANY4 file, that has the heading 'MountainView Business Park' and shows the company names, respective owners and respective numbers of employees.

Assign:

14. the name BUSPARK to the report.

Print:

15. the report.

ASN • Assignment 13

Ticketron Ltd take bookings for various entertainment events. Details of each booking are held on a record card. A blank record card looks like this:

TICKETRON LTD

NAME .... ROAD.....................

AREA .... COUNTY ....

EVENT .... VENUE ....

TYPE .... PRICE ....

DATE .... TICKETS ....

CREDIT CARD ....

The type field shows whether the event is a concert (C), a play (P) or a sporting (S) occasion. The credit card field shows whether the booking was made by credit card (Y/N). Set up a data-base file on your computer and enter the following details of eight separate bookings:

Nolan P	22 Clogher Rd
Crumlin	Dublin 12
The Mai	Peacock
P	£10.00
26/08/96	2
Y	

Hoey A	9 Muirhevna Rd
Dundalk	Co Louth
R.E.M	Slane
C	£25.00
21/07/96	1
Y	

Cahill F	12 Farnham St
Cavan	Co Cavan
Wrestlemania	Point
S	£20.00
29/08/96	1
N	

Keran P	High St
Ballinamore	Co Leitrim
Elton John	RDS
C	£22.00
08/09/96	4
Y	

Daly S	65 Greenlea Rd
Terenure	Dublin 6
The Cranberries	Millstreet
C	£15.00
07/07/96	2
Y	

Murphy M	85 Glanmire Rd
Cork	Co Cork
Big Maggie	Gaeity
P	£8.00
25/06/96	3
Y	

Quinn J	8 Main St
Clifden	Co Galway
Feile	Pairc Ui Caoimh
C	£45.00
21/07/96	2
N	

Fox P	34 Ennis Rd
Limerick	Co Limerick
Sive	Abbey
P	£12.00
19/07/96	2
Y	

Carry out the following tasks:

Save:

1. the file as TICKET1.

Organise (using the sort or indexing facilities):

2. the file into chronological (date) order.

Save:

3. the index or sort file as TICKET2.

Extract:

4. from the organised file all the details of those bookings made by credit card for events in July.

Save:

5. this subset to a new file called VISA.

Print:

6. the VISA file.

Recall:

7. the original TICKET1 file to the screen.

Sort:

8. the file into ascending order of event type (primary key) and alphabetical order of name (secondary key).

Save:

9. this sorted file as TICKET3.

Create:

10. a report format, using the TICKET3 file, that has the heading 'Ticketron Ticket Sales' and shows only the name, road, area, county, event and number of tickets. Do not total the number of tickets in the report.

Save:

11. this report as TICKETRP.

Re-sort:

12. the TICKET3 file into reverse chronological order.

Save:

13. this new sorted file as TICKET4.

Develop:

14. suitable mailing labels (name, road, area and county) from the TICKET4 file with two labels across the page.

Save:

15. the mailing labels to a file called LABELS.

Print:

16. the mailing labels.

A$_N$ • *Assignment 14*

Autoline Insure Direct PLC, based in Cork, provides car insurance for drivers of all ages. Details of each insured driver are currently held in paper files. A blank insurance card from the files would appear as follows:

Autoline Insure Direct PLC
Driver Insurance Card

Name ....   Policy No. ....

Car ....   Model ....

Premium ....   Category ....

Reg. No. ....   Expiry date ....

Claim ....   Full licence ....

Two fields on this card require explanation:
- *Category* — the type of insurance bought. This may be fully comprehensive (Co), third party, fire and theft (Tt) or third party (Tp).
- *Claim* — whether the driver has claimed on a policy during the past five years (Y/N).

You are given the following details on eight different drivers that are insured with the company:

Hughes Mary	MP0987
Nissan	Almera
96-CN-559	12/09/97
£722	Co
N	Y

Silke Sean	MO1009
Volkswagen	Vento
94-LS-6712	31/10/97
£458	Tt
N	Y

Murphy Noel	MP7812
Toyota	Carina
96-D-4599	02/09/97
£1,239	Co
Y	Y

Nugent Kathy	SK2388
Renault	Clio
96-WX-1008	19/04/97
£355	Tp
N	Y

Larkin Brenda	MO7661
Toyota	Starlet
95-MO-812	25/09/97
£640	Tt
N	N

Moore Owen	RD4556
Volkswagen	Passat
96-LM-88	15/08/97
£550	Co
N	Y

Keegan James	SK9948
Ford	Mondeo
95-C-9120	30/09/97
£1,085	Tt
N	N

Evans Sandra	MP8110
Nissan	Micra
94-KE-226	28/06/97
£970	Co
Y	Y

Set up a data-base file on your computer and enter the details given. Your data entry screen should look identical to the record card shown on p. 110 (the border is optional).

Carry out the following tasks:

Save:

1. the file as POLICY1.

Extract:

2. a subset of records from the file that consists of all policies that expire during September **and** October 1997.

Save:

3. this subset to a new file called SOPOLICY.

Sort:

4. the POLICY1 file into alphabetical order of category (primary key) **and** descending order of premium (secondary key).

Save:

5. the sorted file as POLICY2.

Extract:

6. a subset of records from the POLICY2 file that consists of all the details for drivers who have bought either third party **or** third party, fire and theft policies.

Save:

7. this subset to a new file called POLICY3.

Produce:

8. a report format from the POLICY3 file showing all the fields with the heading 'Non Fully Comprehensive Policies'.

Save:

9. this report as POLRPT1.

Retrieve:

10. the POLICY1 file.

Sort:

11. this file into reverse alphabetical order of driver name.

Save:

12. this sorted file as POLICY4.

Extract:

13. from the POLICY4 file all the details of policies on cars that were registered before 1996.

Save:

14. this subset to a new file called PRE96.

Produce:

15. a report format from the PRE96 file that has the heading 'Old Car Policies' and shows the driver's name, car, model, expiry date and premium only. This report should also show the average premium for the listed policies.

Save:

16. this report as OLDERCAR.

Print:

17. this latter report.

A$N · *Assignment 15*

Irish Estates Ltd provides details of farms for sale throughout Ireland. The following details are held on each farm:
- Auctioneer — handling the sale
- County — where the farm is located
- Code — each farm has a unique code
- Acres — number for sale
- Type — Beef, dairy, mixed or tillage farm
- Price — seller's reserve price
- Lots — the farm may be divided into several lots
- Frontage — along the roadside (Fr)
- Dwelling house — on the land (Dw).

Set up a data-base file containing the details in the table below. The data input screen should have the centred title 'Irish Estates Ltd' and there should be three fields per line. Choose appropriate field names.

E C A *Table*

Auctioneer	County	Code	Acres	Type	Price	Lots	Fr	Dw
Trim Agri-sales Ltd	Meath	M244	8	Beef	£25,000	1	N	N
O'Shea Properties	Cork	D397	212	Dairy	£750,000	1	Y	Y
Cody & Daughter	Kilkenny	T098	103	Tillage	£315,000	2	Y	Y
Mahon Estates	Louth	M249	27	Beef	£65,000	1	Y	N
Brady & Co	Cavan	J884	77	Dairy	£190,000	1	Y	N
McHale & Co	Mayo	C452	67	Mixed	£132,000	2	Y	Y
O'Shea Properties	Kerry	D391	45	Mixed	£110,000	3	Y	Y
Mahon Estates	Meath	M230	12	Beef	£45,000	1	N	N
Wilson & Sons	Wexford	H348	52	Tillage	£150,000	2	Y	N
Brady & Co	Cavan	J763	32	Beef	£80,000	1	Y	N
Green Acres Ltd	Tipperary	K019	150	Dairy	£410,000	1	Y	Y
Mahon Estates	Meath	M238	80	Dairy	£225,000	3	N	Y

Carry out the following tasks:
Save:
1. the file as FARM1.
Extract:
2. from the file the county, acres, price and auctioneer fields **only** for any dairy farm listed.
Save:
3. this subset to a new file called MILKFARM.

Print:

4. the MILKFARM file.

Extract:

5. from the original FARM1 file the county, acres, lots, dwelling house and price fields (in that order) for all non-dairy farms costing £150,000 or less.

Save:

6. this subset to a new file called NONMILK1

Sort:

7. the NONMILK1 file into descending order of farm size (acres).

Save:

8. this sorted file as NONMILK2.

Produce:

9. a report format from this file showing the acres and price fields. The report should have the centred heading 'Non-Dairy Farms'. The report should also highlight the price of the cheapest farm listed.

Save:

10. this report as FARMREP1.

Modify:

11. the report to include the dwelling house field.

Save:

12. this modified report as FARMREP2.

Recall:

13. the original FARM1 file to the screen.

Sort:

14. the file into alphabetical order of type (primary key) and descending order of price (secondary key)

Save:

15. this sorted file as FARM2.

Produce:

16. a *grouped* report format based on the type field from the file showing the auctioneer, county, type, price, acres and lots fields (in that order) **only** for each farm listed. The report should have the centred heading 'Farms for Sale'. The report should also include the average size (acres) of each farm type listed.

Save:

17. this report as FARMREP3.

Print:

18. this latter report.

ASN · *Assignment 16*

Mayfield College provide a range of evening classes during the winter months. Elizabeth Gormley, the head of the evening school at Mayfield College, must hold the following details on each course:

- *Course*
- *Code*
- *Day*
- *Time*
- *Weeks* — duration of the course
- *Size* — number in class
- *Teacher*
- *Exam* — Y/N
- *Cost*
- *Room.*

Using the italicised words above as field names, enter the details outlined in the following table into a data-base file:

E C A Table									
Spreadsheets	Wp	Wed	19:00–21:00	10	15	Flynn T	Y	£80	C31
Accounting	Ac	Thu	19:00–20:30	20	25	Cox D	Y	£150	A15
Typing	Ty	Mon	19:00–20:30	10	18	Cahill A	Y	£70	S12
Psychology	At	Mon	20:00–21:00	6	25	Watson B	N	£40	S19
Yoga	Yo	Tue	20:00–22:00	12	10	Wilson M	N	£90	Gym
Economics	Ec	Thu	19:30–21:00	20	20	Moore D	Y	£150	A17
Spanish	Sp	Wed	19:00–21:00	15	15	O'Reilly K	N	£100	L04
Cookery	Co	Mon	19:00–21:00	8	12	Murtagh C	Y	£80	H10
Aerobics	Ae	Thu	20:30–22:00	12	15	Wilson M	N	£80	Gym
Data-bases	Dp	Mon	19:00–21:00	10	18	Flynn T	Y	£90	C31

Carry out the following tasks:

Save:

1. the file as EVENING1.

Make the following alterations to the relevant records:

2. Desmond Cox takes his Accounting class in room A09.
3. Denise Moore's Economics class starts at 19:00 on Wednesday evenings.
4. Caroline Murtagh's Cookery class costs £115.
5. Michael Wilson's Aerobics class has been cancelled. Delete this record from the file.

Enter:

6. the following details on two new courses:

E C A Table									
German	Ge	Thu	20:00–22:00	15	20	Kaltz M	Y	£100	L05
Law	La	Mon	19:00–21:00	18	25	Smyth J	Y	£180	A17

Erase:

7. the Code field from the file.

Enter:

8. a new field called *Dept* to show the department running the course and insert the following details for the relevant records:

◇E◇C◇A◇ **Table**	
Course	**Dept**
Spreadsheets	Computer
Accounting	Business
Typing	Secretarial
Psychology	Fitness
Yoga	Fitness
Economics	Business
Spanish	Language
Cookery	Catering
Aerobics	Fitness
Data-bases	Computer
German	Language
Law	Business

Save:

9. this edited file as EVENING2.

Extract:

10. all the records for courses that are run on Monday evenings **and** cost less than £100.

Save:

11. this subset to a new file called MONCLASS.

Sort:

12. the EVENING2 file into alphabetic order of department (primary key) and descending order of cost (secondary key).

Save:

13. this sorted file as EVENING3.

Produce:

14. a report format using the EVENING3 file that has the heading 'Mayfield College — Evening Classes' and shows only the course, time, day, weeks and cost fields. The duration and cost fields must not be totalled on the report.

Save:

15. this report as CLASSRPT.

Print:

16. the report.

A^SN · *Assignment 17*

The *Evening Echo*, Ireland's fastest growing evening newpaper, carries twelve pages of classified advertisements. Mary McCarthy, the editor, holds nine different items of information on each classified advertisement in the paper:

- *Section* — under which the advertisement is placed
- *Description* — of item or service
- *Words* — number of words in the advertisement
- *Evenings* — number for which the advertisement is carried
- *Date* — of first printing
- *Name* — of person who placed the advertisement
- *Cost* — of placing the advertisement
- *Box no.* — reply (Y/N)
- *Payment* — credit card (Cc), cheque (Ch) or Cash (Ca).

Using the italicised words above as field names, produce a data-base file containing the details in the table below:

E C A Table

Jobs	Secretary	20	2	12/09/96	Logan R	£13.00	Y	Cc
Holidays	Kerry B & B	12	5	14/09/96	Keegan M	£22.00	N	Ch
Pets	Pony	17	4	17/09/96	Byrne A	£25.50	Y	Cc
Lost & Found	Wallet	8	2	10/09/96	Lawlor K	£7.50	Y	Ch
Holidays	Sligo Hotel	30	3	18/09/96	Silke D	£31.75	N	Cc
Equipment	Piano	25	2	13/09/96	Evans H	£16.50	Y	Ca
Pets	Dog	18	2	16/09/96	Joyce C	£12.50	N	Ca
Jobs	Accountant	14	2	14/09/96	Logan R	£10.75	Y	Cc
Equipment	Gas Cooker	22	3	18/09/96	Brogan A	£24.00	N	Cc
Pets	Budgie	14	4	15/09/96	Conway T	£20.00	Y	Ch
Pets	Cat	12	4	12/09/96	O' Dea J	£16.00	Y	Ca
Jobs	Chef	27	2	16/09/96	Foley S	£17.00	Y	Cc
Equipment	Bicycle	20	3	16/09/96	Lynch B	£21.50	N	Ch
Holidays	Cavan Chalet	18	5	11/09/96	O'Reilly P	£30.00	Y	Cc

Carry out the following tasks:

Save:
1. the file as ADVERT1.

Make the following alterations to the relevant records:
2. the cost of advertising for the wallet in the *Lost & Found* section was only £5.00.
3. the piano was advertised in the *Music* section.
4. Susan Foley's advertisement was carried for three evenings, cost £24.00 and was paid for in cash.

Delete:

5. the record containing the details of an advertisement of a cat.

Save:

6. this edited version of the file as ADVERT2.

Extract:

7. all records of those advertisements that cost more than £20.00 and were paid for by credit card.

Save:

8. this subset to a new file called CCPAY.

Sort:

9. the ADVERT2 file into chronological order.

Save:

10. the sorted file as ADVERT3.

Produce:

11. a report format from the file using all the fields with the heading 'Evening Echo — Classifieds'. The cost field **only** must be totalled.

Save:

12. this report as ECHORPT1.

Sort:

13. the ADVERT3 file in ascending order of the number of *evenings* (primary key) and ascending order of *cost* (secondary key).

Save:

14. this sorted file as ADVERT4.

Produce:

15. a *grouped* report format from the file showing the section, description, words, cost and name fields. The report should have the centred heading 'Customer Enquiries'. The report should also include averages for the words **and** cost fields for 2, 3, 4 and 5 evening advertisements.

Save:

16. this report as ECHORPT2.

Print:

17. this latter report.

ASN · *Assignment 18*

NCVA Data-base Methods Sample Paper 1994

Task 1

Set up a data-base structure from supplied structure data (see Figure 1), choosing appropriate data types, print the structure, and save as 'CUSTOMER'.

Note: You may make changes to the suggested field names, if necessitated by your database software, provided they accurately describe the contents of the field.

E C A Figure	**Figure 1**	
Name of field	**Type**	**Width**
Account No.	?	4
Customer Name	?	12
Address 1	?	17
Address 2	?	10
Equipment	?	20
Price	?	5
Invoiced?	?	1
Paid?	?	1

Task 2

Enter the data supplied in Figure 3 accurately, using a formatted Data Entry Screen, (see Figure 2), and save again as 'CUSTOMER'.

E C A Figure	**Figure 2**

Wizzard Computer Sales Tracking System

Customer Account Code: [   ]   Customer Name: [   ]

Customer Address: [   ]   [   ]

Type of Equipment: [   ]   Price: [   ]

Have the Goods Been Invoiced?: [   ]   Has Payment Been Received?: [   ]

Notes on the Data Entry Screen Format (see Figure 2 for suggested format):

a) The screen format should have a centred heading, 'Wizzard Computer Sales Tracking System'.

b) There should be at least two input fields and suitable field labels on each line of the data entry screen.

A/C No.	Customer	Add1	Add2	Equipment	Price	Invoiced	Paid
2378	VCR Supplies	21, Fade St	Dublin 1	33 Mhz 386SX 100 Mb HD	1289	Y	N
2376	Gone West	123, Lagan St	Dundalk	66 Mhz 486DX 350 Mb HD	1974	Y	N
2337	Murphy Ltd	89, Cork St	Dublin 12	66 Mhz 486DX 85 Mb HD	1243	Y	N
2347	Alma Stores	9 Dublin Road	Carlow	33 Mhz 386SX 85 Mb HD	1243	Y	N
2357	Shea Travel	9, Bray Ind Est	Wicklow	33 Mhz 386SX 185 Mb HD	1378	Y	N
2356	People Power	41, Clare St	Cork	66 Mhz 486DX 85 Mb HD	1243	Y	N
2358	Sports Wear	76, Church St	Arklow	33 Mhz 386SX 100 Mb HD	1289	Y	N
2334	Dutch Import	10, Lesson St	Dublin 4	66 Mhz 486DX 170 Mb HD	1624	Y	N
2322	Willy Porter	Main St	Wicklow	66 Mhz 486DX 85 Mb HD	1428	Y	N
2393	ABC Cars Ltd	Hill House	Portrush	33 Mhz 386SX 85 Mb HD	1243	Y	N
2374	Car Valets	91, Pearse St	Dublin 2	33 Mhz 386SX 200 Mb HD	1579	Y	N
2372	New Age Tours	14, Market Square	Kildare	33 Mhz 386SX 120 Mb HD	1320	Y	N

Figure 3

Task 3

a) Change the contents of the PAID field to 'Y' for those customers with the following account numbers: 2337, 2356, 2357, 2322, 2376 and 2374.

b) Print the resulting data-base using a full report format, choosing an appropriate report title, and appropriate column titles for each field, as well as totalling the price field.

Task 4

a) Create a subset of this file, extracting those records where invoices have not been paid, and save the resulting file as 'NOTPAID'.

b) Organise the new file 'NOTPAID' in DESCENDING order of price (primary key field) and customer name (secondary key field), and save as 'NOTPAID2'.

c) Develop and print mailing labels for the customer records in the file 'NOTPAID2' (at least two labels across the printed page).

Task 5

a) Using the original file 'CUSTOMER', make the following alterations:
   I.   change the address of Murphy Ltd from '89, Cork St' to '10, JFK Ind Est'.
   II. change the equipment for Shea Travel to a 66 Mhz 486DX, leaving the hard disk as is, and altering the price to 1768.
   III. delete the record for Willy Porter.

b) Using the updated file, 'CUSTOMER', and an appropriate search string, select only those records for customers who purchased an 85 Mb Hard Disk, and print them.

c) Print the contents of the fields Account No., Customer Name, Address 1, and equipment from the updated file, 'CUSTOMER'.

ASN · Assignment 19

NCVA Data-base Methods Paper 1994

Introduction

Ardara Crafts Distribution Centre collects articles, both hand-made and machine-made, form craftspeople throughout a wide area, for sending on to buyers both overseas and within the country. Some of the articles sent in to the Centre are sent on as they are, because they are made for a single order; while other articles are divided up between a number of buyers. Michael Herrity, the manager of the Centre, requires a data-base to be set up in order to facilitate the handling of the articles and to ensure that the correct articles go to make up the correct orders.

Task 1 (6 marks)

From the data-base structure provided in **Figure 1**, create a data-base to store the data provided in **Figure 2**, using appropriate field names and data types. Write out this structure, and save the resulting data-base as 'CRAFTS'.

Figure 1

Name of Field	Data Type	Width
Name of Worker	?	15
Address	?	25
Method by which Article was Made	?	8
Category of Article	?	11
Size	?	6
Colour of Article(s)	?	12
Quantity	?	3
Are Goods Part of Single Order ?	?	1

Figure 2

Name	Address	How_Made	Category	Size	Colour	Qty	Single Order
Cashin Alma	Ardamin House, Sligo	Handmade	Pullover	M/L	Brown/Blue	12	Y
O'Neill Ian	24, Rock Road, Ardara	Machine	Shawl	M/L	Black/Brown	4	N
Clarke Anne	Glebe House, Carigoe	Handmade	Scarves	M/L	Red/Green	11	N
Buitlear Sean	Carraig Dubh, Ath an Ri	Handmade	Pullover	S/M/L	Grey/Green	8	Y
Fleming Sandra	Barton House, Ardara	Machine	Rug	M	Red/White	3	Y
Walsh Catriona	Rose Cottage, Beltra	Machine	Table-cloth	M/L	White	2	Y
Kinnear Martha	45, Carnlough Rd, Ardara	Machine	Bedspread	L	Red/Blue	3	N
O'Hare Enda	Clonagoe, Sligo	Handmade	Pullover	S/M	Red/Blue	9	N
Kernaghan Sean	Hill Farm, Killybegs	Machine	Socks	S/M	Blue/Grey	14	Y
O'Shea Aine	12, Tymon Way, Ardara	Handmade	Rug	M	Blue/Red	1	Y
Tormey Alan	Craft Shop, Portnoo	Handmade	Pullover	M/L	Brown/Black	7	N
O'Fiach Maire	Dronamore, Donegal	Handmade	Scarves	S/M/L	White/Brown	8	N

Task 2 (13 marks)

Using a suitable data input format screen, enter and save the data in Figure 2 into the data-base 'CRAFTS'.

Notes on data input format screen:

I.   Where possible, there should be at least two fields and suitable field labels on each line of the data entry screen.
II. The entry screen should have a suitable centred heading.
III. No extra marks will be given for borders, highlighting etc.

Task 3 (14 marks)

Mr Herrity requires labels for those deliveries from his suppliers which are **not** part of a single order, in order that he may identify who made the articles, using what method, to what category they belong, in what colour(s) they are provided, and how many there are in each consignment.

a) Extract a suitable subset of the master file for this purpose, saving it to a new file, NOTSING.

b) Organise the file 'NOTSING' in ascending order of colour (primary key field) and descending method of manufacturing (secondary key field), and save this organised file or index as 'NOTSING2' for printing now or later.

c) Develop suitable labels from the file 'NOTSING', for the purpose specified in the introduction to this task, placing at least two labels across the page, for printing now or later.

Task 4 (6 marks)

Using the original data-base 'CRAFTS', develop a report format, containing all fields and all records, which will include a suitable report title, suitable column titles, and a total for the quantities of articles, for printing now or later.

Task 5 (11 marks)

a) Make the following alterations to the data-base 'CRAFTS':
   I.   Delete the records for Ian O'Neill and Martha Kinnear.
   II. Change the colour of Anne Clarke's scarves from red/green to red/grey.
   III. Change the pullover from Enda O'Hare to a bedspread, and the quantity to 3 (three).

b) Using the altered file 'CRAFTS' from 5(a), select only those records for suppliers who can provide articles in small sizes, using an appropriate search string, and saving the results as 'CRAFTS2', for printing now or later.

c) Select the fields containing the name of the suppliers, the manner in which the articles are made, the type of articles, the sizes supplied and the colours, from all the records in the altered file 'CRAFTS' from 5(a), and save as 'CRAFTS3' for printing now or later.

ASN · *Assignment 20*
NCVA Data-base Methods Paper 1995

Introduction

The passport office receives tens of thousands of passport applications each year. On the application form, applicants are asked to specify their name and address, sex, date of birth, place of birth, marital status, number of children, and how long the new passport will last for, among other details. In order to improve the standard of service to the public, the passport office has decided to set up a data-base to record these details. Because the application procedure is simplified if the application type is a renewal type, rather than a first time application, the type of application is also recorded. Additionally, because the fee for a passport varies from year to year and even within the same year (the fee is reduced at off-peak times), details of the fee are also recorded.

Task 1 (6 marks)

From the data-base structure provided in Figure 1, create a data-base to store the data provided in Figure 2, using appropriate field names and data types. Write out the structure on paper. The data-base file should be saved as 'APPLICS'.

ECA Figure	Figure 1	
Name of Field	**Data Type**	**Width**
Name of Applicant	?	15
Address	?	25
Sex	?	1
Date of Birth	?	8
Place of Birth	?	15
Marital Status	?	7
No. of Children	?	2
Duration of passport (years)	?	2
Is this the first passport ?	?	1
Passport fee	?	3

Task 2 (10 marks)

Design and create a data input screen and then use the data input screen to enter the data shown in Figure 2 into the data-base 'APPLICS'. Print this data now or later.

   With regard to the data input screen you should follow these guidelines:
- All fields must have suitable field labels.
- There should be two fields per line on the data input screen.
- The input screen should have a title on top and centred.
- There is no need for borders or other effects.

Name	**Address**	**Sex**	**D.O.B.**	**Place of Birth**	**Marital Status**	**No. of Children**	**Passport Duration**	**First Time**	**Fee**
Duffy John	Finglas Dublin	M	11/12/65	Dublin	Single	0	10	Y	45
Dunne Pat	Swords Dublin	M	03/03/53	Sligo	Married	6	10	N	45
Smith Jane	Naas Kildare	F	05/04/74	Naas	Single	1	3	Y	50
Byrne Joe	Clones Meath	M	13/05/64	Dundalk	Single	0	10	N	30
Rooney Bob	Tralee Kerry	M	12/12/71	Kerry	Married	3	10	Y	45
Duffy John	Drogheda	M	11/12/65	Dublin	Single	4	3	Y	50
Al Saab Sheikh	Clones Meath	M	03/04/53	Riyadh	Single	0	3	Y	50
Rice Anne	Bray Wicklow	F	21/02/65	Dublin	Single	0	10	Y	50
Dyas Martha	Cooley Louth	F	01/11/63	Drogheda	Married	2	10	N	50

Figure 2

Task 3 (14 marks)

The manager of the passport office has decided to write to all the first-time applicants to inform them of a delay in processing their applications. She requires mailing labels for this purpose. You have been asked to do the following:

a) Extract from the Master file all records for first-time applicants. Save this subset to a new file called 'FIRSTIME'.

b) Organise the file 'FIRSTIME' in ascending order of Name of Applicant (primary key) and descending order of Duration of Passport (secondary key). Use either indexes or the SORT command to carry out this task.

c) Develop suitable labels from the sorted file with at least two labels across the page for printing now or later.

Task 4 (10 marks)

Extract a subset of records from the original data-base that consists of all records for applicants who are not first-time applicants. Using this subset, create a report format using all the fields with the heading 'NON FIRST-TIME APPLICANTS' and column titles and a total for the passport fee field. Print this report now or later.

Task 5 (10 marks)

a) Make the following alterations to the data-base 'APPLICS':
   I. Delete the record for **Pat Dunne**.
   II. Change the address for Anne Rice from **Bray Wicklow** to **Wexford**.

b) Create a report format using this modified data-base that has the heading 'PASSPORT APPLICANTS' on it and shows only the name, address, sex, place of birth, number of children, duration, type of application (i.e. first passport or renewal) and fee fields. Print this report now or later.

Chapter 4

INTRODUCTION TO SPREADSHEETS

What is a spreadsheet?

A spreadsheet is a screen image of a form or matrix made up of rows and columns in which automatic and interconnected calculations are made.

In 1978 an American business student named Dan Bricklin got very tired of adding columns of numbers and then adding them again and again when only a few changes had been made. He approached a programming friend for help in solving his problem, and they came up with a program called Visicalc, written for the Apple II computer. There are now many other spreadsheets available, such as Microsoft Excel, Lotus 1-2-3 and Quattro Pro. Most of these programs contain many new features.

What does a spreadsheet look like?

	A	B	C	D	E	F
1		CELL B1				
2						
3						
4						CELL F4
5						
6	CELL A6					
7						
8						
9				CELL D9		
10						
11						
12						
13						
14						
15						
16						
17						
18						
19						
20					CELL E20	

Each **column** in a spreadsheet is usually labelled with a letter, and each **row** with a number. The panel where a column and a row cross each other is a **cell**. Where column A and row 6 meet is cell A6; where column B and row 1 meet is cell B1.

A small spreadsheet might contain 200 rows and 60 columns; this means that it would have 12,000 cells. The size of a computer screen would not allow all these cells to be seen together: usually a screen can show about 6 columns and 20 rows at a time. Any movement outside or below the edge of the screen will mean losing the display of some information from the previous screen.

In fact the display can be considered as a movable window that can view only one 'page' or screen of the spreadsheet at any time.

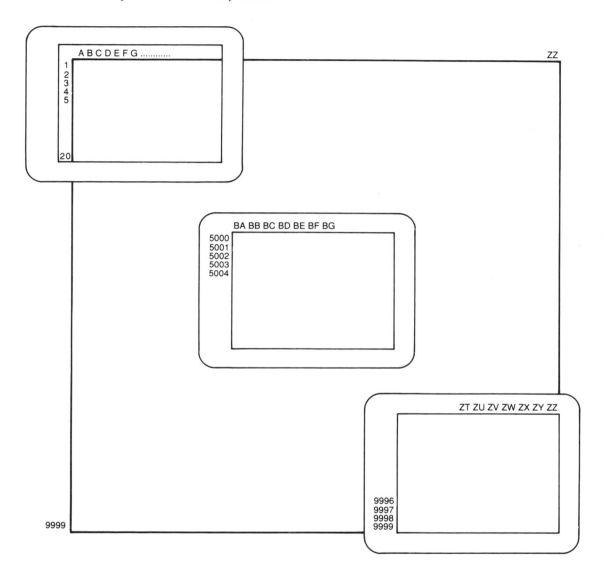

What can be put into a spreadsheet?

Any of three types of data can be entered in a cell: a value, a label, or a formula.

A **value** (or 'numeric') is any number on which calculations can be performed. This excludes dates and times, numbers followed by units of measurement and numbers at the beginning of headings. Also, large numbers must be entered without the traditional comma (or, in modern practice, the space) used as the 'thousand marker', as this would prevent calculations being carried out on them; most spreadsheets, however, can add such markers to the results.

A **label** is any non-numeric data. Normally it is text used as headings, such as the labels INCOME, EXPENSES and PROFIT in the example below, but can also include numbers that are not used for calculation purposes, e.g. year headings.

A **formula** is any algebraic expression used for performing calculations on different cells. In cell C8 in the illustration below, +C5-C6 is a formula that subtracts the contents of cell ·C6 from the contents of cell C5. When a formula is typed into a cell, the result of the calculation is displayed in that cell, not the formula.

Remember to use the asterisk (*) as the multiplication sign, the stroke (/) for division, and the circumflex (^) for 'to the power of', and to leave no spaces between numbers and signs.

Spreadsheet

	A	B	C	D	E	F
1	PROFIT STATEMENT, 1994 TO 1996					
2						
3			1994	1995	1996	
4						
5	INCOME		10000	20000	40000	
6	EXPENSES		5000	8000	17000	
7						
8	PROFIT		+C5-C6	+D5-D6	+E5-E6	
9						
10						

Example 1

Personal budget

The following topics will be discussed using example 1 below:

1. Setting up the spreadsheet
2. Entering formulae
3. The summation function
4. Improving the appearance of the spreadsheet
5. Replication
6. Editing the spreadsheet
7. Considering 'what if?' situations
8. The 'logical if' function
9. Other facilities

Explanation

This example contains a record of personal income and weekly expenditure of a family for four weeks.

Data entry

The only items entered directly are the wages and the various expenses during the week. All other totals and figures are worked out automatically.

	A	B	C	D	E	F
1	PERSONAL BUDGET	WEEK 1	WEEK 2	WEEK 3	WEEK 4	TOTAL
2						
3						
4	OPENING BALANCE	0	12.14	9.82	3.28	
5	WAGES	170	155	150	182	657
6						
7	TOTAL MONEY	170	167.14	159.82	185.28	
8						
9	EXPENSES					
10						
11	CAR EXPENSES	22.45	22	11	18.33	73.78
12	FOOD	40.86	43.77	51.67	35.45	171.75
13	BILLS	13	23	26	33	95
14	ENTERTAINMENT	18	10	5.32	29.55	62.87
15	BANK SAVINGS	8	8	8	8	32
16	MORTGAGE	50.55	50.55	50.55	50.55	202.2
17	MISC.	5	0	4	10	19
18						
19						
20	TOTAL EXPENSES	157.86	157.32	156.54	184.88	656.6
21	CLOSING BAL.	12.14	9.82	3.28	0.4	
22						
23						
24						
25						

1. Setting up the spreadsheet

In this example, column A contains labels that explain the contents of rows 4 to 21. The labels WEEK 1 etc. are column headings that identify which week the figures in the columns relate to.

The width of column A will have to be changed to accommodate the labels in it. This is done by giving the appropriate command. Here the width is changed from the default setting of 9 characters to 18 characters wide. On most spreadsheets it is possible to change all or just one column width.

The labels in the example would be typed into the blank sheet first. Formulas will be used to calculate totals and closing and opening balances. The information on income and expenses would then be typed in each week.

The opening balance in week 1 is any spare money we have. For the other weeks it is the difference between the total we receive in a week and the total expenses, i.e. the previous week's closing balance.

2. Entering formulae

The TOTAL MONEY is the opening balance plus net wages (wages after tax). The formula in B7 would therefore be +B4+B5. (Remember that when a formula is entered in a cell it is the result that is displayed, not the formula.)

To total the expenses we must again use a formula in B20. This would be +B11+B12+B13+B14+B15+B16+B17.

The CLOSING BAL. is the difference between total income and total expenses this week. The formula to be typed in B21 therefore is +B7-B20.

The opening balance for week 2 will be the closing balance for week 1. So in C4 we enter the formula +B21.

For the next three weeks the formulae will be repeated, except for cell references. The formulae for week 2 are:

Cell C4: + B21
Cell C7: + C4 + C5
Cell C20: + C11 + C12 + C13 + C14 + C15 + C16 + C17
Cell C21: + C7 - C20

Similarly the formulae for week 3 will be:

Cell D4: + C21
Cell D7: + D4 + D5
Cell D20: + D11 + D12 + D13 + D14 + D15 + D16 + D17
Cell D21: . . .

Try working out the formulae for week 4 yourself.

Cell E4: . . .
Cell E7: . . .
Cell E20: . . .
Cell E21: . . .

Finally, the totals for the month are entered. The formula for total wages is B5+C5+D5+E5. This will be entered in cell F5. Similarly the formula for total car expenses will be +B11+C11+D11+E11. This would be entered in cell F11. Try working out the formulae for the following cells:

Cell F12: . . .

Cell F13: . . .

Cell F14: . . .

Cell F15: . . .

Cell F17: . . .

Cell F20: . . .

3. The summation function

You may have noticed that the formulae in cells B20, C20, D20 and E20 are very long. They would be even longer if we had any more expenses.

We can use the summation or total function to add up whole columns or rows of numbers.Instead of typing all the parts of the formula we only have to type in the first and last cell references. Using Microsoft Excel the formula in cell B20 would be =SUM(B11:B17); in Lotus 1-2-3 it would be @SUM(B11..B17). Similarly the formula in F5(+B5+C5+D5+E5) would be replaced with SUM(B5,E5) or @SUM(B5..E5). Check your own spreadsheet program for the formula for this function.

Write down on a page all the shorter summation formulae required to add up the rows and columns in this example.

Other mathematical functions are available on most spreadsheets, e.g. the 'average' function, which will find the mean of a range of numbers. Other mathematical functions available include sin, cos, tan, etc. More advanced financial and statistical functions are available on some spreadsheets.

4. Improving the appearance of the spreadsheet

Changing the format of numbers

You will notice that the money amounts in our example are very untidy in appearance. This is because all the numbers do not have the same number of decimal places. For money amounts of course this is usually two. If possible also the pound sign should be displayed in front of the amounts. A special command can be given to change the required range or group of numbers to this style, called 'cash format'.

Aligning the labels

You will notice also that the week labels are not exactly in line with the amounts below them. This is because numbers are automatically displayed **flush right** or aligned on the right (i.e. the last digit is at the extreme right of the cell), whereas text is automatically displayed **flush left** or aligned on the left (i.e. the first character of the label is at the extreme left of the cell). However, it is possible to change the alignment of any cell to flush right, flush left or centred.

Here we will give the command to change the week labels to flush right and change the money amounts to cash format. Our spreadsheet should now look like this:

	A	B	C	D	E	F
		Spreadsheet				
1	PERSONAL BUDGET	WEEK 1	WEEK 2	WEEK 3	WEEK 4	TOTAL
2						
3						
4	OPENING BALANCE	£0.00	£12.14	£9.82	£3.28	
5	WAGES	£170.00	£155.00	£150.00	£182.00	£657.00
6						
7	TOTAL MONEY	£170.00	£167.14	£159.82	£185.28	
8						
9	EXPENSES					
10						
11	CAR EXPENSES	£22.45	£22.00	£11.00	£18.33	£73.78
12	FOOD	£40.86	£43.77	£51.67	£35.45	£171.75
13	BILLS	£13.00	£23.00	£26.00	£33.00	£95.00
14	ENTERTAINMENT	£18.00	£10.00	£5.32	£29.55	£62.87
15	BANK SAVINGS	£8.00	£8.00	£8.00	£8.00	£32.00
16	MORTGAGE	£50.55	£50.55	£50.00	£50.55	£202.20
17	MISC.	£5.00	£0.00	£4.00	£10.00	£19.00
18						
19						
20	TOTAL EXPENSES	£157.86	£157.32	£156.54	£184.88	£656.60
21	CLOSING BAL.	£12.14	£9.82	£3.28	£0.40	
22						
23						
24						
25						

5. Replication

You will have noticed when entering the data in our example that there is a lot of repetitive typing of formulae. If you had to expand the model to accommodate fifty-two weeks you would be very tired after typing in all the formulae! However, all spreadsheets allow you to 'replicate' or copy formulae or text from one area of the spreadsheet to another.

There are three levels of copying or replicating to begin with: straight copying, range copying and formula copying.

Straight copying

This is where one item (whether a number or label) is copied from one cell to another, and can be used when you want to avoid retyping names or headings. It is done by entering the appropriate command and the identification of the cells you want to copy from ('source cells') and copy to ('target cells').

Range copying

This involves entering the 'source range' of cells to be copied and the 'target range' of cells to be copied to.

Formula copying

There are three types of formula copying: **absolute**, where there is no change in the cell references when copied; **relative**, where the copied formulae change cell references according to their position; and **absolute and relative**, where some cell references in the formula do not change when copied and others do. For example, copying down a column:

Absolute	Relative	Absolute-relative	Relative-absolute
A1*B1	A1*B1	A1*B1	A1*B1
A1*B1	A2*B2	A1*B2	A2*B1
A1*B1	A3*B3	A1*B3	A3*B1
A1*B1	A4*B4	A1*B4	A4*B1
A1*B1	A5*B5	A1*B5	A5*B1

(The formula to be copied is the first one in each column. Notice that only the row numbers change by one when copying relative cell references down a column.)

Copying across rows:

Absolute	A1*B1	A1*B1	A1*B1	A1*B1
Relative	A1*B1	B1*C1	C1*D1	D1*E1
Absolute-relative	A1*B1	A1*C1	A1*D1	A1*E1
Relative-absolute	A1*B1	B1*B1	C1*B1	D1*B1

(The formula to be copied is the first one in each row. Notice that only the column letter changes by one when copying relative cell references across a row.)

In the personal budget example above we could have copied most of our formulae. We could have typed the formula +B4+B5 in B7, then copied it across to C7, D7 and E7 using relative cell references, so that each cell reference would change across the row. This would be done by identifying B7 as the cell to copy from and the range C7 to E7 as the range to copy to.

If we were to copy B7 using absolute cell references or a combination of absolute and relative cell references we would get incorrect totals. The results from the different alternatives would be:

Copy	from B7	to C7	to D8	to E7
Absolute	+B4+B5	+B4+B5	+B4+B5	+B4+B5
Relative	+B4+B5	+C4+C5	+D4+D5	+E4+E5
Absolute-relative	+B4+B5	+B4+C5	+B4+D5	+B4+E5
Relative-absolute	+B4+B5	+C4+B5	+D4+B5	+E4+B5
Results	**B7**	**C7**	**D8**	**E7**
Absolute	170	170	170	170
Relative	170	167.14	159.82	185.28
Absolute-relative	170	155	150	182
Relative-absolute	170	182.14	179.82	173.28

Replication could also be used for the formulae in rows 20 and 21. For row 20 we would copy the formula from cell B20 to the cells in the range C20 to F20, using relative cell references. In the same way we would copy the formula in cell B21 (+B7-B20) to the cells in the range C21 to E21.

Copying with relative cell references could also be used for the formulae in column F, from cell F11 to the cells in the range F12 to F16.

The importance of replication

It is the replication function that gives the computer spreadsheet its real power. Once the core or original formulae have been entered it is only a matter of replicating them as far as the memory of your computer will allow. Spreadsheets can be constructed very quickly and easily using replication, which is their main advantage over manual systems. In our example we could expand the model to cover fifty-two weeks by simple replication of the formulae: no new formulae would need to be typed in.

6. Editing the spreadsheet
Simple editing

If we want to change any information on the spreadsheet we simply type over it or use the editing facility to insert or delete some characters. In this example we want to change the contents of cell A5 to read NET WAGES instead of WAGES. We will use the editing facility, type the word NET and then press [enter].

Inserting rows or columns

In our example we might decide to enter a blank row in row 9 to separate the expenses more clearly from other data on the sheet. To do this we use the appropriate command for inserting a row. The result will be that the present contents of row 9 will move down one row; all subsequent rows will also move down one row.

When we do this the computer automatically changes all formulae that are affected by the move. The formula for total expenses will change from @SUM(B11..B16) to @SUM(B12..B17), while the formula to calculate the closing balance will change, from +B21 to +B22. In fact most of the formulae in the spreadsheet will change because of the insertion of the row.

If we insert a new column, the information is moved across to the right, and again any formulae that are affected will change automatically.

Our spreadsheet will look like this after these two changes have been carried out:

	A	B	C	D	E	F
1	PERSONAL BUDGET	WEEK 1	WEEK 2	WEEK 3	WEEK 4	TOTAL
2						
3						
4	OPENING BALANCE	£0.00	£12.14	£9.82	£3.28	
5	NET WAGES	£170.00	£155.00	£150.00	£182.00	£657.00
6						
7	TOTAL MONEY	£170.00	£167.14	£159.82	£185.28	
8						
9						
10	EXPENSES					
11						
12	CAR EXPENSES	£22.45	£22.00	£11.00	£18.33	£73.78
13	FOOD	£40.86	£43.77	£51.67	£35.45	£171.75
14	BILLS	£13.00	£23.00	£26.00	£33.00	£95.00
15	ENTERTAINMENT	£18.00	£10.00	£5.32	£29.55	£62.87
16	BANK SAVINGS	£8.00	£8.00	£8.00	£8.00	£32.00
17	MORTGAGE	£50.55	£50.55	£50.00	£50.55	£202.20
18	MISC.	£5.00	£0.00	£4.00	£10.00	£19.00
19						
20						
21	TOTAL EXPENSES	£157.86	£157.32	£156.54	£184.88	£656.60
22	CLOSING BAL.	£12.14	£9.82	£3.28	£0.40	

Perhaps we forgot to include some expenses. In that case we would need to insert a new row and heading containing the new information. Let us say the forgotten expense was pocket money of £1 a week given to one of the children, and the information is to be inserted after the food expense. When this row is inserted the formulae and amounts will change automatically to reflect this: for example, the total expenses formula will now be @SUM(B12..B19). Note that in week 4 we have overspent by £3.60.

The spreadsheet will look like this after inserting the new pocket money row:

	A	B	C	D	E	F
1	PERSONAL BUDGET	WEEK 1	WEEK 2	WEEK 3	WEEK 4	TOTAL
2						
3						
4	OPENING BALANCE	£0.00	£11.14	£7.82	£0.28	
5	NET WAGES	£170.00	£155.00	£150.00	£182.00	£657.00
6						
7	TOTAL MONEY	£170.00	£166.14	£157.82	£182.28	
8						
9						
10	EXPENSES					
11						
12	CAR EXPENSES	£22.45	£22.00	£11.00	£18.33	£73.78
13	FOOD	£40.86	£43.77	£51.67	£35.45	£171.75
14	POCKET MONEY	£1.00	£1.00	£1.00	£1.00	£4.00
15	BILLS	£13.00	£23.00	£26.00	£33.00	£95.00
16	ENTERTAINMENT	£18.00	£10.00	£5.32	£29.55	£62.87
17	BANK SAVINGS	£8.00	£8.00	£8.00	£8.00	£32.00
18	MORTGAGE	£50.55	£50.55	£50.00	£50.55	£202.20
19	MISC.	£5.00	£0.00	£4.00	£10.00	£19.00
20						
21						
22	TOTAL EXPENSES	£158.86	£158.32	£157.54	£185.88	£660.60
23	CLOSING BAL.	£11.14	£7.82	£0.28	(£3.60)	
24						

7. Considering 'what if?' situations

When the spreadsheet is set up we can experiment with the data to consider the effect of different figure or policy changes. These are called 'what if?' calculations.

In the example above we could ask ourselves, what if we decided not to bring the car to work? This would mean we would only spend £10 a week on car expenses. All we would need to do is type over the amounts in the car expenses row with the new amount, £10. All the totals will be recalculated for us. Note the saving on the weekly balances.

Any number in the spreadsheet can be changed to see what effect it might have on our total budget. On a more complex example involving many thousands of calculations, this ability to recalculate is invaluable for decision-making.

Our spreadsheet will look like this after the car expenses are changed:

	A	B	C	D	E	F
		WEEK 1	WEEK 2	WEEK 3	WEEK 4	TOTAL
1	PERSONAL BUDGET					
2						
3						
4	OPENING BALANCE	£0.00	£12.14	£9.82	£3.28	
5	NET WAGES	£170.00	£155.00	£150.00	£182.00	£657.00
6						
7	TOTAL MONEY	£170.00	£167.14	£159.82	£185.28	
8						
9						
10	EXPENSES					
11						
12	CAR EXPENSES	£10.00	£10.00	£10.00	£10.00	£40.00
13	FOOD	£40.86	£43.77	£51.67	£35.45	£171.75
14	POCKET MONEY	£1.00	£1.00	£1.00	£1.00	£4.00
15	BILLS	£13.00	£23.00	£26.00	£33.00	£95.00
16	ENTERTAINMENT	£18.00	£10.00	£5.32	£29.55	£62.87
17	BANK SAVINGS	£8.00	£8.00	£8.00	£8.00	£32.00
18	MORTGAGE	£50.55	£50.55	£50.00	£50.55	£202.20
19	MISC.	£5.00	£0.00	£4.00	£10.00	£19.00
20						
21						
22	TOTAL EXPENSES	£146.41	£146.32	£156.54	£177.55	£626.82
23	CLOSING BAL.	£23.59	£32.27	£25.73	£30.18	
24						

8. *The 'logical if' function*

Is the profit this year greater than last year? Has the aeroplane been overloaded with luggage? The answers to these questions are either true or false. These are considered logical questions, i.e. those having true or false answers.

Most spreadsheet programs allow you to employ a formula to ask a question and generate a true or false response. The general pattern this formula takes is:

If (*condition, true response, false response*)

This function is very similar to the IF — THEN — ELSE command in the programming language Basic.

In the example above we could get the computer to make a decision for us. We decide to save money based on the previous week's closing balance. We have decided that if the amount left over in the previous week is greater than £10, we will save £6 in the next week; otherwise we will not save anything in the coming week.

The first week's savings will be entered by the user, and all other weeks' savings will be calculated automatically by using the 'if' function. The formula in cell C17 will be as follows:

@IF(B23>10,6,0)

This means that if the content of cell B23 (the closing balance) is greater than £10, £6 will be entered in cell C17; otherwise £0 is entered in cell C17. This formula can then be copied across the row as far as cell E17, using relative cell references.

When the formula is copied the numbers in row 17 will change to reflect this new decision, and other totals that are affected will also change. The spreadsheet will now look like this:

	A	B	C	D	E	F
1	PERSONAL BUDGET	WEEK 1	WEEK 2	WEEK 3	WEEK 4	TOTAL
2						
3						
4	OPENING BALANCE	£0.00	£23.59	£34.27	£29.73	
5	NET WAGES	£170.00	£155.00	£150.00	£182.00	£657.00
6						
7	TOTAL MONEY	£170.00	£178.59	£184.27	£211.73	
8						
9						
10	EXPENSES					
11						
12	CAR EXPENSES	£10.00	£10.00	£10.00	£10.00	£40.00
13	FOOD	£40.86	£43.77	£51.67	£35.45	£171.75
14	POCKET MONEY	£1.00	£1.00	£1.00	£1.00	£4.00
15	BILLS	£13.00	£23.00	£26.00	£33.00	£95.00
16	ENTERTAINMENT	£18.00	£10.00	£5.32	£29.55	£62.87
17	BANK SAVINGS	£8.00	£6.00	£6.00	£6.00	£26.00
18	MORTGAGE	£50.55	£50.55	£50.55	£50.55	£202.20
19	MISC.	£5.00	£0.00	£4.00	£10.00	£19.00
20						
21						
22	TOTAL EXPENSES	£146.41	£144.32	£154.54	£175.55	£620.82
23	CLOSING BAL.	£23.59	£34.27	£29.73	£36.18	
24						

'What if?' again

We could then ask the question, what would the situation be if we used the car again for work, but this time making use of the new saving policy? We would only have to change all car expense amounts back to the original figures: all the other calculations will be done for us, including the amount we would save each week. (Note that we will save nothing on the third week.)

	A	B	C	D	E	F
1	PERSONAL BUDGET	WEEK 1	WEEK 2	WEEK 3	WEEK 4	TOTAL
2						
3						
4	OPENING BALANCE	£0.00	£11.14	£9.82	£10.28	
5	NET WAGES	£170.00	£155.00	£150.00	£182.00	£657.00
6						
7	TOTAL MONEY	£170.00	£166.14	£159.82	£192.28	
8						
9						
10	EXPENSES					
11						
12	CAR EXPENSES	£22.45	£22.00	£11.00	£18.33	£73.78
13	FOOD	£40.86	£43.77	£51.67	£35.45	£171.75
14	POCKET MONEY	£1.00	£1.00	£1.00	£1.00	£4.00
15	BILLS	£13.00	£23.00	£26.00	£33.00	£95.00
16	ENTERTAINMENT	£18.00	£10.00	£5.32	£29.55	£62.87
17	BANK SAVINGS	£8.00	£6.00	£0.00	£6.00	£20.00
18	MORTGAGE	£50.55	£50.55	£50.55	£50.55	£202.20
19	MISC.	£5.00	£0.00	£4.00	£10.00	£19.00
20						
21						
22	TOTAL EXPENSES	£158.86	£156.32	£149.54	£183.88	£648.60
23	CLOSING BAL.	£11.14	£9.82	£10.28	£8.40	
24						

9. Other facilities

Most spreadsheet programs have several other useful features, which we can use to make this application work more effectively.

Quick cursor movement

It is possible on most spreadsheets to move directly to another cell. This is done by giving a command or using a function key. The name of the desired cell is requested, and the cursor moves directly to that cell. This facility is very useful when using a very large spreadsheet.

Non-scrolling titles

Selected rows and columns can be fixed on the screen so that they do not scroll off when we move to another part of the spreadsheet. If we had the budget information for fifty-two weeks in our sample spreadsheet we might need to fix column A so that the labels for each expense would be on display permanently as we go from column to column.

Printing part or all of the spreadsheet

Large spreadsheets can be printed on several sheets and the parts joined together. Selected parts of the spreadsheet can also be printed.

Only columns A and F in the example above might be required on paper, so that the total amount for each expense could be noted separately. This would require copying column A into column G and marking columns F and G to be printed. This would be displayed as follows:

◈E◈C◈A◈ *Spreadsheet*	
Totals	**Personal Budget**
	Opening Balance
£657.00	Net Wager
—————	Total Money
	Expenses
£73.78	Car Expenses
£171.75	Food
£4.00	Pocket Money
£95.00	Bills
£62.87	Entertainment
£20.00	Bank Savings
£202.20	Mortgage
£19.00	Misc.
—————	
£648.60	Total Expenses
	Closing Bal.

Turning off automatic recalculation

When a new number is typed into a spreadsheet the computer automatically recalculates all other cells affected by this change. But recalculation can take a considerable time on small computers. It is possible to turn off automatic recalculation until all changes have been made; then a command can be entered to recalculate.

Using the 'look-up' function

A range of cells that have codes and corresponding values in them can be searched with the 'look-up' function. This will return a value that relates to the code requested. This function is often used to produce invoices, where product codes are entered and the price per unit is 'looked up' by the computer.

Summary of the standard facilities of a spreadsheet program

- The cursor can be moved quickly to anywhere in the spreadsheet
- Rows and columns can be inserted in existing spreadsheets
- Rows and columns and ranges of data can be deleted
- Cell display can be changed to show different formats
- Single items or ranges of data can be copied
- Formulas can be copied or replicated
- Mathematical functions are available, e.g. sum, average, sin, cos, tan (on some spreadsheets other functions are available, such as financial and statistical functions)
- Editing facilities are available, while information is being typed in and afterwards
- Column widths can be changed
- Data can be stored for later retrieval
- Part or all of the spreadsheet can be printed
- Logical decisions can be made on data using the 'if' function
- Coded data can be looked up using the 'look-up' function
- Non-scrolling rows and columns can be fixed on the screen when more than one screen of data is used
- Data in the spreadsheet can be protected to prevent further changes
- Some spreadsheets allow integration or links with other types of program, such as graphics and word-processor programs

Creating a spreadsheet

Before typing in a spreadsheet you should plan what you want to do. This will involve some of the following decisions:

1. What title will I give the spreadsheet?
2. What headings will I use for the rows and columns? These should be concise but descriptive.
3. Will I need to increase or decrease the width of a column, and by how much?
4. Which of the items will be labels and which values?
5. Where will I use a formula, and can I use a built-in function?
6. Can I replicate this formula? If so, will it be relative, absolute or a combination?

7. Should the data be displayed in a special format, e.g. cash format, and where?

8. What file name will I use for the spreadsheet? This name will have to be concise but should remind you of the contents of the spreadsheet when retrieving it later.

Example 2

A more complex spreadsheet

Explanation

A small airline operates a twelve-seater aeroplane between Dublin and Knock. It wants to store passenger information on a spreadsheet. The following conditions apply:

1. The basic price of a ticket is £50.
2. There is VAT at 21 per cent on the basic price of all tickets (excluding discount).
3. There is a 10 per cent discount on the basic price of all tickets for children under 12.
4. A passenger is charged an extra £1 for every 1 kg over the 20 kg luggage allowance. No VAT is charged on this extra charge.

Data entry

The only items to be typed in are the passenger information and the standard data such as ticket price, penalty charge, etc. All other figures are to be automatically calculated by the spreadsheet through the use of formulae.

Questions

1. Set up a spreadsheet for a particular flight, including the following passenger information:

Seat no.	Name	Age	Luggage (kg)
1	Brendan Bradley	45	17
2	Ciarán Collins	5	7
3	Denis Collins	11	9
4	Martin Collins	26	23
5	Aisling Doyle	42	18
6	Kevin Geraghty	7	14
7	Paul Hillery	35	21
8	Brian Laffey	17	16
9	Sean Byrne	27	10
10	Bernadette Ryan	10	20
11	Sheila Ryan	24	17
12	Deirdre White	33	4

2. Use appropriate formulae and replication to show for each passenger the ticket price, discount, VAT and baggage penalty. Use suitable headings.

3. Save the spreadsheet as AIR.

4. Produce a printout of the entire spreadsheet.

Solution

Decide on the following before typing in data:

1. The title: KNOCK AIRLINES. This will be put into cells A1 and B1.

2. The following row headings will be used for the standard data in cells A2 to A5. Column A must be 11 characters wide. The figures will be put opposite this information in cells B2 to B5.

PRICE	50
VAT	.21
DISCOUNT	.10
PENALTY	1

3. Column headings will be needed for the following: SEAT NO., NAME [15 characters wide], AGE, PRICE, DISCOUNT, PRICE LESS DISCOUNT, VAT, PENALTY and TOTAL PRICE.

The spreadsheet should now look like this:

	A	B	C	D	E	F	G	H	I	J
1	KNOCK AIRLINES									
2	PRICE	50								
3	VAT	0.21								
4	DISCOUNT	0.1								
5	PENALTY	1								
6										
7										
8	SEAT NO.	NAME	AGE	LUGGAGE	PRICE	DISCOUNT	PRICE-DIS.	VAT	PENALTY	TOTAL PRICE
9										
10	1	B BRADLEY	45	17						
11	2	C COLLINS	5	7						
12	3	D COLLINS	11	9						
13	4	M COLLINS	26	23						
14	5	A DOYLE	42	18						
15	6	K GERAGHTY	7	14						
16	7	P HILLERY	35	21						
17	8	B LAFFEY	17	16						
18	9	S BYRNE	27	10						
19	10	B RYAN	10	20						
20	11	S RYAN	24	17						
21	12	D WHITE	33	4						

4. Align all headings flush right.

5. All money amounts should be changed to cash format.

6. Decide on formulae. These will be:

E10: +B2. This must be copied down the column, using an absolute cell reference, as everybody has the same basic ticket price before other considerations are taken into account.

F10: @IF(C10<12,e10*B4,0). All parts of this formula will be copied, using relative cell references, except B4, which should remain absolute down the column.

G10:+10-F10. This will be copied down the column, using relative cell references. The formula simply subtracts the discount (if any) from the price.

H10: +G10*B3. G10 will be relative and B3 will be absolute when copied, as the VAT rate remains 21 per cent for all tickets.

I10: @IF(D10>20,(D10-20)*B5,0). All will have relative cell references, except B5 (the penalty amount, £1), which should be absolute. (D10-20) calculates the number of kilograms over the 20 kg limit.

J10: +G10+H10+I10. This gives the total price, and should be copied using relative cell references. It includes the discounted price plus the VAT and penalty charge (if any).

The final spreadsheet should look like this after the editing and copying discussed above:

	A	B	C	D	E	F	G	H	I	J
1	KNOCK AIRLINES									
2	PRICE	50								
3	VAT	0.21								
4	DISCOUNT	0.1								
5	PENALTY	1								
6										
7										
8	SEAT NO.	NAME	AGE	LUGGAGE	PRICE	DISCOUNT	PRICE-DIS.	VAT	PENALTY	TOTAL PRICE
9										
10	1	B BRADLEY	45	17	£50.00	£0.00	£50.00	£10.50	£0.00	£60.50
11	2	C COLLINS	5	7	£50.00	£5.00	£45.00	£9.45	£0.00	£54.45
12	3	D COLLINS	11	9	£50.00	£5.00	£45.00	£9.45	£0.00	£54.45
13	4	M COLLINS	26	23	£50.00	£0.00	£50.00	£10.50	£3.00	£63.50
14	5	A DOYLE	42	18	£50.00	£0.00	£50.00	£10.50	£0.00	£60.50
15	6	K GERAGHTY	7	14	£50.00	£5.00	£45.00	£9.45	£0.00	£54.45
16	7	P HILLERY	35	21	£50.00	£0.00	£50.00	£10.50	£1.00	£61.50
17	8	B LAFFEY	17	16	£50.00	£0.00	£50.00	£10.50	£0.00	£60.50
18	9	S BYRNE	27	10	£50.00	£0.00	£50.00	£10.50	£0.00	£60.50
19	10	B RYAN	10	20	£50.00	£5.00	£45.00	£9.45	£0.00	£54.45
20	11	S RYAN	24	17	£50.00	£0.00	£50.00	£10.50	£0.00	£60.50
21	12	D WHITE	33	4	£50.00	£0.00	£50.00	£10.50	£0.00	£60.50

This spreadsheet could be used again and again by the airline. The person operating the spreadsheet would enter the standard information, including name, age and weight of luggage, and all other figures would be calculated automatically.

Also, the formulae would not need to be changed when ticket prices and other variables changed. For example, if the rate of VAT were to change, the operator would only have to change the actual rate in cell B4: no formulae would need to be altered.

Graphing the data

Most spreadsheet programs allow users to present numerical data on a spreadsheet in graph form.

Example 3

There are currently 402 students enrolled at Leeside College. The following table shows the numbers of students taking the various courses offered at the college:

Course	Number
Accounting	62
Catering	98
Computing	75
Hairdressing	46
Marketing	37
Secretarial	84

The bar graph

Peter Connolly, the college principal, has asked us to produce a bar graph of the data shown in the table. We follow these steps:
1. Enter the data onto a spreadsheet.
2. Select the cells containing the data.
3. Choose the **Create Chart/Graph** command or icon.
4. Indicate where the graph should appear on the spreadsheet.
5. Specify the graph type (bar).
6. Add a graph title.
7. Add labels for the *x* and *y* axes.

The bar graph should appear as follows:

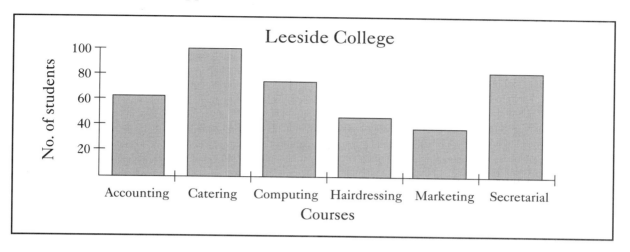

If the data to be graphed is changed, the bar graph will automatically reflect the changes.

The pie graph

In a similar manner, we can produce a pie graph to show the percentage of students taking each course. No axes labels are required. We have, however, included a graph title and a *legend;* the latter is a key that identifies the items shown on the graph by colour, hatch pattern or symbol.

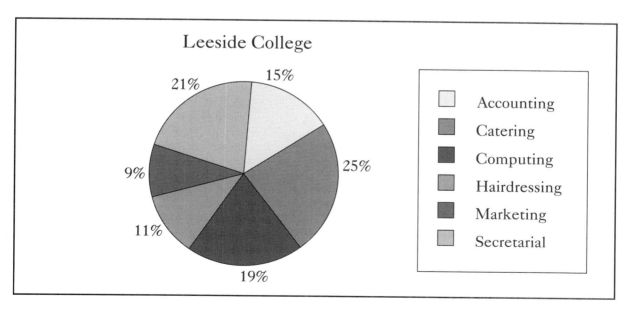

Financial matters

Depreciation

Depreciation is the cost to a business of wear and tear on assets that it owns. There are a variety of methods by which depreciation amounts can be calculated on items purchased. One popular method is known as the fixed-declining balance method. The DB function, in Microsoft EXCEL, returns the real depreciation of an asset for a specific period using the fixed-declining balance method. The syntax of the function is as follows:

$$=DB(cost,salvage,life,period)$$

The four items enclosed in parenthesis are now explained:

1. *Cost* is the initial cost of the asset.
2. *Salvage* is the value of the asset at the end of the life of the asset.
3. *Life* is the number of periods over which the asset is being depreciated. This is frequently known as the useful life of the asset.
4. *Period* is the period for which you want to calculate the depreciation. It must be in the same units as life (e.g. years).

Example 4

Conor Lawlor has just purchased a new car costing $18,000. The estimated life of the car is 12 years. It has been decided that the salvage value of the car in twelve years' time will only be $2000. Conor asked us to produce a spreadsheet to show the depreciation on the car at the end of each year for the first ten years. The completed spreadsheet appears as follows:

	A	B
	Spreadsheet	
1	Depreciation Analysis	
2		
3	Item Purchased =	Car
4	Estimated Life (yrs) =	12
5	Initial Cost =	£18,000.00
6	Salvage Value =	£2,000.00
7		
8	Year	Depreciation
9		Amount
10	1	£3,006.00
11	2	£2,504.00
12	3	£2,085.83
13	4	£1,737.50
14	5	£1,447.33
15	6	£1,205.63
16	7	£1,004.29
17	8	£836.57
18	9	£696.87
19	10	£580.49

The depreciation amounts displayed in column B were obtained as follows:
(a) The formula, =DB(B5,B6,B4,A10), was entered in cell B10.
(b) It was then copied into the range of cells B11:B19.

Loan repayments

Lending agencies frequently use spreadsheets to calculate loan repayments. The PMT function, available on most spreadsheet programs, returns the payment for an investment based on periodic, constant payments and a constant interest rate. The syntax of this function in Microsoft EXCEL is:

$$=PMT(rate, nper, -pv) \text{ where:}$$

1. *rate* is the loan interest rate
2. *nper* is the number of payment periods
3. *pv* is the loan amount.

Make sure that you are consistent about the units you use for specifying *rate* and *nper*. If *rate* is per year then *PMT* returns the number of payments per year and *nper* is the number of years.

Example 5

Patricia O'Leary wishes to borrow $30,000 from the EasyLoan Building Society. Patricia asked us to produce a spreadsheet showing the monthly repayments over the twenty-five year term of the loan for four different interest rates (7%, 8%, 9% and 10%). Our completed spreadsheet is now shown:

	A	B
		Spreadsheet
1	Mortgage Repayments	
2		
3	Years =	25
4	Months =	300
5	Loan =	£30,000.00
6		
7	Interest	Monthly
8	Rate	Repayment
9	7%	£212.03
10	8%	£231.54
11	9%	£251.76
12	10%	£272.61

149

The monthly repayment amounts displayed in column B were obtained as follows:

(a) The formula, *=PMT(A9/12,B4,-B5)*, was entered in cell B9.
(b) It was then copied into the range of cells B10:B12.

As the monthly repayments were required, the rate (i.e. the contents of cell *A9*) was divided by twelve to maintain consistency with the number of repayment periods (i.e. the contents of cell *B4*).

Investment venture

Investors must frequently decide between investing in new ventures or leaving the money on deposit in the bank or building society. A measure of the potential of an investment venture is to compare the projected income with bank interest earnings. Current spreadsheet programs offer the user an efficient means of making this comparison through the use of the Net Present Value (NPV) function.

The syntax of this function in Microsoft EXCEL is:

$$=NPV(rate, range\ of\ values)$$

The function returns the net present value of an investment based on a series of periodic cash flows, *range of values*, and a discount rate equal to *rate*. The cashflow periods must be equally spaced in time.

Example 6

Gerard Clarke, the owner of Breffni Farm Machinery Ltd, is considering investing $1 million in his business. This amount of money must be invested in full at the outset. The projected sales from it are expected to last from 1997 to 2000 inclusive. The corresponding sales for each successive year are $300,000, $500,000, $900,000 and $1,200,000. The Thrifty Building Society, however, are offering 15% interest on all deposits over $750,000. Gerard has asked us to advise him on whether he should go ahead with the venture or simply deposit the money with the Building Society. We have produced the following spreadsheet to aid Gerard in his decision:

	A	B	C	D	E
	◇E◇C◇A◇ *Spreadsheet*				
1	Farm Machinery Ltd				
2					
3	Projected Sales				
4					
5	Investment	1997	1998	1999	2000
6	£1,000,000.00	£300,000.00	£500,000.00	£900,000.00	£1,200,000.00
7					
8	Interest Rate Given =		15%		
9					
10	Net Present Value =		£1,916,809.90		
11	Bank Savings Return =		£1,749,006.25		

The initial investment and the current interest rate are displayed in cells A6 and C8, respectively. The projected incomes from sales over the four-year period have been entered in the range of cells B6:E6.

The net present value, displayed in cell C10, was obtained by entering the formula: *=NPV(C8,B6:E6)*. The bank savings return, displayed in cell C11, was obtained by entering the formula *=A6*1.15^4* (the initial investment plus the compound interest earned). The spreadsheet shows that the return on the investment venture would be better than the deposit earnings at the building society in this particular case.

Using macros

Macro basics

A macro is a sequence of specially phrased instructions which when executed will accomplish a specific task or set of tasks. Macros are frequently used to automate tedious and time-consuming work. A macro is normally assigned a name and a short-cut key; when either is invoked (called upon) the macro is executed.

Let us say that we wish to alter a numeric display in a cell on a Microsoft EXCEL spreadsheet to currency format. We would follow these steps:
1. Place the cell pointer in the appropriate cell.
2. Choose the *Number* option from the *Format* menu.
3. Select *Currency* from the category list presented.
4. Choose the exact currency format required.

151

A macro to automate this procedure, when produced, would appear as follows:

Macro	Comment
Table	
Money (m)	Macro name and key
=FORMAT.NUMBER("£0.00")	Change to currency format
=RETURN()	End of macro

The macro is executed by pressing CRTL+m (Windows version).

Creating a macro

Most current spreadsheet programs offer the user two methods by which a macro can be created:
(a) building a macro manually
(b) recording a macro.

Building a macro manually

The processing of building a macro manually can normally be broken down into six separate stages:

    1. Planning   4. Naming
    2. Entering   5. Executing
    3. Documenting   6. Saving

An editing stage may also be required if the macro is not executing properly.

Example 7

The Adair Arms Hotel offers excellent accommodation to visitors. Each week Karen O'Brien, the hotel manageress, produces a Visitor Category Card using the spreadsheet program on her computer. A completed card is shown opposite:

Spreadsheet

Adair Arms Hotel

Guest Category

	Home	Foreign
Business	27	8
Holiday	31	62
Other	23	11

We will now create a macro, using Microsoft EXCEL, to produce a template based on the above table. When the macro is executed, the following details should appear on the spreadsheet:

	A	B	C
	Spreadsheet		
1	Adair Arms Hotel		
2			
3	Guest Category		
4		Home	Foreign
5	Business		
6	Holiday		
7	Other		

Planning

The following fifteen instructions will go to make up the macro:

Number	Instruction Required
1	Move the cell pointer to cell A1
2	Enter "Adair Arms Hotel"
3	Move the cell pointer to cell A3
4	Enter "Guest Category"
5	Move the cell pointer to cell A5
6	Enter "Business"
7	Move the cell pointer to cell A6
8	Enter "Holiday"
9	Move the cell pointer to cell A7
10	Enter "Other"
11	Move the cell pointer to cell B4
12	Enter "Home"
13	Move the cell pointer to cell C4
14	Enter "Foreign"
15	End macro

Entering

Each of the instructions outlined above should have a corresponding macro instruction. The instructions must be entered, using the appropriate syntax, onto a Microsoft EXCEL macro sheet. The macro sheet is almost identical in appearance to a spreadsheet. The default column widths, however, are a little wider on a macro sheet than those on a spreadsheet.

Documenting

Documenting a macro involves adding comments to explain its purpose and/or its mode of execution. These comments are essential for anyone using a macro that was created by someone else.

Naming

The macro is then assigned a name and/or key. Microsoft EXCEL users place the name and key in the cell above the first macro instruction. The precise command is then given to associate the macro name and key with the list of instructions. We will assign 'template' and 't' as the name and key of our macro.

Our completed macro should appear as follows:

Spreadsheet

Macro	Comments
template (t)	*Macro name and key*
=SELECT(!A1)	
=FORMULA("Adair Arms Hotel")	This macro creates a data entry
=SELECT(!A3)	template for the Adair Arms Hotel
=FORMULA("Guest Category")	to show the number of home and
=SELECT(!A5)	foreign guests, in each guest
=FORMULA("Business")	category, who stayed at the hotel.
=SELECT(!A6)	
=FORMULA("Holiday")	
=SELECT(!A7)	
=FORMULA("Other")	
=SELECT(!B4)	
=FORMULA("Home")	
=SELECT(!C4)	
=FORMULA("Foreign")	
=RETURN()	

Executing

When the macro name or key is invoked, the macro instructions are carried out. Our macro may be executed by pressing the 'CTRL' and 't' keys simultaneously.

Saving

Most current spreadsheet programs allow users to save new macros to a central macro library. This means that a macro originally produced for application on a particular spreadsheet may be used while working on other spreadsheets.

Recording a macro

Macros can also be produced by using the macro recording facility of a spreadsheet program. This facility allows the user to record keystrokes and mouse selections as macro instructions. The latter can then be assigned a name and/or key and can be executed as a macro. Creating macros in this way has a number of advantages:
- It is less time consuming.
- The macros are error-free.
- Complex macros can be produced by novices.

Interactive macros

Interactive macros pause during execution and allow the user to enter input before execution resumes.

Example 8

We will now create an interactive macro to convert any number of inches to centimetres. The macro will pause during execution and allow the user to enter the number of inches.
- Measurements required: 1 inch = 2.54 centimetres

    Our macro will consist of twelve instructions:

Number	Instruction Required
1	Move the cell pointer to the A1 cell
2	Enter "Length Conversion"
3	Move the cell pointer to the A3 cell
4	Enter "Inches ="
5	Move the cell pointer to the B3 cell
6	Pause for input
7	Move the cell pointer to the C3 cell
8	Enter "Centimetres ="
9	Widen column C to 13 to fit the label 'Centimetres ='
10	Move the cell pointer to the D3 cell
11	Enter a formula to multiply the contents of cell B3 by 2.54
12	End the macro

A fully documented macro, in Microsoft EXCEL, to carry out the instructions above should appear as follows:

◇ E ◇ C ◇ A ◇ Spreadsheet

Macro	Comments
Length (l)	*Macro name and key*
=SELECT(!A1)	
=FORMULA("'Length Conversion")	This macro converts any number of inches to the
=SELECT(!A3)	equivalent number of centimetres.
=FORMULA("Inches =")	
=SELECT(!B3)	
=FORMULA(**INPUT("",1)**)	The highlighted instruction pauses execution of
=SELECT(!C3)	the macro and 'expects' input.
=FORMULA("'Centimetres =")	
=COLUMN.WIDTH(13)	
=SELECT(!D3)	
=FORMULA(!B3*2.54)	
=RETURN()	

Conclusion

Spreadsheets are extremely powerful and useful analytical tools. They are used by people in many different occupations, including accountants, statisticians, engineers and scientists. They are easy to use, and complex spreadsheets can be constructed quickly by using replication and the many built-in functions and facilities we have discussed.

In the next chapter you will have an opportunity to practise using spreadsheets by working through the different assignments.

Glossary of spreadsheet terms

absolute cell reference: a cell reference that does not adjust or change when a formula is copied to another cell.

alignment: the cell formatting function that controls the position of labels within a cell.

automatic recalculation mode: a feature whereby cell values are recalculated every time any cell relating to those values is changed.

block: a series of adjacent cells manipulated as an entity; also called a 'range'.

built-in functions: ready-to-use formulae that perform mathematical, statistical and logical calculations, e.g. the summation function.

cash format: a value format in which a number is displayed with two decimal places and usually with a pound sign and thousand markers.

cell: a rectangle formed by the intersection of a row and a column and in which numbers, labels and formulae can be entered and edited.

cell address: a code used to identify a cell by specifying the row and column, e.g. B34.

cell format: the way in which values and labels are displayed in a cell; the more common formats for numbers include integer format, cash format and exponent format; common formats for labels are flush right, flush left and centred.

cell pointer: a rectangular highlight that indicates the current cell, in the same way that the cursor indicates the current position in text.

cell reference: a cell address when used in a formula, e.g. A1 and A10 in the formula @SUM(A1..A10).

cell type: the classification of a cell according to whether it contains a label, a value or a formula.

centred: a label format in which the text is half way between the left and right edges of the column.

column: a vertical series of cells running the full length of the spreadsheet, and usually identified by a letter or letters.

exponent format: a value format in which a number is displayed in the form of a real number between 1 and 9 multiplied by 10 to the power of the appropriate integer.

flush left: a label format in which the text is aligned with the left-hand edge of the column.

flush right: a label format in which the text is aligned with the right-hand edge of the column.

formula: an algebraic expression that defines the relationship between two or ore values, using cell references to represent the values or formulae they contain, e.g. +A2+B7.

integer format: a value format in which a number has no decimal fraction.

non-scrolling titles: a function that allows rows or columns to remain fixed on the display when the rest of the screen scrolls out of view; also called 'fixed titles'.

label: any non-numeric data in the spreadsheet.

real format: a value format in which a number includes a decimal fraction.

relative cell reference: a cell reference that is adjusted or changed when a formula is copied to another cell.

replication: the function that allows labels, values and formulae to be copied to another part of the spreadsheet (also called 'copying').

rounding error: the difference between the exact number and the displayed number.

row: a horizontal series of cells running across the full breadth of the spreadsheet, and usually identified by a number.

spreadsheet: a screen image of a form or matrix made up of rows and columns in which automatic and interconnected calculations are made.

spreadsheet program: the computer program needed to set up a spreadsheet and to allow the use of commands, formulae and special functions.

value: any arithmetic quantity in the spreadsheet.

'what if?' analysis: the manipulation of data so that numeric variables are changed to show the effect of different policies.

window: a rectangular frame in the display that allows other parts of the spreadsheet to be viewed on the same screen.

Chapter 5

PRACTICAL SPREADSHEET ASSIGNMENTS

These assignments are graded, and we advise that you work through them in the order in which they are given.

Functions and commands required

As you progress through these assignments you will need to check on the commands, functions, icons and pull-down menus specific to your spreadsheet program. You will also be practising commands and functions learned in earlier assignments. (Note: If you do not have access to a printer you can display a preview of the printout on the screen.)

The following points should be noted:

• When entering data on amounts of money, do not add the '£' sign as the data item will then be treated by the spreadsheet program as a label. Spreadsheet cells holding details on amounts of money should be formatted to currency display.
• Once constructed, some of the larger spreadsheets in the later assignments may not be entirely visible on the screen. You will need to 'freeze titles' and/or hide certain columns as required.

The new functions and commands encountered in successive assignment are as follows:

ASSIGNMENT 1
• Entering data onto a spreadsheet
• Altering the column width
• Editing the contents of a cell
• Saving a spreadsheet
• Exiting the system

ASSIGNMENT 2
• Recalling a spreadsheet
• Inserting a column of data
• Aligning headings
• Formatting a range of cells to show one decimal place
• Inserting a row of data

ASSIGNMENT 3
• Copying cell contents
• Adding a new column of data
• The summation function
• Finding the average of a row

ASSIGNMENT 4
- Consolidation assignment

ASSIGNMENT 5
- Multiplying the contents of two cells
- Formatting a range of cells to currency display

ASSIGNMENT 6
- Deleting a row of data

ASSIGNMENT 7
- Arithmetic formulae

ASSIGNMENT 8
- Absolute and relative cell references

ASSIGNMENT 9
- Consolidation assignment

ASSIGNMENT 10
- The 'IF' function — one condition
- The date function
- Sorting rows into alphabetical order
- Protecting cell contents
- Printing the entire spreadsheet

ASSIGNMENT 11
- The 'IF' function — two conditions using AND
- Sorting rows into numerical order
- Copying cell displays
- Printing selected columns

ASSIGNMENT 12
- The 'IF' function — nested conditions
- Manual recalculation
- Hiding cell contents
- Printing selected rows

ASSIGNMENT 13
- The horizontal lookup function
- Hiding entire columns

ASSIGNMENT 14
- The vertical lookup function
- Producing a pie graph

ASSIGNMENT 15
- Producing a bar graph

ASSIGNMENT 16
- Financial functions — NPV, PMT and DB

ASSIGNMENT 17
- Simple macros

ASSIGNMENT 18
- Sample NCVA Spreadsheet Methods paper

ASSIGNMENT 19
- 1994 NCVA Spreadsheet Methods paper

ASSIGNMENT 20
- 1995 NCVA Spreadsheet Methods paper

A^S_N · *Assignment 1*

The following spreadsheet shows rainfall (in millimetres) for the months January to June:

	A	B	C	D	E	F	G
1	Rainfall Record (mm)						
2	All						
3	Regions	Jan	Feb	Mar	Apr	May	Jun
4							
5	North	7	9	7	16	12	6
6	West	19	16	11	11	7	3
7	South	3	0	6	3	8	9
8	East	7	8	9	10	5	2
9	N-East	17	17	15	1	9	5
10	S-East	2	2	2	12	4	5
11	N-West	12	9	6	13	13	7
12	S-West	7	13	15	9	14	15

You are required to enter data as shown onto a spreadsheet.

Carry out the following tasks:
Change:
1. the contents of cell A9 to North-East, cell A10 to South-East, cell A11 to North-West and cell A12 to South-West.
Alter:
2. the width of column A to best accommodate the longer labels.

161

Edit:

3. the rainfall value for February in the East region to show 13 and for June in the South-East region to show 15.

Delete:

4. the contents of cell A2.

Save:

5. the spreadsheet as RAIN.

Exit:

6. the spreadsheet program.

ASN · *Assignment 2*

Carry out the following tasks:

Recall:

1. the spreadsheet RAIN.

Add:

2. a new column between the *Regions* column and the *Jan* information column (i.e. a new column B).

Enter:

3. the area of each region in this new column as given in the following table:

ECA Table	
Regions	**Area**
North	4768
West	5674
South	3213
East	4356
N-East	675
S-East	567
N-West	453
S-West	689

Align:

4. all month labels and the *Area* label flush right (if you have not already done so).

Insert:

5. a new row of rainfall data for *West Islands*, to be the new row 9; the present row 9 will move down to become row 10, and all other rows below this will also move down automatically.

The data for this region is:

Regions	Area	Jan	Feb	Mar	Apr	May	Jun
West Islands	345	17	13	19	20	15	12

(Table heading: E C A Table)

Format:

6. the rainfall data on the spreadsheet to show one decimal place.

Save:

7. the edited spreadsheet as NEWRAIN.

Exit:

8. the spreadsheet program.

ASN · *Assignment 3*

Carry out the following tasks:

Recall:

1. the spreadsheet NEWRAIN.

Add:

2. a new *Total* column after the June data to show the total rainfall for each of the nine regions. (Hint: Use the summation function.)

3. a new *Average* column after the *Total* column to show the average rainfall in each region for the six-month period. (Hint: For each region, use a formula that divides the total rainfall for that region by 6.)

Enter:

4. the heading *Total Area* in cell A14.

Show:

5. the total area of all the regions in cell B14.

Enter:

6. your name and today's date in cells A16 and A17, respectively.

Save:

7. the spreadsheet as ENDRAIN.

Exit:

8. the spreadsheet program.

ASN · Assignment 4

The following table shows student results in four tests. The maximum mark possible for each test is 10; the minimum possible is 0.

Spreadsheet

Test Results

Student	Test 1	Test 2	Test 3	Test 4
J Kelly	9	9	7	8
S Nicholl	0	8	5	4
O Browne	2	7	7	7
M Carey	9	10	8	7
C Smyth	9	7	8	9
E Quinn	3	6	0	0
U Daly	3	6	5	3
F Murphy	9	10	8	5

You are required to enter the details in the table onto a spreadsheet.

Carry out the following tasks:

Add a new:
1. *Overall Marks* column to show the total marks obtained by each student in all four tests.
2. *Average Marks* column to show the average mark for each student in the four tests. (Hint: Use the average function.)

Amend:
3. the marks for J. Kelly, O. Browne and F. Murphy in test 3; each mark should be increased by 2.
4. the mark for S. Nicholl in test 4; it should be 7.

Add:
5. a new *Test Average* row to show the average mark for each test.

Save:
6. the spreadsheet as RESULTS.

A$N • *Assignment 5*

The following table shows the cone sales for seven different flavours of ice cream at Mel's Ice Cream Parlour over a five-day period:

Table

Mel's Ice Cream Parlour

Flavour	Mon	Tue	Wed	Thu	Fri
Caramel	18	24	11	19	14
Choc Chip	27	33	25	20	29
Mint	5	4	9	13	8
Orange	12	9	7	5	4
Pistachio	8	11	12	10	13
Strawberry	22	31	17	22	34
Vanilla	35	20	28	25	37

You are required to enter this data onto a spreadsheet.

Carry out the following tasks:
Save:
1. the spreadsheet as ICE1.
Add:
2. a column after Friday's data to show the *total sales* of each ice cream flavour over the five-day period.
Insert:
3. a column between *Friday's data* and *total sales*.
Enter:
4. in the new column the following ice cream sales for Saturday: Caramel — 20, Choc Chip — 26, Mint — 17, Orange — 6, Pistachio — 17, Strawberry — 28, Vanilla — 31. Amend the totals formulae to take account of this insertion.
Add:
5. a column after the *total sales* column to show the *cone cost* for each ice cream flavour: Caramel — £0.80, Choc Chip — £1.05, Mint — £1.15, Orange — £0.75, Pistachio — £1.10, Strawberry — £0.90, Vanilla — £0.65.
6. a column, after the *cone cost* column, to show the *total income* from the sales of each ice cream flavour during the six-day period.
Enter:
7. a formula, in the appropriate cell, to show the *total income* for the week at Mel's Ice Cream Parlour.

Format:

8. the *cone cost* and *total income* columns to currency format.

Save:

9. the spreadsheet as ICE2.

ASN · Assignment 6

The table below shows the sales commission of seven salespersons who sell different products for Annex Ltd. The salespersons are paid their commission at the end of a three-month period.

ECA Table

Annex Ltd
Commission Payments

Name	EE No	Qtr 1	Qtr 2	Qtr 3	Qtr 4
A Behan	901	157	295	10	290
B Collins	264	71	221	130	355
C Daly	745	247	242	256	176
A Nolan	256	39	227	64	297
A Sheils	633	142	24	120	241
T Timmons	908	178	56	67	359
J Wynne	353	335	367	190	186

Enter the details shown in the table onto a spreadsheet.

Carry out the following tasks:

Change:

1. the name C. Daly to C. Davis.
2. the amount for J. Wynne for the second quarter to 153.62.

Format:

3. all money amounts to currency format.

Insert:

4. a new *Division* column between the employee number (EE No) and the first-quarter details to give the following division names:

   A. Behan: Paper
   B. Collins: Equipment
   C. Davis: Paper
   A . Nolan: Stationery

A. Shiels: Equipment

T. Timmons: Stationery

J. Wynne: Paper

Alter:

5. the width of the *Division* column to accommodate the longest entry.

Add:

6. a new *Total Commission* column to show the total commission for each salesperson for the four quarters.

7. a *Bonus* column to show the end-of-year bonus payable to all salespersons; those in the Paper Division are to get £30 extra; all other divisions get a bonus of £20.

8. a *Commission Earnings* column to show the total commission plus bonus for each salesperson

9. a new *Commission Payable* row to display the total commission issued in each quarter.

Insert:

10. (preserving the alphabetical order of employee names) a new row containing the following details for G Ennis who joined the Equipment Division of the company in the third quarter:

Table					
Name	EE No	Qtr 1	Qtr 2	Qtr 3	Qtr 4
G Ennis	449	0	0	200	345

Add:

11. a new row that shows the average commission issued in each quarter.

Delete:

12. the row containing A. Nolan's details.

Save:

13. the spreadsheet as EARNINGS.

A$_S$N • *Assignment 7*

Quality Copiers Ltd, a company that rents photocopiers to many different businesses, has given you the following details:

◇ E C A ◇ **Table**		

Company Name	Last Reading	Current Reading
BC Services Ltd	31977	33668
Brogan & Co	43222	46472
Connolly & Sons	83661	84700
Energywise Ltd	15003	16191
Fastline Ltd	19981	21130
Kitt Packaging	64812	66917
Lee Electrical	36391	38110
Marsden & Co	28901	30121
Safeclean Ltd	18368	21555
Windowland Ltd	51252	54213

Rental bills, issued monthly, are calculated on:
1. a £0.05 per copy charge **and**
2. a £30.00 monthly service charge.
All bills are subject to VAT at 21%.

  You must enter the details in the table above onto a spreadsheet.

Carry out the following tasks:
Save:
1. the spreadsheet as COPY1.
Add:
2. a *Copies Made* column after the *Current Reading* column showing the number of photocopies made since last month's reading of the photocopier counter.
3. a *Unit Cost* column after the *Copies Made* column showing the cost of one copy.
4. a *Copies Cost* column after the *Unit Cost* column showing the actual cost of copying for each business.
5. a *Service Charge* column displaying the amount.
6. a *Bill Total* column showing the cost of copying plus the service charge for each business.
7. a *VAT* column showing the VAT payable on each bill.
8. an *Amount Payable* column showing the actual amount payable by each business.

Format:

9. all columns containing money details to currency format.

Save:

10. the spreadsheet as COPY2.

A𝒮N · *Assignment 8*

Carrigallen Mart hold livestock sales every week. The table below shows the monthly sales of cattle, pigs and sheep for the past year:

◇ E C A ◇ Table			
Month	Cattle	Pigs	Sheep
January	1466	2621	1121
February	1839	3819	1619
March	2844	1726	2144
April	4525	1341	3282
May	2193	1716	2792
June	1153	1205	1844
July	1008	1017	1102
August	1796	1914	1219
September	4377	2838	1372
October	5542	3561	2611
November	3829	4219	2433
December	2081	4532	1518

You are required to enter these details onto a suitably titled spreadsheet.

Carry out the following tasks:

Save:

1. the spreadsheet as MART1.

Insert:

2. a row, labelled *Total Sold*, beneath the December details.

Enter:

3. formulae into this row to obtain the total number of each animal type sold during the year.

Insert:

4. a new column after each of the three livestock columns.

Label:

5. these three new columns — *Cattle (%)*, *Pigs (%)* and *Sheep (%)*, respectively.

Obtain:

6. the percentage of each animal type sold each month as a fraction of the total sales for that particular animal type for the year. (Hint: each formula will have absolute and relative cell references.)

Format:

7. these three percentage columns to percentage format (one decimal place).

Add:

8. a new column, labelled *Total Livestock*, after the last column on the spreadsheet showing the total number of livestock sold each month and obtain the total for the year.

9. a new column, labelled *Total Livestock (%)*, after the *Total Livestock* column showing the percentage of livestock sold each month as a fraction of the yearly total. This column should also be formatted to display percentages (one decimal place).

Save:

10. the spreadsheet as MART2.

ASN • *Assignment 9*

Riversdale Farms Ltd supply fresh vegetables to a number of greengrocers in the Dublin area. The table below shows the number of kilograms of carrots, onions, parsnips and tomatoes delivered to ten different greengrocers' shops on a particular day:

Shop	Carrots	Onions	Parsnips	Tomatoes
J Bean & Sons	80	40	65	50
Cabbage Patch	65	45	40	85
Get Fresh	120	75	70	100
Just In	75	80	30	75
Lentils & Co	90	45	25	70
Picked Today	50	70	40	45
Salad Days	85	35	15	30
SpringFresh Ltd	110	90	100	85
The Runner Bean	70	20	45	55
Vegworld	60	50	10	40

You must enter these details onto a suitably titled spreadsheet.

Carry out the following tasks:

Save:

1. the spreadsheet as VEG1.

Insert:

2. a new column after each of the four weight columns.

Label:

3. these new columns — *Carrots (£), Onions (£), Parsnips (£)* and *Tomatoes (£)*, respectively.

Insert:

4. two new rows between the spreadsheet heading and the column headings.

Enter:

5. the following price details into the two new rows:

E C A Table				
Vegetable	Carrots	Onions	Parsnips	Tomatoes
Price/kg	£0.35	£0.55	£0.40	£0.50

Enter:

6. appropriate formulae into the four new price columns to calculate the total cost of each vegetable type bought by each individual shop. (Hint: each formula will have absolute and relative cell references.)

Insert:

7. a column, labelled *Total Price* after the *Tomatoes (£)* column, showing the total cost of all four vegetable types for each shop.

8. a new row, labelled *Overall Income* below the bottom row on the spreadsheet, showing the total income generated from sales of all four vegetable types to all ten shops.

Format:

9. all columns containing money details to currency format.

Save:

10. this spreadsheet as VEG2.

ASN · Assignment 10

Mac's Tool Hire Company, set up by Susan MacMahon in 1996, provides a wide range of electrical and mechanical tools suitable for use by the professional builder or the DIY enthusiast. A 25% discount is offered on all equipment hired for more than two weeks. Susan needs your expertise in using a spreadsheet program to help in the preparation of customer invoices. You must transfer the following invoice details to a spreadsheet:

ECA Table

Mac's Tool Hire Company

Customer Invoice: Sean Murphy

Tool Hired	Weekly Cost	Weeks Hired
Skill Saw	£5.00	2
Drill	£4.00	4
Cement Mixer	£75.00	5
Electric Plane	£11.00	1
Generator	£25.00	1
Rotovator	£22.00	3
Roofing Torch	£8.00	4
Compressor	£18.00	1
Pressure Washer	£27.00	2
Floor Edger	£13.00	3

Carry out the following tasks:

Save:
1. the spreadsheet as TOOLS1.

Add:
2. a *Total Cost* column showing the total cost of hiring each item listed.
3. a *Discount Given* column showing the discount, if any, available on each item (Hint: Use the IF function.)
4. an *Actual Cost* column showing the amount payable on each item.
5. three rows below the last row of data showing:
   (a) the total of actual costs for all items listed (*Total Bill*);
   (b) the VAT payable at 21% on the bill (*VAT Payable*);
   (c) the total amount payable by the customer (*Amount Payable*).

Insert:
6. a row beneath the row containing the customer's name.
Enter:
7. today's date in this new row. (Use the appropriate date function.)
Sort:
8. the rows containing the equipment details into alphabetical order of equipment name.
Protect:
9. all cells containing formulae.
Save:
10. the spreadsheet as TOOLS2.
Print:
11. the entire spreadsheet.

ASN · *Assignment 11*

Bethany Travel Ltd specialise in organising pilgrimages for Irish parishes to a number of shrines in Europe and the Holy Land. The following table shows booking details for last week:

Parish Name	Pilgrimage Destination	Group Size	Ticket Cost
Ballinteer	Medjugorie	72	£249.00
Clifden	Fatima	29	£283.00
Drumshambo	Fatima	16	£283.00
Ennis	Rome	25	£380.00
Gorey	Lourdes	38	£315.00
Gort	Medjugorie	50	£249.00
Killeshandra	Lourdes	33	£315.00
Kimmage	Lourdes	85	£315.00
Mostrim	Fatima	20	£283.00
Navan	Fatima	12	£283.00
Omagh	The Holy Land	19	£380.00
Thurles	Lourdes	27	£315.00

A 20% reduction was given to parish groups where the pilgrimage destination was not Lourdes **and** the group consisted of more than thirty people, otherwise a 10% reduction was given.

A 5% government tax was levied on all bookings.

You must enter the details in the table onto a suitably titled spreadsheet.

Carry out the following tasks:
Save:
1. the spreadsheet as PILGRIM1.
Add:
2. a *Group Cost* column showing the total ticket costs for each parish group.
3. a *Group Reduction* column showing the total reductions for each parish group. (Hint: Use a compound IF statement.)
4. a *Govt Tax* column showing the total government tax levied on each parish group. (Hint: This is calculated on the group cost.)
5. a *Group Total* column showing the actual amount paid by each parish group after the appropriate reduction was made and the government tax levied.
6. an *Individual Cost* column showing the actual amount paid by each member of the parish group.
Sort:
7. the rows on the spreadsheet into descending order of parish group size.
Copy:
8. the details displayed in the *Parish Name* column and the corresponding details in the *Individual Cost* column to Columns L and M, respectively, on the spreadsheet.
Protect:
9. all cells containing formulae.
Save:
10. this spreadsheet as PILGRIM2.
Print:
11. the contents of columns L and M.

ASN · Assignment 12

Ashton Electrical Ltd, based in Cork, are one of Ireland's leading importers of electrical goods. The company supplies electrical shops throughout the country with a wide variety of modern domestic appliances. A new shipment of goods is due at the company's warehouses next week and it has been decided to hold a sale in order to clear the existing stock.

The following percentage reductions are available during the sale of existing stock:

Individual items costing:
£200 or less — 20%
between £200 and £400 — 25%
£400 or more — 30%

The company's fleet of lorries delivers the goods to the individual shops. If the delivery distance is more than 20 miles then the charge is £3.00 per mile, otherwise the charge is £2.50 per mile.

JD Abbot, the head of Sales at Ashton Electrical, has employed you for the sale period to produce customer invoices on a spreadsheet. The following incomplete invoice has just been given to you:

◇E◇C◇A◇ Table			

Ashton Electrical Ltd

Customer:	Harry Murphy & Co	Address:	4 Main St, Athlone
Date:	Today's Date	Delivery Distance:	32

Electrical Item	Usual Price	Units Bought
Cooker	£450.00	5
Deep fat fryer	£40.00	18
Dish washer	£150.00	3
Fridge freezer	£240.00	6
Microwave	£80.00	9
Stereo	£220.00	7
Television	£300.00	4
Tumble dryer	£110.00	2
Vacuum cleaner	£100.00	12
Video	£270.00	10
Washer dryer	£410.00	7
Washing machine	£320.00	3

Enter the invoice details given onto a spreadsheet. Use the appropriate function to include *today's date*.

Carry out the following tasks:
Save:
1. the spreadsheet as SALE1.
Add:
2. a *Total Price* column showing the total price of all the units bought of each item **before** any sales reduction.

3. a *Reduction Available* column showing the total reduction on all the units bought of each item. (Hint: Use a nested IF statement.)

4. a *Total Sale Price* column showing the total price of all the units bought of each item **after** the sales reductions are made.

Add:

5. a *Total Charge* row beneath the bottom row of the spreadsheet showing a total for the *Total Sales Price* column.

6. a *VAT Payable* row showing the VAT due on this invoice (VAT is charged at 21%).

7. a *Delivery Charge* row showing the total cost of delivering the items listed to *Harry Murphy & Co.* (Hint: Use a simple IF statement.)

8. a *Total Amount Payable* row showing the actual amount payable on this current delivery to *Harry Murphy & Co.*

Save:

9. the file as SALE2.

Switch:

10. to manual recalculation mode.

Make:

11. alterations to the contents of the appropriate cells to take account of the following:
    - 4 dishwashers and 9 vacuum cleaners were bought;
    - the usual price of a washer dryer is £430.

Switch:

12. to automatic recalculation mode.

Sort:

13. the rows containing the item details into descending order of *Total Sales Price*.

Protect and hide:

14. the contents of all cells containing formulae.

Save:

15. the spreadsheet as SALE3.

Print:

16. the cell displays for the *Total Charge*, *VAT Payable*, *Delivery Charge* and *Total Amount Payable* rows only.

A$N · *Assignment 13*

CareFree Car Rentals, established in 1995, have given you the following table showing rental details for ten tourists who have hired cars from the company:

E C A **Table**

CareFree Car Rentals

Daily Car Hire Rates

Category	A	B	C	D	E
Rate	£35.00	£30.00	£25.00	£20.00	£15.00

Customer Name	Car Type	Car Category	Days Hired
Pierre Almont	Mazda 323F	C	8
Maria Bonetti	Nissan Micra	D	5
Daniel Davies	VW Passat	B	4
Keith Frazier	Toyota Starlet	D	9
Petra Lamvelt	Toyota Carina	B	4
Ida Luff	Ford Mondeo	B	6
Shari McKenzie	Puegot 106	E	7
Carlo Ponti	Mazda 626	B	8
Sven Stonson	Mitsubishi Pajero	A	4
Hillary Wallace	VW Golf	C	6

You are required to enter the details shown in the table onto a spreadsheet.

Carry out the following tasks:
Save:
1. the spreadsheet as CARHIRE1.

Add:
2. a *Basic Cost* column showing the basic cost of car rental for each of the customers listed. (Hint: Use the horizontal lookup function.)
3. an *Extra Days Reduction* column showing the reduction amount, if any, that each customer receives. This reduction amount of £5.00 per day is given for each extra day that a car is rented over the standard five-day rental period. (Hint: Use a simple IF statement.)
4. an *Amount Payable* column showing the actual rental payable by each customer after the correct reduction, if any, has been made on the *Basic Cost*.

Save:

5. the spreadsheet as CARHIRE2.

Switch:

6. to manual recalculation mode.

Make the following alterations to the appropriate cells:

7. the daily car rental costs have increased by £2.50 for all categories.

8. the VW Passat and Toyota Carina were hired for 3 and 7 days, respectively.

9. The reduction amount has been increased to £7.50 per day for each extra day that a car is rented over the standard five-day rental period.

Switch:

10. to automatic recalculation mode.

Hide:

11. all columns except the *Customer Name* and *Amount Payable* columns.

Save:

12. the spreadsheet as CARHIRE3.

Print:

13. the customer names and corresponding amounts payable from the two columns that are visible on the spreadsheet. This printout should show column and row identifiers.

ᴬˢᴺ ∙ *Assignment 14*

The Corn Mill Theatre caters for a wide range of theatrical tastes. The current play running at the theatre is John B. Keane's *'Sive'*. The table below shows the audience attendances in the four different categories for the three areas of the theatre for last evening:

◇ECA◇ *Table*			
Corn Mill Theatre — Audience Receipts			
Audience Category	Base Level	Lower Circle	Upper Circle
Adult	51	35	42
Child	14	22	27
Student	28	19	23
Unwaged	20	12	17

You are required to enter the details shown in the table onto a spreadsheet.

Carry out the following tasks:
Save:
1. the spreadsheet as THEATRE1.
Insert a column labelled:
2. *Base Level (£)* after the *Base Level* column.
3. *Lower Circle (£)* after the *Lower Circle* column.
4. *Upper Circle (£)* after the *Upper Circle* column.
Insert:
5. eight rows between the spreadsheet heading and the column headings.
Enter:
6. the following details concerning ticket prices into the new rows. (Use the correct date function to enter *Today's Date*):

E C A	Table		
Today's Date			
Ticket Prices			
	Base Level	Lower Circle	Upper Circle
Adult	£12.00	£15.00	£18.00
Child	£5.00	£6.50	£8.00
Student	£7.50	£10.00	£13.00
Unwaged	£9.00	£12.00	£15.50

The details from this table can be used as a lookup table.

Enter:
7. formulae in the three new columns to calculate the receipts taken in the various audience categories for each section of the theatre. (Hint: Using the ticket price details in the lookup table and the attendance figures, construct the formulae using the vertical lookup function).
Add:
8. a column, labelled *Total Receipts*, showing the total receipts taken in each of the four audience categories for the whole theatre.
Insert:
9. a formula in the appropriate cell to show the total receipts taken for last evening.
Add:
10. a column, labelled *% Receipts*, showing the percentage of total receipts taken in each of the four audience categories.
Format:
11. the display, in this latter column, to percentage format (one decimal place).

Copy:

12. the cell displays in the *Audience Category* and *% Receipts* columns to the L and M columns, respectively.

Protect and hide:

13. the contents of all cells containing formulae.

Save:

14. the spreadsheet as THEATRE2.

Produce:

15. a pie graph, titled *Corn Mill Theatre — Audience Receipts*, showing the percentage breakdown of audience receipts.

Save:

16. the graph as CORNMILL.

Print:

17. the graph.

A$N · *Assignment 15*

Wheel World Ltd, a shop specialising in the sale of new bicycles and cycling accessories, has been in existence for over twenty years. Susan Kelly, the owner of the shop, provides a hire purchase method of payment to any customer who has just bought a new bicycle at the shop. Different rates of interest are charged depending on the number of agreed monthly payments. The interest payable is calculated as a percentage of the cost of the bicycle. The interest rate categories are as follows:

Table						
Monthly Payments	2	6	10	12	18	24
Interest Rate	0%	3%	6%	7%	10%	15%

If the customer uses Susan's hire purchase method of payment, an initial deposit must be paid. The deposit is calculated as 20% of the cost on all bicycles over £250, otherwise the deposit payable is only 15% of the cost of the bicycle.

Susan has given you the following details on ten new customers who have opted for her hire purchase system:

◇E◇C◇A◇	*Table*			

Customer Name	Bicycle Make	Bicycle Cost	Number of Payments
Sandra Allen	Falcon 65	£160.00	10
Seamus Cullen	Townsend G5	£145.00	6
John Dunne	Alexa MB4	£275.00	2
Marie Higgins	President CX	£320.00	24
Linda Logan	Alexa MB1	£235.00	12
Martin Murphy	Saracen 96	£185.00	18
Noel O'Brien	Falcon 105	£335.00	10
Carol O'Gorman	Marlboro DT	£250.00	2
Brian Ryan	Diamond 109	£170.00	6
Margaret Tracy	Saracen 98	£215.00	12

Enter the details in this table onto a suitably titled spreadsheet.

Carry out the following tasks:
Save:
1. the spreadsheet as CYCLE1.
Insert:
2. two new rows between the spreadsheet title and the column titles.
Enter:
3. the details on monthly payments and interest rates outlined earlier into the two new rows.
Add:
4. an *Interest Payable* column showing the actual amount of interest due on each purchase. (Hint: Use the most suitable lookup function in the construction of the formula.)
5. a *Total Payable* column showing the actual amount of money that each customer must pay.
6. a *Deposit Due* column showing the deposit that must be paid by each customer.
7. a *Monthly Amount* column showing the actual amount of money that must be paid monthly by each customer **after** the initial deposit has been paid.
Save:
8. the spreadsheet as CYCLE2.
Change:
9. the interest rates, in the lookup table, for 2, 6, 10, 12, 18 and 24 monthly payments to 5%, 10%, 15%, 20%, 25% and 30%, respectively.

Copy:

10. the details in the *Customer Name* column and the corresponding details in the *Interest Payable* column to the K and L columns, respectively.

Protect and hide:

11. the contents of all cells containing formulae.

Save:

12. the spreadsheet as CYCLE3.

Produce:

13. a bar graph of the details in columns K and L. The graph should have a suitable title and should show the customer names along the *x*-axis and the interest payable amounts along the *y*-axis.

Save:

14. the graph as INTEREST.

Print:

15. the graph.

ASN · *Assignment 16*

Section A — Investment venture

Mervyn Richardson, the owner of Jetwash Ltd, is considering an investment venture costing £250,000 which must be paid in advance. The projected sales from the venture, expected to last for 1997, 1998 and 1999 are £120,000, £140,000 and £160,000 respectively. Mervyn wishes to know if it is better to invest in the venture or to leave the money in the bank at the current interest rate of 12% over the same period.

You must enter the details given below onto a spreadsheet:

ECA Table

Jetwash Ltd

Projected Sales

Investment	1997	1998	1999
£250,000.00	£120,000.00	£140,000.00	£160,000.00

Interest Rate Given =   12%

Net Present Value =
Bank Savings Return =
Worthwhile Investment =

182

Carry out the following tasks:
Enter a formula in the cell to the right of:
1. the *'Net Present Value ='* label to show the net present value of the investment at a rate of 12%. (Hint: Use the NPV function in constructing the formula.)
2. the *'Bank Savings Return ='* label to show the compound interest that the money would earn over the same period.
3. the *'Worthwhile Investment ='* label to show whether the investment is worthwhile or not (Yes/No). (*Hint:* the investment is worthwhile if the *Net Present Value* is greater than the *Bank Savings Return.*)

Save:
4. the spreadsheet as JETWASH.

Section B — Mortgage repayments

Patrick Doyle, the manager of the EasyLoan Building Society, wishes to produce a mortgage repayments table to show the monthly repayments on a £30,000, a £50,000 and a £70,000 mortgage. The table must show repayments for varying interest rates (from 7 to 9% in increments of 0.5%). All mortgages are for 20 years.

   You are required to enter the details in the following incomplete table onto a spreadsheet:

◇C◇ Table			
EasyLoan Building Society			
Monthly Repayments Table			
Loan Term			
Years	20		
Months	240		
Interest Rate	£30,000.00	£50,000.00	£70,000.00
7.0%			
7.5%			
8.0%			
8.5%			
9.0%			

Carry out the following tasks:
Enter:
1. suitable formulae in the appropriate cells to show the monthly repayment for each mortage amount and interest rate. (Hint: Use the PMT function in constructing the formulae.)

Save:
2. the spreadsheet as MORTGAGE.
Print:
3. the spreadsheet showing the actual formulae used.

Section C — Depreciation

Office Machines Ltd supply businesses nationwide with a range of modern office equipment. Sean O'Gorman, the managing director, is intensely interested in the amounts of depreciation on equipment over a number of years.

Sean has given you the following incomplete table showing details of an autoprinter that has just been sold by the company:

◇E◇C◇A◇ **Table**			
Office Machines Ltd			
Equipment Sold =	Autoprinter	Cost =	£40,000.00
Estimated Life (yrs) =	8	Salvage Value =	£5,000.00
Year Number	Depreciation Amount	Cumulative Depreciation	Net Book Value

You are required to enter these details onto a spreadsheet.

Carry out the following tasks:
Enter:
1. the values 1 to 8 in the eight cells beneath the *Year Number* column heading.
2. a formula in the *Depreciation Amount* column to calculate the depreciation at the end of the first year. (Hint: Use the DB function, i.e. the fixed-declining balance function.)
Copy:
3. this formula down the column to show the depreciation amounts for years 2 to 8.
Enter suitable formulae in the:
4. *Cumulative Depreciation* column to show the total depreciation on the autoprinter at the end of each year.
5. *Net Book Value* column to show the actual value of the printer at the end of each year.
Save:
6. the spreadsheet as PRINTER.
Print:
7. the spreadsheet showing the actual formulae used.

A^S_N · *Assignment 17*

Section A

Produce:

1. a macro that widens a column to 'best fit' the longest entry.

Save:

2. the macro as COLWIDEN.

Section B

Produce:

1. a macro that, upon execution, produces the following template:

	A	B	C	D
	E C A Spreadsheet			
1	Claire's Cake Shop			
2				
3	Cake	Day 1	Day 2	Day 3
4				
5	Carrot			
6	Cheese			
7	Coffee			

Save:

2. the macro as CAKESHOP.

Section C

Produce:

1. an interactive macro that accepts any number of Irish pounds and returns the equivalent amounts of US dollars and German Marks. Use the following exchange rates:
    IR£1.00 = $1.57 = 2.32DM

Save:

2. the macro as MONEY.

When the macro is executed and IR£25 is entered; you should obtain the following:

	A	B	C
	◇E◇C◇A◇ *Spreadsheet*		
	A	B	C
1	Exchange Rate		
2			
3	Irish Punt	US Dollar	German Mark
4	25.00	39.25	58.00

A$N • *Assignment 18*

NCVA Spreadsheet Methods Sample Paper

Task 1 (30 marks)

1. Set up the spreadsheet and input the data as shown in Figure 1.

   a. The *Selling Price* is calculated as 1.3 times the *Cost Price* and should be displayed in currency format.

   b. The *Total* is calculated as the *Selling Price × Qty* and should be displayed in currency format.

   c. The *Sub Total*, *VAT @ 21%* and the *Total Incl. VAT* should be calculated values and displayed in currency format.

2. Insert your name and the date in the positions indicated.

3. Save the spreadsheet under the filename SREPORT1, for printing now or later.

Computer Wizards

September Sales Report

Item Description	Cost Price	Selling Price	Qty	Total
Printer DM9	£180.00		13	
Printer DM 24	£230.00		6	
Printer IJ Model 1	£220.00		15	
Printer IJ Model 2	£250.00		8	
Printer L Model 1	£340.00		6	
Printer L Model 2	£430.00		9	
Plotter A4	£660.00		4	
Plotter A3	£760.00		3	
Disk DD (Box 10)	£4.00		22	
Disk HD (Box 10)	£5.50		18	

Sub Total
VAT @ 21%
Total Incl. VAT

Name:

Date:

Task 2 (25 marks)

1. Input the additional information shown in Figure 2.
   a. Change the subheading to *October Sales Report*.
   b. Insert extra columns as required.
   c. The Disc.% should be calculated on the following basis:
      i. if the *Qty* is less than 5 then the *Disc.%* is 0%.
      ii. if the *Qty* is between 5 and 9 inclusive then the *Disc.%* is 2%.
      iii. if the *Qty* is 10 or greater then the *Disc.%* is 5%.
   d. The *Disc.%* should be displayed in percentage format.
   e. The *Disc. Price* is calculated as *Selling Price* - the discount allowed.
   f. Reposition the *Sub Total*, *VAT @ 21%* and *Total incl. VAT* headings.
2. Recalculate the *Total* to use the *Disc. Price* for the calculation.
3. Save the spreadsheet under the filename SREPORT2 for printing now or later.

Computer Wizards

September Sales Report

Item Description	Cost Price	Selling Price	Qty	Disc%	Disc Price	Total
Printer DM9	£180.00		13			
Printer DM 24	£230.00		6			
Printer IJ Model 1	£220.00		15			
Printer IJ Model 2	£250.00		8			
Printer L Model 1	£340.00		6			
Printer L Model 2	£430.00		9			
Plotter A4	£660.00		4			
Plotter A3	£760.00		3			
Disk DD (Box 10)	£4.00		22			
Disk HD (Box 10)	£5.50		18			

Sub Total
VAT @ 21%
Total Incl. VAT

Name:
Date:

Task 3 (35 marks)
1. Input the additional information as shown in Figure 3.
   a. Change the subheading to *November Sales Report*.
   b. Insert the table of *Computer Type*, *Model* and *Prices* under the subheading
      i. The *Selling Price* should be calculated as 1.3 times the *Cost Price* and displayed in currency format.
   c. Delete the **Disks** from the spreadsheet.
   d. Insert the five *Computer Types*.
      i. Use the LOOKUP function to insert the *Cost Price* form the table into the *Cost Price* column.
      ii. Use the LOOKUP function to insert the *Selling Price* from the table into the *Selling Price* column.
   e. Change the quantities sold as indicated in Figure 3.

f. The *Average Quantity Sold* should be the average of the *Qty* column and should be an integer.

g. The *Average Disc. on Computers* should take account of the quantity of each type of computer sold. The value should be rounded to one decimal place and should be in percentage format.

2. Sort the spreadsheet into alphabetical order on the *Item Description*.

3. Save the spreadsheet under the filename SREPORT3 for printing now or later. This printout will require formulae to be printed.

Spreadsheet **Figure 3**

Computer Wizards

November Sales Report

Computer Type	1	2	3	4	5
Model	386sx 20	386dx 20	386 sx 25	486 sx 33	486 dx 33
Cost Price	£580.00	£620.00	£650.00	£720.00	£760.00
Selling Price					

Item Description	Cost Price	Selling Price	Qty	Disc%	Disc Price	Total
Computer Type 1			12			
Computer Type 2			11			
Computer Type 3			8			
Computer Type 4			5			
Computer Type 5			3			
Plotter A3	£760.00		6			
Plotter A4	£660.00		5			
Printer DM 24	£230.00		2			
Printer DM9	£180.00		8			
Printer IJ Model 1	£220.00		9			
Printer IJ Model 2	£250.00		11			
Printer L Model 1	£340.00		3			
Printer L Model 2	£430.00		12			

Sub Total
VAT @ 21%
Total Incl. VAT

Average Quantity Sold
Average Disc on Computers

Name:
Date:

Task 4 (10 marks)

1. Produce a *Bar Chart* to show the quantity of computers sold:
   a. The quantity should be taken from the *Qty* column.
   b. The *Bar Chart* should have the heading *Sales Figures - Computers by Quantity*.
   c. The *x*-axis should show *Type 1* under the first bar, *Type 2* under the second etc. and should have the label *Computer* underneath.
   d. The *y*-axis should show the *Quantity* in figures and have the label *Quantity*.
2. Save the *Bar Chart* under the filename SGRAPH for printing now or later.

Printing:

Printouts of the following files are required:
- SREPORT1
- SREPORT2
- SREPORT3
- SGRAPH.

A$N · Assignment 19

NCVA Spreadsheet Methods Paper 1994

Task 1(30 marks)

1. Set up the spreadsheet and input the data as shown in **Figure 1**.
   a. Align main heading (Hi-Tech Production) and subheading (Production Report - January 1994) centrally over the data.
   b. Set column widths to appropriate values.
   c. Column 1 heading and values should be centrally aligned.
   d. Column 2 heading and values should be left aligned.
   e. Column 3, 4, 5 and 6 headings and values should be right aligned.
   f. The profit figures should be the profit for the quantity produced in each factory and should be calculated values.
   g. The values in columns 4, 5 and 6 should be displayed in currency format.
   h. The *Total:* and *Total Profit:* should be calculated values. They should be aligned and displayed in the same format as the column in which they appear.
2. Insert the labels *Name:*, *Examination No:* and *Date:* in the positions indicated and insert the appropriate information after each.
3. Save the spreadsheet under the filename 94TASK1, for printing now or later. (The printout should show borders — Row/Column labels.)

◆E◆C◆A◆ *Spreadsheet*	*Figure 1*

Hi-Tech Productions

Production Report - January 1994

No.	Factory	Factory Production Quantity	Unit Production Price	Unit Selling Price	Profit
1	Clondalkin	2500	£0.28	£0.48	
2	Santry	3400	£0.25	£0.46	
3	Cork	2800	£0.30	£0.49	
4	Galway	2300	£0.26	£0.52	
5	Limerick	4400	£0.32	£0.53	
6	Athlone	800	£0.28	£0.46	
7	Sligo	1800	£0.29	£0.51	
8	Waterford	3500	£0.30	£0.50	
9	Dundalk	2700	£0.33	£0.52	

Total: Total Profit:

Name:

Examination No:

Date:

Task 2 (25 marks)

4. Input the additional information shown in **Figure 2**.
   a. Change the month in the subheading to *February*.
   b. Insert an extra column where required.
   c. Insert the heading *Royalty Fee* in the new column and align to the right.
   d. Re-align the main and subheadings centrally over the data.
   e. The *Royalty Fee* should be calculated on the following basis and displayed in the column as a percentage (i.e. 6%, 4%, 2%): if the production quantity is greater than 2000 then the royalty fee is 6%, if the quantity is between 1000 and 2000 inclusive then the royalty fee is 4% and if the quantity is less than 1000 then the fee is 2%.
   f. The *Royalty Fee* should be displayed in percentage format and right aligned.

2. Reposition the *Total Profit:* heading.
3. Recalculate the profit on the following basis: the royalty fee is a percentage of the *Unit Selling Price* and reduces the profit by that amount.
4. Save the spreadsheet under the filename 94TASK2, for printing now or later. (The printout should show borders — Row/Column labels.)

<table>
<tr><td colspan="2">◇◈◇ *Spreadsheet*</td><td colspan="4">*Figure 2*</td></tr>
</table>

Hi-Tech Productions

Production Report - January 1994

No.	Factory	Factory Production Quantity	Unit Production Price	Unit Selling Price	Royalty Fee	Profit
1	Clondalkin	2500	£0.28	£0.48		
2	Santry	3400	£0.25	£0.46		
3	Cork	2800	£0.30	£0.49		
4	Galway	2300	£0.26	£0.52		
5	Limerick	4400	£0.32	£0.53		
6	Athlone	800	£0.28	£0.46		
7	Sligo	1800	£0.29	£0.51		
8	Waterford	3500	£0.30	£0.50		
9	Dundalk	2700	£0.33	£0.52		

Total: Total Profit:

Name:

Examination No:

Date:

Task 3 (35 marks)

1. Input the additional information shown in Figure 3.
    a. Change the month to *March*.
    b. Delete the *Athlone*, *Sligo*, *Waterford* and *Dundalk* factories from the spreadsheet.
    c. Insert the *Blackrock* factory into the spreadsheet.
    d. Change the production quantities as shown.
    e. Insert the headings *Spare Capacity:* and *Value of Spare Capacity:* in the positions shown.
    f. Insert an extra column for the *Factory Production Capacity* and place this heading in the position shown.
    g. Right align the new column and heading.
    h. Re-align the main and subheadings centrally over the data.
    i. Insert the table: *No.*, *Manager* and *Capacity* in the position shown and fill in the information in the table, aligned as in Figure 3.
2. Use the LOOKUP function to insert the *Factory Production Capacity* for each factory in the *Factory Production Capacity* column, from the table in (1) above.
3. Calculate the total production capacity and place it in the position indicated at the bottom of that column.
4. The *Spare Capacity* should be the difference between the sum of the factory production capacities and the sum of the factory production quantities.
5. The *Value of Spare Capacity* should be calculated using the selling price only.
6. Sort the spreadsheet into alphabetical order on the *Factory* names.
7. Save the spreadsheet under the filename 94TASK3, for printing now or later. (Make two printouts of 94TASK3 to show (1) values and (2) formulae and cell references.)

Hi-Tech Productions

Production Report   -   March 1994

No.	Factory	Factory Production Capacity	Factory Production Quantity	Unit Production Price	Unit Selling Price	Royalty Fee	Profit
6	Blackrock		5000	£0.23	£0.51		
1	Clondalkin		900	£0.28	£0.48		
2	Santry		1800	£0.25	£0.46		
3	Cork		3200	£0.30	£0.49		
4	Galway		2300	£0.26	£0.52		
5	Limerick		3500	£0.32	£0.53		

Total: Total Profit:

Spare Capacity: Value of Spare
                                                            Capacity:

No.	1	2	3	4	5	6
Manager:	M. Murphy	P. Doyle	J. Daly	B. Walsh	H. Byrne	N. Cleary
Capacity:	4000	4500	4000	3000	4500	6000

Name:
Examination No:
Date:

Task 4 (10 marks)

1. Produce a **Bar Chart** from spreadsheet 94TASK3 to show the quantities produced in each factory:
   a. The quantities should be taken from the *Factory Production Quantity* column.
   b. The bar chart should have the heading *Production Quantities*.
   c. The *x* -axis should the factory name under each bar and have the word *Factory* as the *x*-axis label.
   d. The *y*-axis should show the quantities in figures and have the word *Quantity* as the *y*-axis label.
2. Save the Bar Chart under the filename 94GRAPH (either separately or as part of the spreadsheet 94TASK3), for printing now or later.

ASN · *Assignment 20*

NCVA Spreadsheet Methods Paper 1995

Task 1 (30marks)

1. Set up the spreadsheet and input the data as shown in **Figure 1**.
   a. Align the main heading (*Long-Life Insurance Company*) and the subheading (*Salaries Report 1994*) centrally over the data.
   b. Set column widths to appropriate values.
   c. Column headings and contents should be as shown.
   d. Insert the headings *Area 1* and *Area 2* in the positions shown.
   e. All monetary values should be displayed in currency format, whole pounds only (i.e. no decimal places).
2. Calculate the *Commission* as 12% of *Sales* and display in the column under the heading Commission.
3. Calculate the *Gross Salary* as *Basic Salary* plus *Commission*, and display in the column under the heading Gross Salary.
4. Calculate the *Totals* for *Basic Salary*, *Sales*, *Commission* and *Gross Salary* using the SUM function and display in the *Totals* row, in the appropriate column.
5. Insert your *Name*, *Examination Number* and *Date of Examination* in the second column, beside the appropriate label.
6. Save the spreadsheet under the filename **95TASK1**, for printing now or later. (The printout should show borders - Row/Column labels.)

	Spreadsheet	**Figure 1**

Long-Life Insurance Company

Salaries Report 1994

Employ. Number	Name	Basic Salary	Sales	Commission	Gross Salary
Area 1					
201	Murphy, James	£8,560	£25,600		
205	Byrne, Margaret	£8,340	£36,300		
206	Doyle, Pauline	£10,230	£43,800		
208	Hughes, Edward	£7,620	£37,200		
210	O'Brien, Sally	£9,760	£52,890		
215	Collins Declan	£6,890	£15,200		
Area 2					
202	Brady, Liam	£8,620	£35,700		
203	Evans, Jacinta	£7,950	£32,600		
204	Falvey, Ann	£11,400	£56,350		
207	Pender, Mark	£8,260	£34,300		
	Totals				

Name:

Exam. No:

Date:

Task 2 (25 marks)

1. Input the additional information as shown in **Figure 2**.
   a. Hide the 3rd, 4th and 5th columns with the headings *Basic Salary*, *Sales* and *Commission*.
   b. Change the subheadings to read *Area 1 - Salaries and Expenses Report 1994* and maintain its central alignment over the column headings.
   c. Delete the row containing the heading *Area 1*.
   d. Delete the rows containing *Area 2* and its **associated data**, leaving one blank row between the *Area 1* data and the *Totals* row.
   e. Insert the column headings *Distance/Miles*, *Rate* and *Expenses/Paid* as shown.

f. Insert the rate £0.58 for each employee under the *Rate* column heading.

g. Insert an extra row between the subheading and the column headings.

h. Insert the heading *Expenses Calculations* and align it centrally over the three column headings in 1(e) above.

i. Insert the table *Emp. No.* and *Distance* in the position shown and fill in the information in the table, aligning as shown.

2. You must:

a. Use the LOOKUP function to insert the *Distance* from the table in 1(i) into the column under the *Distance/Miles* column heading.

b. Display the *Distance/Miles* data centrally in the column.

3. You are required to:

a. Calculate the *Expenses Paid* as the *Distance/Miles* multiplied by the *Rate* and display in the column under the *Expenses/Paid* column heading.

b. Display the *Expenses Paid* in currency format with two decimal places.

4. Use the SUM function to calculate the *Totals* for *Distance/Miles* and *Expenses Paid* and display in the *Totals* row in the appropriate column.

5. Save the spreadsheet under the filename **95TASK2**, for printing now or later. (The printout should show borders - Row/Column labels.)

E C A Spreadsheet   Figure 2

Long-Life Insurance Company

Area 1 - Salaries and Expenses Report 1994

Expenses Calculations

Employ. Number	Name	Gross Salary	Distance/ Miles	Rate	Expenses Paid
201	Murphy, James			£0.58	
205	Byrne, Margaret			£0.58	
206	Doyle, Pauline			£0.58	
208	Hughes, Edward			£0.58	
210	O'Brien, Sally			£0.58	
215	Collins Declan			£0.58	

Totals

Emp. No.	201	205	206	208	210	215
Distance	10340	13900	15890	9850	10340	8200

Name:
Exam. No:
Date:

Task 3 (35 marks)

1. Input the additional information as shown in **Figure 3**.
   a. Insert an extra column between the *Gross Salary* and **D**istance/*Miles* columns, ensuring that the table at the bottom is not disrupted.
   b. Insert the column heading *Car Type* in two rows of the new column and align it centrally as shown.
   c. Align the heading *Expenses Calculations* centrally across the four columns as shown.
   d. Insert an extra row between the *Totals* row and the table.
   e. Insert the heading *Average Rate per Mile* in the position shown.
   f. Insert an extra row between the table and your name at the bottom of the spread sheet.
   g. Insert the side heading *Car Type* and associated data in the table as shown. (**N.B.** Ensure that the distances are adjusted to the new values.)
   h. Ensure that the main heading and subheading are centrally aligned across all column headings.
2. You are required to:
   a. Use the LOOKUP function to insert the *Car Type* from the table in 1(g) above, into the column under the *Car Type* column heading.
   b. Align the *Car Type* column contents centrally in the column.
3. You must:
   a. Delete the values £0.58 from the *Rate* column.
   b. Use the IF function to calculate the rate for each employee as follows:
      i. If the *Car Type* is **A** and the *Distance/Miles* is less than **10,000** then the *Rate* is £0.60.
      ii. If the *Car Type* is **B** and the *Distance/Miles* is less than **10,000** then the *Rate* is £0.55.
      iii. The *Rate* for all other combinations of *Car Type* and *Distance/Miles* is £0.50.
4. Calculate the average rate per mile and insert it in the *Rate* column beside the heading *Average Rate per Mile*.
5. Sort the spreadsheet into alphabetical order on the employee *Name*.
6. Save the spreadsheet under the filename **95TASK3** for printing now or later. (Produce two printouts of **95TASK3** to show (a) **values** and (b) **formulae** and **cell references**, both with borders - Row/Column labels.)

Long-Life Insurance Company

Area 1 - Salaries and Expenses Report 1994

Employ. Number	Name	Gross Salary	Car Type	Expenses Calculations		Expenses Paid
				Distance/ Miles	Rate	
205	Byrne, Margaret					
215	Collins Declan					
206	Doyle, Pauline					
208	Hughes, Edward					
201	Murphy, James					
210	O'Brien, Sally					
	Totals					
	Average Rate per Mile					

Emp. No.	201	205	206	208	210	215
Distance	9580	12068	16350	11670	9560	7940
Car Type	A	A	B	A	B	C

Name:

Exam. No:

Date:

Task 4 (10 marks)

1. Produce a *Pie Chart* (either 2D or 3D) from the spreadsheet **95TASK3** to show the *Expenses Paid* to each employee.
   a. The values should be taken from the *Expenses Paid* column.
   b. The pie chart should have the heading *Expenses Paid - Area 1 1994*.
   c. Each section of the pie chart should be labelled with the **employee's name** and the **percentage of the total expenses** which s/he receives.
2. Save the chart under the filename **95GRAPH** (either separately or as part of the spreadsheet **95TASK3**), for printing now or later.

Chapter 6

COMPUTER APPLICATIONS PROJECTS

Introduction

The production of a good project demands the use of expressive and creative abilities as well as an understanding of how to use a particular computer program. Many students erroneously believe that they must be 'tapping away' on their computer keyboards for the entire duration of a project. A builder will only commence work on a house after he has received detailed house plans from an architect. Similarly, a project idea must be planned accurately and written up as an in-depth design. This project design must then be marked by your teacher **before** you embark on implementing the design using a computer program. In short, your tools during the design phase of your project are pen and paper and **not** a computer equipped with a particular applications program. It is recommended that you spend twice as much time on project design as you do on implementing the design on your computer.

A project idea

The starting point is a period of quiet reflection to decide on a suitable topic for the project. Sources of project ideas are many and varied; some popular sources are:
* your work experience *(do not use real data)*
* hobbies.

A good guide to the suitability of an idea for a data-base project is to ask yourself the following questions:
* *Will the completed project be useful to others?*
* *How many fields will go to make up a record?*
* *Are all the fields relevant?*
* *Can suitable queries and reports be generated?*

Some popular topics for data-base projects include:

Club membership	Concert bookings
Employee details	Car rental
Dentistry patients	Student profiles
Product orders	Restaurant reservations
Shop stocks	Veterinary surgery — pet details

Similarly, a good guide to the suitability of an idea for a spreadsheet project is to ask yourself the following questions:

Will the completed project be useful to others?
Will the final spreadsheet be easy to use?
How many rows and columns will go to make up the spreadsheet?
Will cumbersome formulae be required? (If so, it may not be a suitable project idea.)

Some popular topics for spreadsheet projects include:

Employee salaries	Customer invoices
Cashflow projections	Insurance quotes
Pension schemes	Sales analysis
Stock re-ordering	Equipment hire
Budget forecasting	Loan repayments

A golden rule is to keep the project specifications before you while you work on the project.

Producing a data-base project

This can be broken down into three distinct phases: the design phase, the implementation phase and the conclusion phase.

Design phase

A data-base project design should include:

1. An outline of the problem to be solved including document analysis, e.g. data capture forms
2. Identification of:
   * record structure
   * relevant key fields for sorting and/or indexing the file
   * likely queries, reports and labels to be generated.
3. Design of the data entry screen layout (ideally this should be based on the data capture form to aid data entry).

Implementation phase

During this phase, a computer equipped with a suitable data-base program is required. Hard copy will obviously be produced using a printer. Ability to carry out the following should be demonstrated:

1. Create the record structure and data entry screen
2. Input data accurately
3. Modify the structure and amend data
4. Handle a variety of data types
5. Query the data-base on a variety of data types

6. Organise the data on different field types
7. Create relevant reports and labels.

Conclusion phase

The conclusion should include an evaluation of the project in terms of:
1. its usefulness
2. all necessary modifications
3. any likely improvements.

Common questions

How big should my data-base file be?
The completed data-base file should contain at least five fields and a minimum of twenty five records.

What field types should I use?
Field types should consist of at least character, numeric and one other (e.g. date or logical).

Should I generate query files?
Two relevant queries should be produced as a minimum. Each resulting query file should contain at least four records. One of the queries should contain a logical operator (e.g. AND, OR, NOT).

Must the file be sorted?
The file must be sorted on a minimum of two separate fields and two printouts should be produced using the appropriate report format.

What should the finished project look like?
It should be of a professional standard, typed and bound, within the constraints of the equipment available.

Producing a spreadsheet project

This can also be broken down into the same three distinct phases.

Design phase

A spreadsheet project design should include:
1. A concise description of the problem and a proposed solution, identifying a source of data.

2. Identification of:
    - input data
    - the processing required (in words)
    - output data generated.

    An example of each should be given.
3. Design of the screen layout, which should be based on a data capture form.
4. Specification of:
    - data format (e.g. alignment, currency, decimal places)
    - column widths
    - data to be hidden, frozen and or protected.

Implementation phase

During this phase, a computer equipped with a suitable spreadsheet program is required. Again, hard copy will obviously be produced using a printer. Ability to carry out the following should be demonstrated:

1. Create the spreadsheet
2. Print the spreadsheet
3. Print the spreadsheet showing formulae
4. Change a variable and print the altered spreadsheet.

Conclusion phase

The conclusion should include an evaluation of the project in terms of:

1. its usefulness
2. all necessary modifications
3. any likely improvements.

Common questions

How big should my spreadsheet be?
It is generally accepted that the completed spreadsheet should contain enough data to fill a monitor screen.

How complex should my formulae be?
This depends greatly on the problem which you are solving. The NCVA spreadsheet project guidelines suggest that a simple IF function should be included in at least one column of formulae as the basic minimum.

What should the finished project look like?
It should be of a professional standard, typed and bound, within the constraints of the equipment available.

Chapter 7

INTRODUCTION TO WORD-PROCESSING

A word-processor is a program that makes it possible to use a microcomputer for entering, storing and manipulating text.

In typing a document we usually make some mistakes: spelling errors, missing or duplicated words, and paragraphs in the wrong order, or even omitted. A word-processor allows us to correct these errors and to make any other changes before the document is printed. It also allows us to store a copy of the document onto disk and to recall it later and edit it as required.

Facilities of a word-processor

In this chapter we will examine the following facilities of a word-processor:
1. Elementary editing: deleting and inserting
2. More advanced editing: moving text
3. Enhancing the appearance of a document
4. The 'find and replace' facility
5. Setting tabs
6. Stored paragraphs
7. Merge printing

1. Elementary editing: deleting and inserting

Patrick Matthews is secretary to the managing director of a company that manufactures building insulation: Cavityfoam Enterprises Ltd. he produces all documents on his micro-computer, which is equipped with a word-processor program.

This is the first draft of a document describing the company and its products:

> Cavityfoam Enterprises Ltd was founded in 1981 by John Hall and Fionnuala O'Connor. The aim of the company was to produce good-quality home insulation products at a competitive price.
>
> The company initially employed only twelve people. As markets were quickly established, the number of people employed by the firm grew rapidly. In 1985 the company employed forty-three people, and by 1995 the workforce numbered seventy-eight.

In response to a need in the market, the company directors decided to branch into factory farm building insulation products. John Hall spent nine months in Toronto observing the manufacture and testing of Canadian insulation products.

Today Cavityfoam enterprises Ltd is one of Ireland's leading companies in the manufacture of insulation building products. The Company employs 265 people, and last year's profits were £1.7 million.

Fionnuala now edits this first draft. There are standard ways of indicating what changes are to be made: the most important of these are shown here:

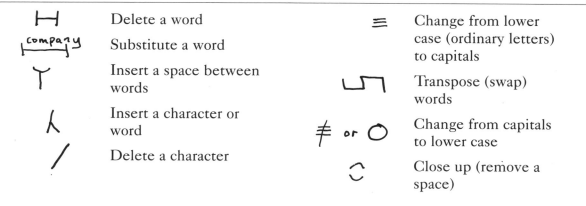

Cavityfoam Enterprises Ltd was founded in 1981 by John Hall and Fionnuala O'Connor. The aim of the company was to produce good-quality home insulation products at a competitive price.

The company initially employed only twelve people. As markets were quickly established, the number of people employed by the firm grew rapidly. In 1985 the company employed forty-three people, and by 1995 the workforce numbered seventy-eight.

In response to a need in the market, the company directors decided to branch into factory farm building insulation products. John Hall spent nine months in Toronto observing the manufacture and testing of Canadian insulation products.

Today Cavityfoam enterprises Ltd is one of Ireland's leading companies in the manufacture of insulation building products. The Company employs 265 people, and last year's profits were £1.7 million.

⊢	Delete a word	=	Change from lower case (ordinary letters) to capitals
company	Substitute a word		
Y	Insert a space between words	⊔⌐	Transpose (swap) words
ʌ	Insert a character or word	≢ or ○	Change from capitals to lower case
/	Delete a character	⌣	Close up (remove a space)

New text can be inserted into a document by moving the cursor to the correct position and simply typing the text. Unwanted text can be deleted by positioning the cursor at the appropriate place and giving one of the delete commands. Word-processors have commands to delete a character, word, line or block of text.

The word-processor will rearrange the text after you have edited a line so that the remainder of the text will move forwards or back to fill the space.
The corrected text will now appear as follows:

Cavityfoam Enterprises Ltd was founded in 1981 by John Hall and Fionnuala O'Connor. The aim of the company was to produce good-quality home insulation products at a competitive price.

The company initially employed twelve people. As markets were quickly established, the number of people employed by the company grew rapidly. In 1985 the company employed forty-three people, and by 1995 the work-force numbered seventy-eight.

In response to a need in the market, the company directors decided to branch into factory and farm building insulation products. John Hall spent nine months in Toronto observing the manufacture and testing of Canadian insulation products.

Today Cavityfoam Enterprises Ltd is one of Ireland's leading companies in the manufacture of building insulation products. The company employs 265 people, and last year's profits were £1.7 million.

---

2. More advanced editing: moving text

The managing director has asked Patrick to draw up a letter to the wholesalers who stock Cavity-foam products. The letter should tell them of future price increases on some products and of the development of a new insulation material suitable for bungalows. Here is his draft:

Dear wholesaler,

We regret to inform you that, because of spiralling raw material costs, we have increased the price of some products. Our very popular Astrofoam has been increased from £11.75 to £12.50 per cubic metre. Our insulation foam for farm buildings, Agrifoam, has been increased from £8.50 to £9.20 per cubic metre. The company has decided to extend its guarantee from ten to fifteen years on all of its insulation products. This fact should be made clear to the retailers, as our largest competitors only guarantee their products for seven years.

We are introducing a new insulation product called Bungafoam onto the market. This is suitable for bungalows, and is competitively priced at £11.50 per cubic metre.

Our sales representative will be calling on you on 28 March. He will furnish you with all the details of our other insulation products and will accept your order this month.

I wish to remind you of our 5 per cent discount on all products that are paid for in full on the delivery date.

> I am confident that you will continue to stock the Cavityfoam range of insulation products. Yours faithfully,
>
> Fionnuala O'Connor
> Managing Director

Fionnuala feels that some changes need to be made to this letter.

- Paragraph 2 should be moved so that it becomes the first paragraph of the letter. This is achieved by marking the paragraph to be moved and positioning the cursor at the new position in the document. The command to move a marked block of text must then be given.
- One paragraph should be divided into two. The paragraph that starts 'We regret to inform you . . . ' should be split at the point that begins 'The company has decided to extend . . .' This is achieved by inserting two carriage returns (pressing the 'enter' key twice) at the appropriate position in the text.
- Two separate paragraphs should be joined together. The paragraph that starts 'Our sales representative will be calling . . . ' and the one that starts 'I wish to remind you . . . ' should be run together. This is achieved by deleting the carriage returns between the paragraphs.

Fionnuala marks the draft with the following symbols:

> **Ⓐ** Dear wholesaler,
>
> We regret to inform you that, because of spiralling raw material costs, we have increased the price of some products. Our very popular Astrofoam has been increased from £11.75 to £12.50 per cubic metre. Our insulation foam for farm buildings, Agrifoam, has been increased from £8.50 to £9.20 per cubic metre. **Ⓑ** The company has decided to extend its guarantee from ten to fifteen years on all of its insulation products. This fact should be made clear to the retailers, as our largest competitors only guarantee their products for seven years.
>
> We are introducing a new insulation product called Bungafoam onto the market. This is suitable for bungalows, and is competitively priced at £11.50 per cubic metre.
>
> Our sales representative will be calling on you on 28 March. He will furnish you with all the details of our other insulation products and will accept your order this month.
>
> **Ⓒ** I wish to remind you of our 5 per cent discount on all products that are paid for in full on the delivery date.
>
> I am confident that you will continue to stock the Cavityfoam range of insulation products. Yours faithfully,
>
> Fionnuala O'Connor
> Managing Director

A Move text to new position
B Start new paragraph
C Run on (not a new paragraph)

The letter will appear as follows after all these changes have been made:

Dear wholesaler,

We are introducing a new insulation product called Bungafoam onto the market. This is suitable for bungalows, and is competitively priced at £11.50 per cubic metre.

We regret to inform you that, because of spiralling raw material costs, we have increased the price of some products. Our very popular Astrofoam has been increased from £11.75 to £12.50 per cubic metre. Our insulation foam for farm buildings, Agrifoam, has been increased from £8.50 to £9.20 per cubic metre.

The company has decided to extend its guarantee from ten to fifteen years on all of its insulation products. This fact should be made clear to the retailers, as our largest competitors only guarantee their products for seven years.

Our sales representative will be calling on you on 28 March. He will furnish you with all the details of our other insulation products and will accept your order this month. I wish to remind you of our 5 per cent discount on all products that are paid for in full on the delivery date.

I am confident that you will continue to stock the Cavityfoam range of insulation products.
Yours faithfully

Fionnuala O'Connor
Managing Director

It is obvious that these changes could not have been carried out on an ordinary typewriter without retyping the whole document.

3. *Enhancing the appearance of a document*

Most word-processors offer the user a number of features to enhance the appearance of the text — although these should be used sparingly in business documents, especially by a beginner. They include:

- changing the font and font size
- centring and underlining key words and phrases
- altering the line spacing
- setting new margins and rearranging text accordingly.

Changing the font and font size

Wordprocessors allow the use of different fonts. A font is a set of characters with a consistent and identifiable typeface. Each font has a name which you can use to select the font and apply it to text. Times Roman and Dom Casual are examples of fonts. Further examples of common fonts are given in the table. The size of the font, known as the point size, can also be changed, as shown in the table.

◇ E ◇ C ◇ A ◇ *Table*	*Table of common fonts*	
10 point size	**12 point size**	**16 point size**
Times	Times	Times
Caslon 540	Caslon 540	Caslon 540
Stone Serif	Stone Serif	Stone Serif
Futura Book	Futura Book	Futura Book
Brush Script	*Brush Script*	*Brush Script*
Bodoni	Bodoni	Bodoni
Helvetica	Helvetica	Helvetica
Baskerville	Baskerville	Baskerville
Freestyle Script	*Freestyle Script*	*Freestyle Script*
Optima	Optima	Optima

Centring and underlining

Centring a line means moving it so that it is half way between the left and right margins, making it stand out more clearly. This is very commonly used for headings.

Underlining a section of text means that a continuous line will be printed under this area.

Word-processors also allow selected words to be printed in **bold type**. On dot-matrix printers this is usually achieved by printing over the same letters two or more times.

To enhance a piece of text using one of these features, the text is usually first marked, and then the command to centre, underline or change to bold must be given.

Word-processors also have a feature called **justification**, where the shorter lines of a document are spread out towards the right margin to make all the lines the same length (as in this paragraph). In business documents this is rarely an improvement over ordinary ('flush left') alignment, and it is never appropriate for letters.

The default setting on most word-processors for justification is off (i.e. flush left alignment), and for line spacing is 1. These settings can be altered by using the correct commands before text is entered. It is also possible to alter justification and line spacing settings after the text has been entered: the text can then be realigned to the new settings.

Patrick has prepared a statement describing the company's plans for overseas expansion. He has centred the heading at the top of the document and changed its font (Caslon 540) and size (11.5pt) , and he has also used bold type, italics and underlining for key phrases:

New Project

Cavityfoam Enterprises Ltd has decided to open a <u>new plant at Reims in France for the production of building insulation materials.</u> The outlay is projected to be £7.8 million, and at first the plant will employ thirty-five people. The town council has given **approval** for the construction of the factory, and it is hoped that production at the new plant will start in eighteen months. This venture will allow *Cavityfoam Enterprises* to gain a foothold in the European market for insulation products.

Altering the line spacing
The amount of spacing between the lines can also be altered on your word-processor. Letters and statements for publication in newspapers often have 'double line spacing' — with approximately the depth of another line of type between each line — as printers prefer to receive text in this form.

Setting new margins
The managing director may wish to have the statement submitted to the local newspaper for publication in the next edition. Newspapers sometimes like text for publication to be formatted in newspaper style. Patrick can reset the margins on his word-processor to allow a maximum line width of 5 cm, as well as changing to double line spacing and justifying the text (straight right and left margins). Centring, underlining and other enhancements are not used.

The document would now appear as follows:

New project
Cavityfoam Enterprises Ltd has decided to open a new plant at Reims in France for the production of building insulation materials. The outlay is projected to be £7.8 million, and at first the plant will employ thirty-five people. The town council has given approval for the construc-

> tion of the factory, and it is hoped that production at the new plant will start in eighteen months. This venture will allow Cavityfoam Enterprises to gain a foothold in the European market for insulation products.

4. The 'find and replace' facility

Sometimes you may have used a word in the course of typing a document and then decide to replace it with another. A word-processor offers you a facility with which you can replace one word with another, at one place in the document or at every occurrence of that word in the document.

In the document above, Patrick has used the word 'plant' three times. He can easily replace it with the word 'factory' by using the 'find and replace' facility on his word-processor. The document would now appear as follows:

The 'find and replace' facility also allows you to replace entire phrases with alternative phrases. The length of phrase permitted may be limited, however.

> New project
>
> Cavityfoam Enterprises Ltd has decided to open a new factory at Reims in France for the production of building insulation materials. The outlay is projected to be £7.8 million, and at first the factory will employ thirty-five people. The town council has given approval for the construction of the factory, and it is hoped that production at the new factory will start in eighteen months. This venture will allow Cavityfoam Enterprises to gain a foothold in the European market for insulation products.

5. Setting tabs

All keyboards have a 'tab' key (short for 'tabulation'). When this key is pressed the cursor will jump a number of spaces horizontally. This saves the inconvenience of continually using the space bar to get to a certain position in the text.

There are a number of positions or 'tabs' already set at equal distances across the line. We can abandon these, however, and set our own tabs. This is an essential facility when we want to enter text in columns.

Tabs can be set quite easily on a word-processor. You can change the number of tabs and their positions, thus varying the widths of columns and the space between them.

Patrick has been asked to list the prices of Cavityfoam products for the last three years in columns. The document appears as follows:

Product	1993	1994	1995
Agrifoam	7.80	8.50	9.20
Astrofoam	10.50	11.75	12.50
Bungafoam	—	—	11.50
Chip carpet	4.99	5.50	5.50
Floor seal	3.60	4.20	4.20
Mason tiles	1.80	2.20	2.20
Shedfoam	7.20	7.20	7.20

Patrick realises that the columns are too close together. He resets the tabs to adjust the distances between the columns. The document would now appear as follows:

Product	1993	1994	1995
Agrifoam	7.80	8.50	9.20
Astrofoam	10.50	11.75	12.50
Bungafoam	—	—	11.50
Chip carpet	4.99	5.50	5.50
Floor seal	3.60	4.20	4.20
Mason tiles	1.80	2.20	2.20
Shedfoam	7.20	7.20	7.20

An alternative is to set up a table. The gridlines on the table can be set to on or off. The main advantage of the table is that it can be easily changed. An example of a table is given below (gridlines are set on):

◇E◇C◇A *Table*						
Product		**1993**		**1994**		**1995**
Agrifoam		7.80		8.50		9.20
Astrofoam		10.50		11.75		12.50
Bungafoam		—		—		11.50
Chip carpet		4.99		5.50		5.50
Floor seal		3.60		4.20		4.20
Mason tiles		1.80		2.20		2.20
Shedfoam		7.20		7.20		7.20

6. Stored paragraphs

One of the most useful features of a word processor is the ability to store frequently used paragraphs in separate files on disk. When we are entering text into a file on our word-processor we can copy one of the stored paragraphs into the file as required.

Many letters and documents produced on word-processors are the result of 'pasting together' a number of stored paragraphs (sometimes called 'boilerplate paragraphs'). Cavityfoam Enterprises Ltd interviewed five suitably qualified people for two positions in the quality control department. The interview board has made its selection and has asked Patrick to send letters to the applicants, telling them of the board's decision. Patrick will store the following paragraphs in separate files on disk:

[Paragraph 1]

We should like to thank you for attending for interview on Thursday last. We were very impressed by your qualifications and experience.

[Paragraph 2]

We wish to offer you the position of quality control assistant. Please confirm your acceptance of the position as soon as possible so that we can organise a suitable date for a medical examination. We look forward to hearing from you.

[Paragraph 3]

We are, however, unable to offer you a position with our company at the present time. We wish you every success in your future career.

[Paragraph 4]
Yours faithfully,

Fionnuala O'Connor
Managing Director

Patrick can open individual documents on his word-processor and use these paragraphs to compose appropriate letters.

Two of the applicants for jobs were Anne Breen and John Cuddy. Anne's efforts have been successful; John, however, has been unsuccessful. Both applicants will receive appropriate letters. The texts of these letters are as follows:

Letter 1: comprising stored paragraphs 1, 2 and 4

18 June 1995

Ms Anne Breen
4 Oakwood Road
Castle Bawn, Co. Donegal

Dear Ms Breen
    We should like to thank you for attending for interview on Thursday last. We were very impressed by your qualifications and experience.
    We wish to offer you the position of quality control assistant. Please confirm your acceptance of the position as soon as possible so that we can organise a suitable date for a medical examination. We look forward to hearing from you.
Yours faithfully,

Fionnuala O'Connor
Managing Director

Letter 2: comprising stored paragraphs 1, 3 and 4

18 June 1995

Mr John Cuddy
31 Eskermore Terrace
Castlebawn, Co. Donegal

Dear Mr Cuddy
    We should like to thank you for attending for interview on Thursday last. We were very impressed by your qualifications and experience.
    We are, however, unable to offer you a position with our company at the present time. We wish you every success in your future career.
Yours faithfully,

Fionnuala O'Connor
Managing Director

The other three applicants would receive replies identical to one or other of the above letters.

This method of composing letters and documents from a set of stored paragraphs is widely used by people who use word-processors as a central part of their work. A lawyer's secretary may store on disk a range of paragraphs relating to contracts and other legal documents. Different sets of paragraphs can then be combined in a document, depending on the nature of the contract being drawn up.

7. Merge printing

One of the most powerful features of a word-processor is the merge printing facility. This allows you to draw up a **source file**, which usually consists of a single document or letter containing **variables**. The precise information to be included instead of the variables is entered in a **data file**. When you invoke merge printing, the various sets of data from the data file are merged into copies of the source file.

The managing director of Cavityfoam Enterprises Ltd has asked Patrick to send letters to wholesalers in three regions — south-west, south-east, and central — informing them of a demonstration of the new insulation product, Bungafoam. The details of the demonstration in each region are as follows:

Region	Time	Date	Venue
South-west	2 p.m.	3 April	Whiterock Hotel
South-east	3 p.m.	5 April	Silver Swan Hotel
Central	2 p.m.	10 April	Kilmore Hotel

Patrick would enter a source file in his word-processor like the one shown below:

---

19 March 1995

Dear Wholesaler,

You are invited to a demonstration of our new insulation product for bungalows, called Bungafoam, at &time& on &date& in the &hotel&. This demonstration is for the benefit of all wholesalers in the &area& region.

There will be time after the demonstration for a discussion on the product. Any opinions or criticisms of the product will be welcome.

We look forward to seeing you at the demonstration.

Yours sincerely

Fionnuala O'Connor
Managing Director

Patrick would then set up a data file and include the times, dates, hotels and regions in a manner similar to that outlined below.

---

2 p.m., 3 April, Whiterock Hotel, south-west

3 p.m., 5 April, Silver Swan Hotel, south-east

2 p.m., 10 April, Kilmore Hotel, central

You should check the exact format on your particular word-processor for variables in the source file and for data in the data file.

When Patrick invokes the merge printing facility, the details from the data file will be merged with the source file, and three separate documents will be produced for the three regions. The three letters should appear as follows:

Letter 1: South-west region

19 March 1995

Dear Wholesaler,

You are invited to a demonstration of our new insulation product for bungalows, called Bungafoam, at 2 p.m. on 3 April in the Whiterock Hotel. This demonstration is for the benefit of all wholesalers in the south-west region.

There will be time after the demonstration for a discussion on the product. Any opinions or criticisms of the product will be welcome.

We look forward to seeing you at the demonstration.
Yours sincerely

Fionnuala O'Connor
Managing Director

Letter 2: South-east region

19 March 1995

Dear Wholesaler,

You are invited to a demonstration of our new insulation product for bungalows, called Bungafoam, at 3 p.m. on 5 April in the Silver Swan Hotel. This demonstration is for the benefit of all wholesalers in the south-east region.

There will be time after the demonstration for a discussion on the product. Any opinions or criticisms of the product will be welcome.

We look forward to seeing you at the demonstration.
Yours sincerely

Fionnuala O'Connor
Managing Director

Letter 3: Central region

19 March 1995

Dear Wholesaler,

You are invited to a demonstration of our new insulation product for bungalows, called Bungafoam, at 2 p.m. on 10 April in the Kilmore Hotel. This demonstration is for the benefit of all wholesalers in the central region.

There will be time after the demonstration for a discussion on the product. Any opinions or criticisms of the product will be welcome.

We look forward to seeing you at the demonstration.

Yours sincerely

Fionnuala O'Connor
Managing Director

We have examined some of the most frequently used facilities of word-processor programs. You can gain practice in using these facilities by attempting the assignments in the following chapter.

Applications of word-processing

Almost any application requiring the manipulation of text can be handled efficiently with a word-processor. Only a few of the most common applications are described here.

Standard letters

These are letters containing the same information that are sent to many customers. With the merge printing facility the letters can be 'personalised', i.e. the name and address of the customer can be added to the letter. Matching envelope labels can also be printed.

Contracts and agreements

Most legal contracts contain standard information. When a solicitor's secretary prepares a contract, some of these paragraphs can be read into the document by using the stored paragraphs facility. The paragraphs need only be typed in once and can then be used any number of times.

Reports

Reports usually require a variety of styles of presentation. Some of the various text enhancement facilities can be used here, as well as the ability of most word-processors to read text into the report from other sources, e.g. from a spreadsheet or data-base.

Mail shots

These are regular advertising leaflets posted to a compiled list of customers. The information may need to be changed from time to time, and word-processor editing facilities will help here. More importantly, the word-processor will produce printed labels showing the name and address of each customer.

Regularly updated lists

Lists of all kinds that require regular updating can be produced, such as price lists, directories, customer lists, inventories and catalogues.

Advantages of word-processor use

We have already examined many of the advantages of word-processors in the creation and editing of documents of all kinds. Some of the most important advantages are summarised here.

Storage of text

The ability to store and retrieve text means that it can be used again, either exactly as first used or with changes. Magnetic storage media are also less bulky and easier to retrieve than paper copies.

Time savings

The ability to edit easily, both while entering text and subsequently, means a very significant saving in time, which is of great importance to a business.

Quality

The layout and general appearance of documents can be enhanced by changing typefaces, margins, alignment, and line spacing, as well as by other enhancement features, particularly if a high-quality printer such as a laser printer is available.

Security

Confidential documents are easily protected on word-processor files, which can be secured against accidental viewing or changing by use of the 'protect' tab on diskettes or programmed to require a password to permit viewing or changing them. Magnetic media can be easily stored in fireproof safes.

Ease of use

Most word-processor programs are easy to operate and learn. Good programs have a key that provides on-screen help when you are entering text.

Disadvantages of word-processor use

Despite their many advantages, word-processors have a number of drawbacks that should also be taken into account.

Cost

Business-quality computers and peripherals can be expensive, and the rapid pace of technological change can make systems obsolete very quickly and frequent updates are required.

Staff training

Staff must be trained to use the computers and the word-processor programs. Equipment and programs will need to be upgraded occasionally and the staff retrained in their use. This can be a considerable cost for a business.

Poor checking

Because so many editing facilities are available during the typing of text, there may be a temptation to be less thorough in correcting the final print-out.

Health

There is some evidence that prolonged use of monitors can have adverse physical effects (e.g. eye strain, migraine).

Conclusion

In this section we have examined the main features of a word-processor, and we hope that you will work through all the assignments in the next chapter on your own equipment and using your own programs. The word-processor is by far the most widely used computer application, and the ability to operate one is essential in many occupations as the trend away from the use of typewriters continues.

Questions

M^CQ • *Multi-choice questions*

1. Word-processing is:
   (a) the sending of text from a microcomputer to a large mainframe computer for processing
   (b) the use of microelectronic equipment to increase the amount of work carried out by office staff in a given time
   (c) the use of microelectronic equipment to enter, edit and store text
   (d) the use of microelectronic equipment to eliminate errors in writing

2. Which of the following could be carried out just as efficiently using a typewriter as using a word-processor?
   (a) producing customised letters
   (b) producing short occasional letters
   (c) producing long legal documents with many identical clauses
   (d) producing complex medical documents containing many pharmaceutical terms

3. Centred text in a document may help to highlight:
   (a) text that has to be moved
   (b) the start of a new section
   (c) text that contains errors
   (d) where we must justify the text

4. A triple-underline symbol on a corrected document means that we must:
   (a) start a new paragraph
   (b) use a capital letter
   (c) use a lower-case letter
   (d) correct the spelling of a word

5. The 'find and replace' facility —
   (a) finds all occurrences of words longer than eight characters and offers a list of alternatives from the thesaurus
   (b) finds a block of text you may have marked for moving and allows you to replace the markers with 'move' symbols
   (c) searches for all words at the beginning of sentences and checks that they start with a capital letter
   (d) finds one or all occurrences of the given text and changes it to the given replacement

6. The term 'text' means:
   (a) letters, numbers and symbols (excluding pictures and diagrams) that make up a document
   (b) documents that consist of letters only
   (c) all documents (excluding business letters)
   (d) a document that does not contain any typing errors?

7   A font is the same as
    (a) the pitch
    (b) the typeface
    (c) the size of the characters
    (d) none of the above

SAQ · *Short-answer questions*

1. Briefly describe the main text editing facilities of a word-processor.
2. Suggest three advantages and two disadvantages of a word-processor compared with a typewriter.
3. Briefly describe the main features you would look for in buying a word-processor program.
4. Describe the following styles of text alignment, and give examples of where each one might be used: justified, flush left, flush right and centred.
5. Illustrate, by means of an example, the 'stored paragraphs' facility of a word-processor.
6. What is merge printing? Give an example of an application where it might be used.
7. Distinguish between the spelling check and thesaurus facilities of a word-processor.

Glossary of word-processing terms

alignment: the way in which the text of a document is adjusted relative to the left and right margins, whether flush left, flush right, justified, or centred.

bold type: a typeface design matching the one in normal use but made up of thicker lines to give emphasis; on dot-matrix printers, bold type is simulated by overstriking the same characters two or more times.

carriage return: the keystroke or command that ends the current line of text and sends the cursor to the first character position on the next line, invoked in word-processing by pressing the 'enter' key.

centred: the style of alignment in which the text is placed half way between the left and right margins of the document.

data file: a computer file on disk that contains text or other data that the user has created and stored, as distinct from program files, which contain the computer code that runs the program.

editing: making corrections and other changes to a text, including substitutions, deletions, and insertions.

'find and replace': a facility that automatically replaces a selected word or phrase with an alternative word or phrase, at selected occurrences or at every occurrence in the document.

flush left: the style of alignment in which lines are of different length and the text has a straight left margin and uneven right margin, exactly as it was typed into the word-processor.

flush right: the style of alignment in which lines are of different length and the text has a straight right margin and uneven left margin.

font: a special type of program file that contains instructions for creating a particular type-face on the printer, usually with a separate font for each size.

justification: the style of alignment is which all the lines are forced out to equal length by increasing the space between words, with straight left and right margins.

line spacing: the adjustable vertical distance between lines of text.

menu: a list of the options available at any stage in the execution of a program.

merge printing: a facility that allows the user to customise standard documents by automatically reading in variable data.

page break: a code in a word-processor file that causes the printer to start printing on a new page: it may be a 'forced page break' entered by the user or one that occurs automatically when the amount of text entered would fill the defined page size.

spelling check: a facility of most word-processors that checks the spelling of words in a document by comparing them against a list of words in one of the program files.

stored paragraph: a paragraph stored in a separate file on disk that can be combined with other paragraphs to make up a composite document.

tab key: a key that causes the cursor to jump a number of spaces horizontally to user-defined positions on the typing line in order to set the width of columns and the space between them.

thesaurus: a facility that allows the user to choose alternative words from lists of words with a related meaning.

typeface: a distinctive style of type with its own name.

underlining: the printing of a continuous line under a selected group of words to emphasise them.

word-processor: a computer program used in the creating, editing and printing of text.

word wraparound: a feature of a word-processor that causes the cursor to move automatically to the beginning of the next line in the display when the end of a line is reached.

work area: the area of the display excluding the status line, menu and ruler line, where text is typed and edited.

WYSIWG (What You See Is What you Get): this means that the image on the screen is very close to how it will appear when printed.

C h a p t e r   8

P R A C T I C A L   W O R D - P R O C E S S I N G   A S S I G N M E N T S

These assignments are graded, and we advise that you work through them in the order in which they are given. Unless otherwise stated, set up the document for A4 page size with one inch left and right borders for all assignments. Justification should be off unless otherwise stated.

Functions and commands required

As you progress through these assignments you will need to check on the functions and commands specific to your word-processor program. You will also be practising commands and functions learned in earlier assignments. (Note: If you do not have access to a printer, you can display the results of that task instead.)

The functions and commands required for each assignment are as follows:

ASSIGNMENT 1
• Text entry in a document file
• Cursor movement
• Saving a document to disk

ASSIGNMENT 2
• Deleting and inserting text

ASSIGNMENT 3
• Consolidation assignment

ASSIGNMENT 4
• Moving a block of text

ASSIGNMENT 5
• Dividing and joining paragraphs

ASSIGNMENT 6
• Consolidation assignment

ASSIGNMENT 7
• Centring

ASSIGNMENT 8
• Underlining and bold

ASSIGNMENT 9
• Setting margins

ASSIGNMENT 10
- Consolidation assignment

ASSIGNMENT 11
- Find and replace

ASSIGNMENT 12
- Setting tabs

ASSIGNMENT 13
- Tabs and tables, layout

ASSIGNMENT 14
- Decimal tabs, tables

ASSIGNMENT 15
- Stored paragraphs: block reading

ASSIGNMENT 16
- Merge printing: document layout and merge print commands

ASSIGNMENT 17
- Merge printing: and merge print commands

ASSIGNMENT 18
- Consolidation assignment

ASSIGNMENT 19
- Consolidation assignment— NCVA Examination 1994

ASSIGNMENT 20
- Consolidation assignment— NCVA Examination 1995

A^Sn · *Assignment 1*

• You are required to enter the text below in your word-processor. When you have finished you should save the work onto disk in a file called LOCHHUNT and exit the system.

Nessie lies low

A prize of £1,500 in the Loch Ness monster hunt was won yesterday by Oceanscan, an American survey company. The prize, however, feel far short of the £250,000 on offer for conclusive proof of Nessie's existence.

Oceanscan made sonar contact on Saturday with a large unidentified object measuring up to 8 m long. The sonar contact was made near the loch's northern shore, where most sightings of Nessie have been reported.

Andy James (42), the team leader, said yesterday: 'We are thrilled to win the prize for the best search method. The object, which showed up on Saturday, registered as two blips on the sonar screen, but it moved out of range quickly.'

The organising committee of the hunt have decided to hold the event again next year. It will be held over a ten-day period in July, and the prize money for conclusive proof of Nessie's existence will be increased to £300,000. Many teams, including those from Canada and the United States, have agreed to participate again.

Carry out the following tasks:

Recall LOCHHUNT to the screen and practise the various cursor movement commands for your word-processor.

A$N • *Assignment 2*

You are required to enter the news extract below in your word-processor and save it on disk, using OILFIND1 as the file name and exit the system.

New oil reserves

Saudi Arabia has discovered extensive new crude oil reserves in previously unexplored areas, according to a report from Reuters news agency today.

One Saudi government source said that the new find was bigger than the total known reserves of some other OPEC member-states. The Saudi state company has reportedly been drilling in areas well away from its existing oil pipeline network.

The agency quotes unnamed Saudi officials as saying that the find could boost the country's oil reserves by as much as 20 per cent. The discovery could have a significant impact on oil markets, in lowering the price of crude oil from its recent record price of around $40 per barrel.

This is good news for the consumer, who has recently been experiencing steadily increasing prices on all oil products. Increased oil prices automatically lead to increased inflation and invariably to increases in unemployment.

Carry out the following tasks:

1. Recall OILFIND1 to the screen.
2. Edit the file by making the alterations shown below.

New oil reserves

Saudi Arabia has discovered extensive new crude oil reserves in previously unexplored areas, according to a report from Reuters news agency ~~today~~. *yesterday*

One Saudi government source said that the new find was bigger than the total known reserves of some other OPEC member-states. The Saudi state *oil* company has reportedly been drilling in areas well away from its existing oil pipeline network.

discovery

The agency quotes unnamed Saudi officials as saying that the ~~find~~ could boost the country's oil reserves by as much as 20 per cent. The discovery could have a significant impact on *world* oil markets, in lowering the price of crude oil from its recent record price of around $40 per barrel.

This is good news for the consumer, who has recently been experiencing steadily increasing prices on all oil products. Increased oil prices ~~automatically~~ lead to increased inflation and invariably to increases in unemployment.

---

3. Save this edited version of the file onto your disk, using OILFIND2 as the file name.
4. Print OILFIND1 and OILFIND2.

ASN • *Assignment 3*

Following the inaugural meeting of Dunbeg Residents' Association, a set of proposals was drawn up for the attention of the county council. The proposals are outlined in the document below. You are required to enter this document in your word-processor and save it onto your disk, using DUNBEG1 as the file name.

Dunbeg development proposals

There is an immediate need for a children's playground in the area. The association considers Knockmore Meadow as a suitable site for a playground, as it is close to Dunbeg swimming pool and gymnasium. The association is prepared to organise and supervise sports events and barbecues during the summer holidays.

There is an immediate need for a pedestrian crossing on Castledean Road near the shopping arcade. Residents of Beechwood Road and Fitzgerald Avenue have great difficulty crossing Castledean Road during working hours.

The association urges the county council to honour its 1988 commitment to install street lights on Bishopstown Road and Gasfinn Road. These roads are close to the railway station, and the lack of adequate street lighting, especially during winter months, is a problem for those who commute to Castledean every day.

Carry out the following tasks:

1. Recall DUNBEG1 to the screen
2. Edit the document by making the alterations shown below.

Dunbeg development proposals

There is an ~~immediate~~ *urgent* need for a children's playground in the area. The association considers Knockmore Meadow ~~as~~ *to be* a suitable site for a playground, as it is close to Dunbeg swimming pool and gymnasium. The association is prepared to organise and supervise sports events and barbecues *at the playground* during the summer holidays.

There is an immediate need for a pedestrian crossing on Castledean Road near the shopping ~~arcade~~ *centre*. Residents of Beechwood Road and Fitzgerald Avenue have great difficulty crossing Castledean Road during working hours.

The association urges the county council to honour its 198*9* commitment to install street light*ing* on Bishopstown Road and Gasfinn Road. These roads are close to the railway station, and the lack of adequate street lighting, especially during winter months, is a problem for those who commute *by rail* to Castledean every day.

---

3. Save the edited version of the file to disk, using DUNBEG2 as the file name.
4. Print DUNBEG1 and DUNBEG2.

ASN · *Assignment 4*

You are required to enter the document below in your word-processor. You should then save the document onto your disk, using NEWS as the file name.

Mason & Co.

COMPANY NEWSLETTER

INTERCOMPANY FOOTBALL. The annual intercompany football tournament took place at Murrenstown football grounds. Many local firms entered a team. The tournament was eventually won by Slaney Meats PLC. Our team reached the semi-final but was beaten by Marymount Electrical Ltd.

FISHING TRIP. Twenty-five people have enlisted for the fishing trip to the Slane valley on Saturday next. A coach will leave from the town hall at 10 a.m. A limited number of places is still available; if you are interested, please forward your name to John Martin or Susan Conway.

NEW ARRIVAL. Best wishes to Andrew and Niamh Boylan on the birth of their first child, a baby girl. She is to be called Ciara.

DRAMA SECTION. Mary McEvoy would like to hear from anyone who would be willing to participate in this year's drama production of John B. Keane's 'Many Young Men of Twenty'. Performances would be in late March of next year.

SECURE PARKING. In the light of last month's vandalism of two cars in the company car park, a new gate has been installed at the entrance to the car park. This gate will be locked from 10 a.m. to 1 p.m. and from 2.15 to 4.45 p.m. each day.

Carry out the following tasks:

1. Produce a print-out of NEWS (or use the text above).
2. Recall NEWS to the screen and make the alterations shown below.

Mason & Co.

* Position here

COMPANY NEWSLETTER

INTERCOMPANY FOOTBALL. The annual intercompany football tournament took place at Murrenstown ~~football~~ sports grounds. Many local firms entered a team. The tournament was eventually won by Slaney Meats PLC. Our team reached the semi-final but was beaten by in a penalty shoot out Marymount Electrical Ltd.

FISHING TRIP. Twenty-five people have enlisted for the fishing trip to the ~~Bland~~ *Boyne* valley on Saturday next. A coach will leave from the town hall at 10 a.m. A limited number of places is still available; if you are interested, please forward your name *and address* to John Martin or Susan Conway.

NEW ARRIVAL. Best wishes to Andrew and Niamh Boylan on the birth of their first child, a baby girl. She is to be called Ciara.

DRAMA SECTION. Mary McEvoy would like to hear from anyone who would be willing to participate in this year's drama production of John B. Keane's 'Many Young Men of Twenty'. Performances would be in ~~late March~~ *early April* of next year.

SECURE PARKING. In the light of last month's vandalism of two cars in the company car park, a new gate has been installed at the entrance to the car park. This gate will be locked from 10 a.m. to 1 p.m. and from 2.15 to 4.45 p.m. each day. → *Take back to previous page. Position where shown by asterix* ✳

3. Save the edited version of the file to your disk, using NEWS 1 as the file name.
4. Produce a print-out of NEWS1.

ASN · *Assignment 5*

You are required to enter the following letter in your word-processor and save it to disk, using CARSALE1 as the file name.

Cox Motors Ltd
Gort Road
Ballymore, Co. Tipperary

Our ref.: TD/ARE

11 May 1995

Mr Ruairi O'Connell
25 Golden Vale Road
Ballymore, Co. Tipperary

Dear Mr O'Connell,

Thank you for your enquiry about the Astra car range.

As requested, we are sending you a brochure giving full details of all six cars in the range.

You will notice that the fuel consumption is excellent and that all models can use unleaded petrol. It is also worth noting that each new Astra has a three-year warranty on all parts. All Astras are equipped with stereo radio and compact disc player, central locking, and rear window wipers. A sun-roof and metallic paint are optional extras.

A leaflet is also enclosed outlining the retail prices of our new cars, together with a comprehensive list of prices of quality used Astra cars in stock.

Please feel free to drop into the garage at any time for a test drive in an Astra.

Yours faithfully,

Desmond Cox
Sales Department

Carry out the following tasks:

1. Produce a print-out of the file (or use the text on the previous page).
2. Edit the letter by marking it with the symbols you have learnt, making the following changes:
   (a) replace the date given with today's date;
   (b) in paragraph 2, replace 'car' with 'model';
   (c) delete the word 'also' in paragraph 3;
   (d) insert the word 'now' before 'in stock' at the end of paragraph 4;
   (e) replace 'drop' with 'call' in paragraph 5;
   (f) join the first two paragraphs together;
   (g) make the sentence that begins 'All Astras are equipped . . .' the start of a new paragraph.
3. Recall CARSALE1 to the screen and make these alterations to the file.
4. Save this version of the letter to your disk, using CARSALE2 as the file name.
5. Produce a print-out of CARSALE2.

AS_N • *Assignment 6*

You are required to enter the following document in your word-processor and save it to disk, using AGM1 as the file name:

Minutes of the annual general meeting of members of Corrugated Steel Products Ltd, held at 34 Riverside Road, Navan, on Tuesday 30 October 1995.

Mr Aidan Dooley, Chairman of the Board, presided.

1. The Secretary read the notice convening the meeting, and the auditors' report.

2. The Chairman addressed the meeting, and proposed: That the directors' report and the accounts for the year ending 30 September 1995 produced at the meeting be hereby received and adopted, and that a dividend of 15 per cent less income tax be declared, to be payable to members on 20 November 1995.

3. The Chairman proposed that Mr Patrick Matthews, the director retiring by rotation, be re-elected as a director of the company, Mr Declan Murphy seconded the motion, which was put to the meeting and carried unanimously.

4. Ms Niamh Sheridan, a shareholder, proposed that Jackson, Brady and Company, having agreed to continue in office as auditors for a further year, receive a fixed fee of £17,000. This was seconded by Mr Seán Moran, another shareholder, put to the meeting, and carried unanimously.

5. There was no other business.

Chairman
7 November 1995

Carry out the following tasks:

1. Produce a print-out of AGM1 (or use the text above).
2. Edit the minutes by marking the print-out with the symbols you have learnt, making the following changes:
   (a) the correct name of the company is Corrugated Iron Products Ltd;
   (b) the dividend declared was 18 per cent, not 15 per cent;
   (c) the dividend will be paid to members one week later than the date given above;
   (d) the motion to re-elect Patrick Matthews was not carried unanimously but by nine votes to two;
   (e) change the order of items 3 and 4 as they appear in the document (remember to change the numbers).
3. recall AGM1 to the screen and make these alterations to the file.
4. Save the altered document to disk, using AGM2 as the file name.
5. Produce a print-out of AGM2.

A^{S}N · *Assignment 7*

You are required to type in the following menu for the Ideal Hotel. Call this file MENU.

IDEAL HOTEL
14 Rose Garden Mews
Rathgannon, Co. Cork

MENU

Mandarin & grapefruit cocktail
or
Chicken and mushroom vol-au-vent
***
Prime cut of roast beef with horseradish sauce
or
Loin of pork rolled with savory stuffing & Cucumber
or
Roast turkey with onion and sage stuffing and baked Limerick ham
or
Prime sirloin of steak bordelaise
or
Poached Moy salmon hollandaise
***
Selection of fresh seasonal vegetables

***
Baked alaska
or
Peach Melba & ice cream
or
Home-made apple tart and fresh cream
or
Sherry trifle chantilly
***
Tea or coffee
After-dinner mints
£14.75 per person

Carry out the following tasks:

1. The menu is to be displayed outside the hotel, but the manager is not pleased with the format. He has asked you to centre all the text, including the hotel name and address and to use fonts to enhance the appearance of the menu. Recall the file MENU and make this change.
2. Save the centred menu to disk, using MENUC as the file name.
3. Produce a print-out of MENUC.

A^S_N · *Assignment 8*

You are required to type in the following report on the decline of sales in the south of the country, and save it as REPORT.

REPORT OF THE SUBCOMMITTEE

This is the report of the subcommittee appointed according to the terms of the Board resolution of 5 July 1995 'that a subcommittee be appointed to investigate and report on the decline of sales in the southern region for the period ending 30 November 1995, and to make recommendations.'

Subcommittee members
   Frank Brady (chairman)
   Valerie Byrne
   Ian Caprani
   Ciarán Dunne
   Madeleine Dunne
   Dermot Moyne
   Mary Purcell

Summary
The full report is in the hands of the marketing manager. Some of the more important findings are:

(a) Competition has increased considerably, especially with the entry into the market of Reprotext Ltd.

(b) Two of our reliable customers have ceased trading in the last twelve months: Southprint Ltd and Speedprint Ltd.

(c) There is a cheaper imported paper on the market, which is affecting sales from department C.

(d) Because of the high rate of absenteeism in the dispatch department some orders were cancelled.

(e) The haulier for the southern region is less reliable than those of any of the other regions.

Recommendations
1. Find a new haulier for the southern region.

2. Obtain more information on possible cheaper sources of paper.

3. Assign two more sales representatives to the region.

4. Establish the reason for the absenteeism in the dispatch department.

5. Make a closer examination of the activities of Reprotext Ltd.

Data
Details of data relevant to this report are attached.

Signed: ....
1 December 1995

Carry out the following tasks:

1. Recall this document and make the following changes to make the report more attractive-looking.
   (a) underline all subheadings in the document;
   (b) change the heading of the report to bold, and centre it.
   (c) change any company name in the document to bold.
2. Save the document as REPORTA.

A$N · Assignment 9

You are required to type in the following letter, which was sent to the *Irish Daily* by a reader. Save the document as OUTDOOR.

---

91 St Peter's Drive
Dublin 24

5 July 1995

Dear Sir,

I am writing to describe a recent experience that might be of interest to your readers.

I decided to do something different for my holidays this year. I booked an adventure holiday at the Slievemore Mountain Lodge adventure centre in Co. Wicklow. From the very minute I arrived at the centre I began to unwind. The scenery was beautiful, with peaceful lakes, rolling heather-covered hills, and sparkling streams.

The centre has a choice of daily activities, including hill walking, canoeing, sailing, orienteering, and rock climbing, to mention only a few. I tried nearly all of these activities during the week. The walks covered an area where we saw no signs of human habitation, which made a pleasant contrast with the 'concrete jungle' I am used to most of the year! The accommodation was very comfortable: it was a real pleasure to return from a day's activity to a roaring log fire and a hot meal.

We hear so much about disappointed holidaymakers nowadays. This was the best holiday of my life, and I would wholeheartedly recommend such a holiday to anyone who wants a real break from it all.

Yours sincerely,

Pádraig Whelan

Carry out the following tasks:

1. To make it more acceptable to the editor of the paper, the letter should be put into a narrow column. Recall the file OUTDOOR and change the margin settings to: left, 10 characters; right, 40 characters (30 characters wide), and realign the text within the new margins.
2. Save the letter as OUTDOOR1.

A$_N^S$ • *Assignment 10*

You are required to enter the following text into your word-processor and save it to disk, using SURVEY as the file name.

HEART DISEASE SURVEY

More than half of a group of patients screened for heart disease risk factors were found to be overweight, and nearly a quarter had high blood pressure, it emerged today.

The researchers looked at forty patients in the Dún Laoghaire area. GPs screened the patients for such things as excess weight, high blood pressure, and high cholesterol levels.

Now researchers are planning a second screening project, to study a larger number of patients, following the disturbing results of the pilot study carried out by the Department of Preventive Medicine in University College, Dublin.

Nearly 60 per cent of the people examined were overweight, according to the 'Irish Medical Times'. A quarter had high cholesterol levels, while 20 to 30 per cent had high blood pressure.

Now, GPs in the wider area of south-east Co. Dublin are to become involved in a second trial to screen a larger number of patients.

Carry out the following tasks:

1. Produce a print-out of SURVEY (or use the text above).
2. Edit the print-out, using the symbols you have already learnt, to make the following alterations to the text:
    (a) change the heading to bold;
    (b) in paragraph 1, 'nearly a quarter' should read 'nearly a third';
    (c) in paragraph 2, 'researchers looked at forty patients' should read ' researchers examined medical reports on forty patients';
    (d) in paragraph 2 also, change 'Dún Laoghaire area' to bold;
    (e) in paragraph 3, 'researchers are planning' should read 'researchers are already planning';
    (f) in paragraph 3 also, underline 'Department of Preventive Medicine';
    (g) in paragraph 5, 'south-east Co. Dublin' should read 'south Co. Dublin';
    (h) change the order of paragraphs 2 and 3.
3. Recall SURVEY to the screen and make these changes to the file.
4. Alter the margins to 5 and 60, and realign the text within the new margins.
5. Save the edited version of the file to your disk, using SURVEY2 as the file name.
6. Produce a print-out of SURVEY2.

A^S_N • *Assignment 11*

You are required to type in the following letter informing a customer of a new product. Save the letter as NEWPROD.

MOUNTAINGEAR LTD
Glenview, Co. Kildare
Telephone (048) 52345

19 April 1995

The Outdoor Shop
62 Fleet Street
Dublin 2

Dear Sir,

We are writing to inform you of a new product in our range, the Eiger storm tent.

The shape of the Eiger has been designed to give top performance in fierce weather. Tensions have been carefully worked out so that all strains are equally distributed over the whole surface. The tunnel shape, formed by two supporting hoops, is chosen because of its aerodynamic efficiency and because it offers more usable volume inside than all other tent shapes. Further stability is created by the canting of the two poles at an angle. This improves Eiger performance under a snow load.

The interior space of Eiger is remarkable for a relatively small tent. This allows for greater comfort when using the Eiger for long periods in extreme weather. The front bell end has plenty of working space and has two zips, giving a choice of entry.

Ease of setting up the tent was another important consideration in developing Eiger. The tent can be erected in less than two minutes by one person, even in a strong wind.

Enclosed is a detailed specification and photograph of the Eiger. A display tent can be delivered if requested.

Yours faithfully,

Liam Burns
Sales Manager

Carry out the following tasks:

1. Before sending these letters to different customers, the marketing manager decided to change the name of the product: the new name is Everest. Use the 'find and replace' facility (if available) to make this change anywhere the name Eiger is mentioned in the letter.
2. Save this version of the letter as NEWPROD1.

A^{S}N • *Assignment 12*

You are required to type in the following daily timetable for an introductory computer course. You should use tabs or a table to help in the aligning of the text.

ECA *Table*

Course: Introduction to computing

Time	Details	Tutor	Room
9:30	Introduction to computer hardware	Ms M. Purcell	Com1
10:30	Coffee break		
10:50	Introduction to computer software	Dr D. Cox	Com1
11:30	Keyboarding	Mr G. Coakley	Com2
12:30	Lunch		
1:30	Hands-on word-processing	Prof. J. O'Brien	Com2
2:30	Hands-on spreadsheets	Dr A. Clifford	Com2
3:30	Coffee		
3:50	Hands-on data-base	Dr D. Cooney	Com2
4:30	Networking; electronic mail; computer safety	Mr M. Keenan	Com2
5:30	Review		

Save the document as TABS, and print it.

A$N • *Assignment 13*

You are required to set up the following survey questionnaire which will be sent to colleges. You should use tabs or a table to help in the aligning of the text.

Questionnaire

A. Personal Profile

Q1. Sex | Male | | Female | |

Q2. Number of years teaching   [   ]   Number of years teaching with computers   [   ]

Q3. Number of years as computer/IT coordinator   [   ]

Q4. Qualifications   [   ]

Q5   Age | 20-30 | | 31-40 | | 41-50 | | 50+ | |

Q6   Computer owner | No | | Yes | |

B. School Profile

Q7

1	Location of school (e.g. Dublin 12)	
2	School type (e.g. vocational)	
3	Is your school coeducational? (Y/N)	
4	Number of students in the school	

C. Hardware Facilities

Q8   Please indicate the number of each of the following computers in your school.

	No.	Networked (Y/N)
IBMs or compatibles		
Apples		
Nimbus		
BBCs		
Commodores		

Thank you for your cooperation!

ASN • Assignment 14

You are required to set up the following tax deduction card for an employee. You should use tabs or a table to help in the aligning of the text.

Tax Deduction Card for: Mary Woods

Week No.	Gross Pay	Cumulative Gross Pay	PAYE tax
	£	£	£
1	200.34	200.34	28.75
2	200.34	400.68	28.75
3	184.77	585.45	23.77
4	73.91	659.36	0.00
5	0.00	659.36	0.00
6	0.00	659.36	0.00
7	73.91	733.27	0.00
8	248.96	982.23	31.43
9	195.47	1,177.70	27.19
10	0.00	1,177.70	0.00
11	200.34	1,378.04	28.75
12	200.34	1,578.38	28.75
13	200.34	1,778.72	28.75
14	200.34	1,979.06	28.75
15	200.34	2,179.40	28.75

A^{S}N · *Assignment 15*

You have just been appointed to the complaints department of Hewson Electrical Ltd. Your duties include responding to letters of complaint from dissatisfied customers.

You are required to save each of the following paragraphs in separate files on your disk. The files should be named PT1, PT2, PT3 PT4 and PT5, respectively.

[File 1]
We have received your letter concerning the item that you bought at our store. We are sorry to hear that it is causing problems.

[File 2]
As the goods are still under guarantee, please call our maintenance department to arrange a suitable time for our repair technician to call to you.

[File 3]
As the goods are no longer under guarantee, repair work cannot be carried out free of charge. Our repair technician, however, can call to you to give a quotation for the cost of repairs.

[File 4]
As this is an old model, parts are extremely difficult to obtain. We have an excellent range of new models in our showrooms, and we would be happy to offer you a reasonable trade-in discount off the cost of a new model.

[File 5]
Your faithfully,

Desmond Joyce
Repair Control Department

Carry out the following tasks:

Use the correct combination of stored paragraphs and today's date to compose letters of reply to the following customers. Your are also given suitable names for your letter files.

E C A Table		
Letter	**Person**	**Stored paragraphs**
LTR1	Ms Joyce Noonan 55 Kilmore Road Castlebawn, Co. Donegal	Files: PT1, PT2, PT5
LTR2	Mr Seán Ryan 73 Ormond Road Invermore, Co. Limerick	Files: PT1, PT3, PT5
LTR3	Ms Róisín Nestor 6 Mount Nugent Road Dunfinn, Co. Cavan	Files: PT1, PT4, PT5

ASN · *Assignment 16*

As personnel manager of Green Valley Foods Ltd you must recruit a new secretary for the managing director of the company. You have advertised the position in the local press and have received a large number of applications.

You have decided to call three suitably qualified people for interview, and to use the merge printing facility of your word-processor to compose letters to these three people requesting them to attend for interview.

The standard letter is as follows:

<merged name>
<merged address>

17 May 1995

Dear <merged name>,

We are pleased to invite you to an interview for the post of secretary to the managing director of our company, on <merged date> at <merged time>.

You should call at the reception desk in the front hall. The receptionist will direct you to <merged location>.

Please confirm that you will be able to attend at that time.

Yours faithfully,

Mary Thompson
Personnel Manager

Carry out the following tasks:

1. Enter the text of the letter as given above. Here the symbol '<>' is used to enclose the variables: different indicators may be required on your word-processor. Save the letter in a file called NEWJOB.
2. Create a data file called PEOPLE, using the data given on p. 243.

Table

person:	Ms Aisling Downey	Mr Paul Ryan	Ms Patricia Burke
address1:	3 Willowbrook Rd	45 Collins Pk	12 Rosslee Rd
address2:	Kilpatrick,	Kilpatrick,	Kilpatrick,
	Co. Cork	Co. Cork	Co. Cork
name:	Ms Downey	Mr Ryan	Ms Burke
date:	26 May 1995	26 May 1995	26 May 1995
time:	10:30 a.m.	2:15 p.m.	3:30 p.m.
location:	room 19	room 22	room 22

3. Use the merge printing facility on your word-processor to merge the data from the file PEOPLE with the standard letter in the file NEWJOB.

ASN · *Assignment 17*

As personnel manager of Green Valley Foods Ltd you must organise and confirm the holiday arrangements for three members of staff. You will use the merge printing facility of your word-processor to compose the letters. Set up two files, the standard letter and the data file and merge print them.

The standard letter is as follows:

01/05/95

<merged name>
<merged address>

Dear <merged name>

Re: Summer Holidays 1995

I have received your request for holiday leave and I am pleased to be able to confirm the following dates from <merged dates> inclusive.

Yours sincerely

Joe Manning
Personnel Manager

The holiday rota is as follows:

◇E◇C◇Λ◇ *Table*		
Brenda Clancy	Paul Cusack	Sean Whelan
13 Willows Lodge	11 Rathdown Rd	23 Marley Close
Killiney	Bray	Rathfarnham
Co. Dublin	Co. Wicklow	Dublin 14
11/06/95 to 27/06/95	17/07/95 to 31/07/95	28/07/95 to 11/08/95

ASN • *Assignment 18*

You are required to type in the following document, which is a report on the valuation and condition of a property that a client is thinking of buying. The appropriate tab settings should also be used in typing the columns in the 'Accommodation' section.

SHOWPIECE AUCTIONEERS
3 Ringsend Green
Dublin 4

VALUATION REPORT

Property: 76 Mountain Road
Dublin 16
Clients: Mr Peter Flanagan and Ms Mary Flanagan
8 Terenure Drive
Dublin 6

In accordance with your instructions we inspected the above property to ascertain the current market value and condition. Our report follows:

Location
The property is situated within a modern residential development beside St Peter's Park and all other amenities. It is approximately 4 km from Rathgar centre and approximately 10 km south of Dublin city centre.

Description
The gross internal floor area is approximately 114 square metres. The property comprises a two-storey mainly blockbuilt semi-detached house with maple timber floors. Windows throughout are double-glazed in all rooms. The roof is concrete-tiled and pitched. The house has a half-brick front elevation, otherwise Tyrolean front, rear and side elevations.

Accommodation
Glazed entrance porch.
Spacious hallway with telephone.
Sitting-room: 4.5 × 4.2 m, with inset fireplace. Double doors to:
Dining-room: 3.75 × 4.5 m, with patio doors.
Kitchen: 3.75 × 3.5 m, with stainless sink unit and oak fitted presses.
 Upstairs there are three bedrooms:
Bedroom 1: 4.25 × 4 m, with double built-in wardrobes, and bathroom with shower en suite.
Bedroom 2: 2.75 × 4.25 m, with built-in wardrobe.
Bedroom 3: 2.75 × 2.75 m, with fitted shelving.
Bathroom: with three-piece suite.
Hot press with dual immersion heater.

Outside
Mature landscaped gardens to front and rear; garage with fuse-box and gas meter.

Services
All main services are available, including gas-fired central heating.

Title
Freehold

Condition of the property
In our surveyor's report it is noted that the property is in excellent structural order, but some attention should be given to the maintenance of the fascia and soffit sheeting at the rear of the property. A small crack at the gable wall under the window-sill needs to be repaired immediately.

Valuation
In or opinion the present market value of the property, subject to the foregoing work being carried out, is in the region of

£62,000.00
(sixty-two thousand pounds)

Signed ....
Date ....

Carry out the following tasks:

1. Save the report as VALUE, and print it (or use the text above).
2. Edit the print-out, using the symbols you have already learnt, to make the following alterations to the text:

(a) change the headings 'Property' and 'Clients' to bold;

(b) centre and underline the subheadings 'Location' to 'Valuation';

(c) in the section headed 'Location' delete the word 'modern', and change 'Rathgar' to 'Rathmines';

(d) in the section headed 'Description' change 'maple' to 'pine' and delete the words 'in all rooms'; move the first sentence of this paragraph so that it becomes the last sentence;

(e) change the names of the rooms in the 'Accommodation' section, from 'Sitting-room' to 'Bathroom', to bold;

(f) in the section headed 'Condition of the property' insert 'wooden' before 'fascia'; make the last sentence the beginning of a new paragraph.

3. Recall VALUE to the screen and make these changes to the file.

4. Save the report as VALUE1, and print it.

ASN • Assignment 19

NCVA Word Processing Practical Level 2 1994

Operator please replace staff with employees throughout

SECURITY SURVEY — *Spaced caps & US*

A security consultant was recently contracted to survey and report on various aspects of security within our Company. The survey was undertaken over a period of three to 4 weeks and included regular discussions with all grades and groups of staff, workshops and personal observation by the consultant at all times of the night and day covering the full seven days.

All groups of staff responded positively and the result is a fairly comprehensive report which identifies both problem areas and offers solutions to minimise the risk to both staff and resources. To put the position of the Co. into context the report draws comparison with a division of a large Public Company with similar turnover and manpower. That Company employs a multi-manned security force, a radio communication system, specialised alarm and patrol equipment. Our Company relies upon individual managers and portering staff as its deterrent.

The latter *Contracted* *and regular access to security advice*

NP

us

Specific comment has been made on the following:

<u>Staff Ide-tification</u>

Identification badges (including photograph) shld. be issued to all staff without delay. A start has already been made - a firm has been commissioned to photograph all ~~members of~~ staff & issue them with *DEL* sealed perspex badges displaying relevant details concerning their employment with the Co.

<u>Access to Site</u>

Multi-point access to all sites should be reviewed and recommendations are made in the report regarding immediate improvement. 3

<u>Access to Buildings</u>

Specific recommendations were ~~were~~ made regarding control of access to all buildings.

<u>Key Control</u> ⟵ Leave 1 clear line space
A number of examples were given of inadequate key control and recommendations made to improve the situation.

<u>**Parking**</u>

Certain recommendations ⟨have been⟩ ~~are made~~ which are designed to help in the control of parking.

Staff Safety Certain groups of staff have been ~~identified~~ *chosen* as being in a higher risk capacity. These include on-call staff working in ⟨remote⟩ *stet* ⟦REMOTE⟧ areas of the building and all staff concerned with the movement of cash ~~within~~ and outside the various premises.

Theft

Various examples of potential risk were cited from personal observation. Emphasis must be made of staff responsibilities to safeguard ~~personnel~~ *PERSONAL* and Company property.

The Solar System ⟵ (CAPS, CENTRE, BOLD + u/s)

PLANET	DIAMETER (KILOMETRES)	DISTANCE[1] FROM SUN	ORBITAL[2] PERIOD	ROTATION[3] PERIOD
Mercury	4,880	57.9	88 days	59 days
Venus	12,104	108.2	224 days	243 days
Earth	12,750	149.6	365 days	23 hrs 56 mins
Mars	6,760	227.9	687 days	24 hrs 37 mins
Jupiter	142,700	778.3	11 years	9 hrs 45 mins
Saturn	67,600	1,427.0	29 years	10 hrs 15 mins
Uranus	120,840	2,869.6	84 years	16 hrs
Neptune	46,570	4,496.6	164 years	18 hrs
Pluto	3,000	5,900.0	247 years	6 days 9 hrs

⟨retain abbreviations in final column⟩

Operator:

Please put planet names in caps. and column headings in lower case with initial capitals.

1. In millions of kilometres.
2. Time taken for the planet to complete one orbit of the sun. All planets orbit in the same direction.
3. Time taken for the planet to rotate on its own axis.

[1]

[2]

Dear [3]

REMOVAL EXPENSES ← (EMBOLDEN)

Congratulations on yr promotion to [4] which
NP will take effect from [5]. [As you may be
aware Company policy is to assist employees
with removal expenses when moving to a new
area as a result of promotion. An initial
sum of [6] will be made available
immediately, but to enable me to reimburse
you your full entitlement I need you
to complete the enclosed Removal Expenses
Claim Form. (in full)
Once you have completed the R E C F sign
the bottom, ~~and~~ have it authorised and
return it to this office at your earliest
NP convenience. [On behalf of the Co. I would
like to take this opp. to wish you every
success in your new position.

Yours faithfully

FC Fuller
Chief Accountant

VARIABLES

LETTER 1
[1]   Today's date
[2]   Mr Michael Greene
         9 Main Street
         ROSCOMMON
[3]   Mr Greene
[4]   Area Manager for Galway
[5]   1 June 1994
[6]   £500

LETTER 2
[1]   Today's date
[2]   Mr John Murphy
         High Street
         TUBBERCURRY
         Co Sligo
[3]   Mr Murphy
[4]   Sales Director
[5]   Monday next
[6]   £650

LETTER 3
[1]   Today's date
[2]   Miss Helen O'Brien
         22 Patrick Street
         LETTERKENNY
         Co Donegal
[3]   Miss O'Brien
[4]   Public Relations Officer for Cork and Limerick
[5]   1 September 1994
[6]   £900

ASN • Assignment 20
NCVA Word Processing Practical Level 2 1995
Practical Assignment 1 (25%)

1 Recall the document stored on your system as TASK1.
2 Proof-read and correct where necessary, and make the amendments as indicated.
3 Ragged or justified line endings are accepted.
4 Take great care with pagination.
5 Save your document for printing as instructed by your Specialist Teacher.
• All abbreviations should be typed in full where appropriate.
• Block or centre style is acceptable once used consistently throughout the assignment.
• Dictionaries are allowed.

Mackey's Garden Centre
Garden Centre of the year

Evening events for June 1995
all welcome - all free

Tuesday	June	7	Hanging Basket	Demonstration Paul Murray
"	"	13	Water Gardening	Frank Fanning
"	"	20	Spring Bulbs	Peter O'Brien
"	"	27	Conservatories	Bob West

(Operator - enforce page break here + display above text attractively)

Caps Bold

Flower Arranging

It is important that you have the correct tools and equipment when arranging flowers. There is nothing worse than finding you are short of something when you are halfway through an arrangement. Your hobby does not seem *is not quite* so expensive when you first begin if you start with just one or two basic tools and add to them.

SCISSORS

There are several very good makes available and ~~it is up to you to find ones~~ *you must choose ones* that ~~are of a~~ *slet*
suitable size and weight for you. Make sure that the rings are comfortable and do not trap your
fingers

SECATEURS

These will be necessary when you wish to cut heavy stems of plant material or wire.

KNIFE

A sharp knife is essential. It can be used for trimming all kinds of stems, removing thorns and
leaves from stems and for cutting floral foam. *This need not cost a lot of money.*

FLORAL FOAM

There are two main types - green for using with fresh flowers, pale brown for using with dried
and fabric flowers. The green type must be thoroughly soaked before use.

The foam comes in many shapes and sizes - bricks, cylinders, squares, etc. All shapes can be
cut to the appropriate sizes. We stock a full range.

ADHESIVE TAPE

This may be used for securely fixing the foam to the container especially for large designs.
You must make sure that the surface is completely dry.

Remember to browse through the items in our extensive display of equipment for flower arrangers. Our stocks are usually complete but, if you cannot find what you need, please ask at the Information Desk.

*Operator:
Replace "foam" with "oasis" throughout,
please number pages at bottom right-hand side*

Practical Assignment 2 (25%)

1 Key in and display this Memorandum attractively.
2 Tabulate the table of events.
3 Save your document for printing as instructed by your Specialist Teacher.
- All abbreviations should be typed in full where appropriate.
- Block or centre style is acceptable once used consistently throughout an assignment.
- Dictionaries are allowed.

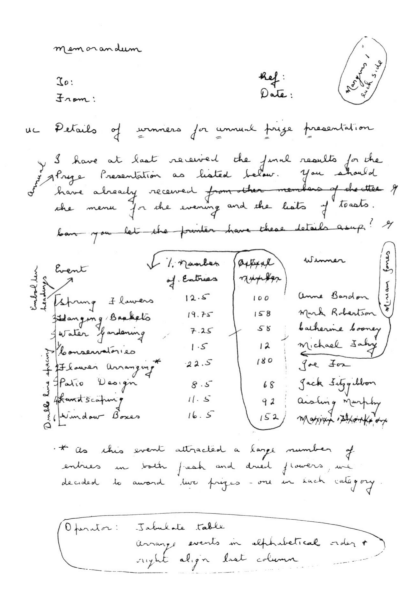

Practical Assignment 3 (30%)

1 You are required to reply to three applicants for a position with the Winning Widget Co.
2 Using the standard paragraphs stored on your diskette, please send the appropriate letter in reply. Your teacher will inform you of the names and location of the paragraphs.
3 Save each of the letters for printing out as instructed by your Specialist Teacher.

Use the Paragraphs as follows:

Call for interview   -   **paragraphs 1, 2 and 4.**

Decline   -   **paragraphs 1, 3 and 4.**

Applicants for post of   **Supervisor**   in   **our Garden Centre**

They should arrive   **9.30 a.m.**   on   **30 June 1995**

Call for Interview: **Decline:**

Ms Jane Maguire   Mr Liam Delaney
34 Main Street   Old Mill Street
ATHLONE   SWINFORD
Co Westmeath   Co Mayo

Mr Michael Scully
Society Street
BALLINASLOE
Co Galway

- All abbreviations should be typed in full where appropriate.
- Block or centre style is acceptable once used consistently throughout an assignment.
- Dictionaries are allowed.

Chapter 9

CONCLUSION

Integrated packages

Microcomputer programs can be divided into three types according to the way in which they can be used in conjunction with other programs.

A 'standalone' program can be used for one application only — for example, word-processing — and cannot incorporate files from other programs.

A 'non-standalone' program can also be used for only one application but has an 'import facility', which allows the user to include files from certain other applications: for example, to import a spreadsheet from a spreadsheet program into a word-processor program in compiling a report.

An 'integrated package', on the other hand, contains a number of different applications, all within the same main program. Typical combinations include a word-processor, a database, and a spreadsheet, and sometimes a communications program and a graphics program. These packages allow the user to import or export data files between applications; and — unlike the non-standalone programs — if data is changed in one application, the data change will be reflected in all related applications, so that, for example, a graph made up from spreadsheet data would change automatically to reflect recalculations on the spreadsheet.

Advantages of integrated packages

Integrated packages have a number of advantages over other types of program.

One program for most essential applications

An integrated package allows the user to produce all the usual business documents using only one program.

Easy to learn and use

Instead of having to become familiar with the conventions and commands of four or five different programs, the user has the advantage of a common method of entering commands; for example, the command to save data to a disk would be the same for all the applications in the program. Once the commands and conventions of the program are mastered the user will only have to learn the underlying concepts of the different applications to use the program.

Cost

There can be a large cost saving with an integrated package compared with the cost of purchasing four or five standalone application programs.

Disadvantages of integrated package use

Integrated packages also have a number of significant disadvantages, however.

Less advanced features

Applications in an integrated package contain less advanced features than standalone programs. Integrated packages never have enough memory to contain all the advanced features of standalone programs.

Limited space for data files

The packages occupy a large amount of RAM, limiting the size of data files that can be used.

ASN • Assignment

In this book so far, one particular application has been used to carry out each assignment: a data-base, spreadsheet or word-processor program. There are, however, many situations where the computer user may use a combination of all three to carry out a particular task.

The following assignment is an example, where all three applications are used to generate a useful report. You may use standalone programs, non-standalone programs or an integrated package to complete the assignment.

Comfort Footwear PLC was established in Cork in 1979 by Peter Casey. The company manufactures a mid-range sports training shoe: the Marathon Marvel. Market research shows that it is bought mainly by people under the age of 25. The sales price is £25.50.

The company has its head office in Cork, but it supplies its product to retail shops throughout the country. The following market information is available to the marketing director of the company.

1. Competitors' sales

There are five competitor companies importing a similar type of sports shoe. Table 1 outlines the number of pairs of mid-range sports training shoes sold by Comfort Footwear and each of the competitor companies during the past year.

Table 1				
Company	**Connacht**	**Leinster**	**Munster**	**Ulster**
Comfort Footwear	4,400	32,200	21,200	3,500
Allweather Shoes	4,400	38,000	8,200	8,400
John Martin	8,700	46,000	17,800	18,600
Easyfeet Now	1,700	9,400	12,100	6,900
J.K. Williams and Son	5,500	24,000	4,800	44,500
Footwear Supplies	700	5,600	4,200	2,450

2. Market population structure

Table 2 shows a percentage breakdown of the population of Ireland by province and age group for 1995.

Table 2				
Age group	**Connacht**	**Leinster**	**Munster**	**Ulster**
Under 15	2	12	4	3
16 to 25	2	20	3	7
26 to 60	4	13	7	10
Over 60	1	6	3	

3. Company sales trends

Table 3 shows the total number of units sold by each of the six companies in four consecutive years.

Table 3				
Company	**1992**	**1993**	**1994**	**1995**
Comfort Footwear	33,000	34,550	47,800	61,300
Allweather Shoes	45,000	38,700	47,400	58,600
John Martin	30,000	80,500	62,000	49,700
Easyfeet Now	20,000	29,600	31,800	30,100
J.K. Williams and Son	45,000	92,500	83,600	78,800
Footwear Supplies	13,400	12,300	12,950	

4. *The sales team*

The company's sales team consists of the following twelve members:

Seán McCarthy has been with the company since its foundation. He is based in Cork. His sales for the past year were 8,300 units. The total distance covered by Seán to achieve these sales was 93,000 km, and he incurred £6,200 in expenses.

Ronan Byrne joined the company at the beginning of the year after completing his Sales and Management Diploma at the College of Commerce in Rathmines, Dublin. Ronan is based in the Carlow-Kilkenny region. The total distance covered in the course of his work was 45,000 km, and his expenses amounted to £3,400. For the past year Ronan's total sales amounted to 3,600 units.

Catherine Stephens joined the company in 1993 after gaining three years' experience in sales with John Martin Ltd. She is attached to the company's Dublin office, and her sales for the past year amounted to 7,500 units. Catherine's total travelling amounted to 35,000 km, and she had £2,400 of expenses.

Linda O'Connor has been with the company since 1990, and is responsible for sales in north Leinster. She was ill for three months during the year but still managed to sell 4,800 units. She had £3,900 of expenses and she travelled 29,000 km in the course of her work. Brian Ward, a native of Castlebar, is the sole sales representative in Connacht. He joined the company in 1987 after three years as a member of the Garda Síochána. His sales for the past year were 4,400 units. During the year Brian travelled 75,000 km to achieve his sales, and had expenses of £35,100.

Claire Conroy joined the company in 1991 after returning from the United states, where she gained two years' valuable experience in selling and sales management with a large pharmaceutical company in San Francisco. She is attached to the company's Dublin office, and her sales for the past year were 6,800 units. She covered 50,000 km in making her sales, and her expenses were £5,800.

Liam Dolan, a native of Co. Kerry but now living in Waterford, has been with the company since 1993. His sales for the past year in Munster were 5,700 units. Liam travelled 145,000 km to make his sales, and he had expenses of £5,900.

Kevin Molloy is the sole sales representative in Ulster. He joined the company in 1986 after resigning his teaching position at a secondary school in Omagh. He was a successful member of the Leinster sales team, and this year he has been redeployed to the Ulster region. This is the first year that the company is selling the product in Ulster. Kevin's sales in Ulster amounted to 3,500 units for the past year. Kevin had expenses of £2,700, and he covered 38,000 km in the course of his work.

Peter McNicholl is another member of the Leinster sales team. He has been with the company since 1984, and his sales for the past year were 5,300 units. Peter had £4,100 expenses during the year and covered 50,000 km to achieve his sales.

Rachel Doyle, a native of Dublin but now living in Co. Tipperary, is responsible for sales in north Munster. She joined the company in 1990 on her return from Glasgow, where she worked for one year as a member of the sales team of a cosmetics company. She was attached to Comfort Footwear's Dublin office until 1994. Her sales amounted to 4,000 units for the past year. Rachel's travelling for the company during the year was 42,000 km, and her expenses amounted to £3,300.

Jim Ellis joined the company in 1992 after spending three years with Allweather Shoes as a member of their sales team. His sales in Munster for the past year were 3,200 units. Jim had to travel 37,000 km for the company during the year, and his expenses were £3,600.

Brenda Scott joined the company in 1989 as a secretary to the managing director, and in 1987 she joined the sales team, of which she is now an effective member. She operates in Kildare, Wicklow and Wexford, and her sales for the past year were 4,200 units. Brenda's travelling for the company during the year totalled 35,000 km, and she had expenses of £2,400.

Carry out the following tasks:

You are required to generate a report for the managing director of Comfort Footwear, using the following applications programs: data-base, spreadsheet, graphics (if available) and word-processor.

Outputs from the data-base, spreadsheet and graphics programs are to be included in the appendices of the report (if you are using standalone programs). Comments and explanations marked with an asterisk (*) are to be produced using the word-processor program, making reference to the appendices. (If you are using an integrated package, the word 'output' will refer to output files that will be integrated into the report. If you are using standalone programs, 'output' will refer to print-outs obtained.)

The report must be divided into two sections:

Section A: general sales report

In compiling the general sales report you must take the following steps:
1. Enter the data from Table 3 into a spreadsheet; you should then use this spreadsheet to show:
   (a) the overall sales in Ireland of mid-range sports training shoes for each year, and
   (b) the percentage market share for each company for each year, using the overall sales calculated above.
2. Produce two line graphs, one showing the number of units sold for each company and the other showing the percentage market share for each company for the four-year period. These graphs can be obtained by using the graphics capability of your spreadsheet program, or otherwise.
3. Include this spreadsheet and these graphs as Appendix A in the report.
*4. Comment on the percentage market share for each company and the changing trend in units sold.
5. Enter the data from Table 1 into a spreadsheet, showing total units sold in each province, and show the percentage market share in each province for each company during the past year.
6. Include this spreadsheet as Appendix B in the report
*7. With reference to Appendix B:
   (a) indicate the company with the highest market share in each province, and

(b) show how the companies have spread their sales across the provinces, and which seems the most successful policy.

Section B: Sales team report

In compiling the sales team report you must take the following steps:

1. Enter the information on Comfort Footwear's sales team into a data-base file. Each record in the file should contain the following fields for each salesperson as given in the sales personnel data above:

   (a) name (surname first);

   (b) province;

   (c) sales (units) during 1995;

   (d) expenses incurred during 1995;

   (e) distance travelled for 1995;

   (f) number of years' sales experience (including experience with other companies) to the end of 1995.

2. Extract from this data-base file an output list of the sales personnel, sorted in descending order of the number of units sold by each salesperson in 1995, together with their respective province and number of years' experience.

3. Include this output list as Appendix C in the report.

*4. Comment on the relationship between unit sales achieved and the number of years' sales experience of the members of the sales team.

5. Extract from the data-base file an output list showing name, sales and province of all sales staff who did not reach the company's sales quota of 5,000 units during 1995, sorted into alphabetical order of name. Include this list as Appendix D in the report.

*6. In each case where the sales quota was not reached, comment on possible reasons, other than sales experience, with particular reference to population structure (Table 2) and competition in each region (Table 1 and Appendices A and B).

7. Extract from the data-base file an output list showing the name, distance travelled, sales and province of the entire sales team, sorted in descending order of distance travelled. Include this list as Appendix E in the report.

*8. After you have examined Appendix E, consider whether there is a stronger relationship between distance travelled and sales in certain provinces.

9. Extract from the data-base file an output list showing the name and distance travelled, in descending order of distance covered during 1995, of those sales personnel who are exempt from 'benefit in kind' tax (see question 12 below). Include this list as Appendix F in the report. *Explain that the sales personnel in Appendix F are exempt from benefit-in-kind tax, and explain why.

10. Produce an output list in alphabetical order of surname for each member of the sales team showing name, sales experience, distance travelled and unit sales (Appendix G).

11. Using the output list from Appendix G above, enter on a spreadsheet the name, sales experience, distance travelled and unit sales for each member of the sales team for 1995.

12. Sales representatives using company cars can be liable for 'benefit in kind' tax. The

aim of this tax is to discourage people from registering cars for business purposes and then using them largely for private purposes.

The tax is calculated as a percentage of the value of the car. Those who travel more than 40,234 km (25,000 miles) in one year are exempt from this tax. For those whose annual travelling was less than 40,234 km the tax is calculated as follows:

For each successive 1,609 km (1,000 miles) less than 40,234 an extra 2 per cent of the car's value is charged as tax; for example, a salesperson who has a car valued at £10,000 and a total travelling distance in one year of 37,000 km would pay £400 tax:

Rate of tax = $((40{,}234 - 37{,}000) \div 1{,}609) \times 0.02 = 0.04$

Amount of tax = $0.04 \times 10{,}000 = £400$

The following general formulae can be used:

Tax rate = $((40234 - \text{distance})/1609)*0.02$

Tax amount = tax rate*value of car

Set up a new column showing the 'benefit in kind' tax for each member of Comfort Footwear's sales team. (Assume each salesperson drives a car valued £12,500.)

13 Set up a SALES VALUE column in the spreadsheet, showing the total sales value for each salesperson by multiplying the number of units sold by the unit retail price.

14. Set up a VARIANCE column, to contain the difference in unit sales and the company's 1995 sales quota (5,000 units) for each of the sales personnel.

15. As an incentive to its sales team the company operates the following bonus scheme: those who sell more than the sales quota will receive 5 per cent of the unit price as a bonus for each unit sold over the quota. Set up a BONUS column to display the total bonus, if any, paid to each member of the sales team.

16. Each member of the sales team receives a basic salary of £10,000 and a further £500 for each year's sales experience. Set up a SALARY column to include these salary details.

17. Commission is calculated on the basis of 1 per cent of sales value. Set up a COMMISSION column to show the commission paid to each of the sales personnel.

18. The total income of each salesperson is calculated by adding the salary, commission and any bonus earned. Include an INCOME column to show the total income of each member of the sales team in the past year.

19. Include this spreadsheet as appendix H in the report.

*20. Outline in the report the method of calculating the bonus, salary and commission, and give a full explanation of 'benefit in kind' tax.